SEARCHING FOR CHARLOTTE

A romantic self-portrait of Charlotte Waring in
September 1826, *wrapped in Mr Atkinson's
plaid cloak,* from Charlotte's 1848 sketchbook,
held in the Mitchell Library.

For all the strong, determined and loving women
in our family, especially our mother Gillian Evans,
our daughters Emily Murrell and Ella Forsyth,
and our niece Meg Humphrey

SEARCHING FOR CHARLOTTE

The Fascinating Story of
Australia's First Children's Author

KATE FORSYTH & BELINDA MURRELL

NLA PUBLISHING

The publishing imprint of the
National Library of Australia

Title: *Searching for Charlotte: The Fascinating Story
of Australia's First Children's Author*
Authors: Kate Forsyth and Belinda Murrell
ISBN: 9780642279699
Published by NLA Publishing
Canberra ACT 2600

**Books published by the National Library of Australia further the Library's objectives
to produce publications that interpret the Library's collection and contribute to the
vitality of Australian culture and history.**

Commissioning publisher: Susan Hall
Managing editors: Amelia Hartney and Katherine Crane
Editor: Diana Hill
Designer: Lisa White
Typesetter: transformer.com.au
Image coordinator: Jemma Posch
Production coordinator: Dian Gargano
Printed in Australia by CanPrint Communications Pty Limited

Find out more about NLA Publishing at nla.gov.au/national-library-publishing.

I dare say there are many wonderful things yet undiscovered

Charlotte Waring Atkinson,
A Mother's Offering to Her Children

CONTENTS

Prologue

A FAMILY OF STORYTELLERS

Written by Belinda

for that is the use of all learning:
to make us wiser and better

Charlotte Waring Atkinson

———⟫◆⟪———

I first fell in love with Charlotte as a child. My maternal grandparents, Nonnie and Papa, would tell us enthralling stories about our great-great-great-great-grandmother Charlotte de Waring Atkinson and her family. In my memory, Charlotte always shines as being clever, beautiful, rebellious and fiercely independent. Like a Jane Austen heroine. Even her name was romantic—de Waring, a reminder of her French aristocratic forebears. It was only later that we discovered that the 'de' in de Waring hadn't actually been used in centuries, but family stories are like that: romanticised, exaggerated and embellished.

We grew up in a family of storytellers and book lovers. Both my parents would tell fascinating, colourful anecdotes about their lives, their adventures and the people they met. My grandparents also told tantalising tales of long ago. Famously, our family motto was 'Never let the truth get in the way of a good story'.

Our mother, Gilly, always encouraged us to write. Almost from the time we could hold a pen, we wrote poems, plays, stories and novels, which we illustrated by hand in exercise books or typed up on our clackety old typewriter. Mum commissioned us to write poems for dinner party guests or stories for our grandparents for Christmas presents.

My sister Kate and I played wildly imaginative games, where we dressed up as characters from our favourite books and had sword fights up and down the stairs, or raided our mother's wardrobe for costumes for our theatre productions. Nick, our long-suffering younger brother, was dressed up and ordered to play the parts we required.

As tiny children we all had imaginary friends and made up exciting adventures for them. A favourite family story is that when I was three I caused a major ruckus on the Manly ferry when I insisted that my friend Sharn had been left behind. The captain was preparing to turn the ferry back when Mum, with the greatest embarrassment, had to confess to him that Sharn was a figment of my overactive imagination. Kate also had a whole family of magical siblings, while if any mischief was discovered, my brother Nick was very quick to blame it on the invisible and exceptionally naughty Andrew.

Undoubtedly it was this richly creative childhood that encouraged all three of us to become writers. Many people have suggested that writing must be in our blood. Or perhaps growing up in a family where there had been a history of multiple published authors gave us the confidence and courage to follow our dreams?

In the school holidays, Kate and I would often go and stay with Nonnie and Papa. We adored staying with them because, naturally, they spoiled us rotten. While normally we dressed in practical jeans and T-shirts, perfect for climbing trees and getting dirty, with our grandparents we always dressed in our very best clothes. We might be adorned in floaty floral sundresses or matching Mackenzie kilts to celebrate our Scottish ancestry. Our faces were scrubbed clean and our hair brushed and curled.

Nonnie and Papa often took us on a journey down to Sutton Forest in the Southern Highlands, to show us our family history and where we came from. On the long drive down, through Mittagong and Moss Vale, they would tell us romantic stories about our ancestors, the Atkinson family, who had once owned great swathes of this beautiful rolling countryside. They were fascinating stories of adventure, bravery, tragedy, determination and defiance.

In hindsight, there was a theme that ran through many of my grandmother's stories, and it was about the strong and clever women from whom we were descended. Women who faced almost impossible difficulties but who tackled them with courage, strength and dignity, and managed to live rich and meaningful lives. These stories were truly inspirational.

When at last we arrived at Sutton Forest, a small English-style village built around the church and an inn, we bumped along a rough dirt road until we came to an ancient line of elm trees and the locked gates of Oldbury. We would peer through the prickly hawthorn hedges at the grand old house that had been built by our great-great-great-great-grandparents Charlotte and James Atkinson in 1828. During our childhood, the golden sandstone house was surrounded by overgrown gardens and looked neglected and forlorn. It seemed like something out of a fairytale—romantic, forgotten by time.

We would visit the churchyard where the family were buried and try to read the faint script on the family vault. The elaborate stone vault had subsided into the marshy ground. It was so sad to think of those long-ago ancestors struck down by their various tragedies and misadventures.

My grandparents' stories of the Atkinsons were so vivid that it seemed as though we knew them all personally: artistic Charlotte, her first husband James, their three daughters Charlotte Elizabeth (our great-great-great-grandmother), Emily and Louisa, and their son James John. We felt we knew their personalities, their talents and weaknesses, their romances and their griefs and their triumphs. These stories had all been passed down from mother to child for over 150 years.

We heard about the romance between James and Charlotte, who met on board the ship that carried her from England to Australia to be a governess for the Macarthur family. He tipped his hat to her as he climbed the gangplank, and only three weeks later they were engaged to be married. It was love at first sight. They built their home together and named it 'Oldbury' after James' birthplace in Kent. For many years, Kate and I dreamed of travelling to England together to discover the special places in our family history. One of our many joys in researching this book was visiting the beautiful stone-and-red-brick Oldbury House, near Ightham, with its ancient oak trees and rambling gardens.

Charlotte was an outstanding teacher and schooled all four of her children herself, educating them to a standard that was extremely rare in the colony and indeed in England. Her passion for natural history was unusual for a woman of this time, and her scientific interests were wide ranging, covering zoology, ornithology, etymology, conchology, mineralogy, geology and botany. According to an article in *The Sydney Morning Herald*, she was *one of the most accomplished women of her era*.

When Charlotte was in dire financial straits and desperately needed funds to support her children, she wrote a book—the first children's book to be published in Australia. It may well have been inspired by her frustration that there were no children's books portraying Australian experiences for her children to read.

A Mother's Offering to Her Children was published anonymously in 1841 and is written as a dialogue between a mother and her four children. The book was released to critical acclaim and was immediately successful. To us now it may seem quaint and old-fashioned, with its early nineteenth-century conversation format, but it is important for so many reasons. It was the first time that an author wrote stories set in Australia featuring Australian children and adventures, historic events, natural science and Aboriginal culture. The book gives a rare insight into colonial domestic life and the unique role played by mothers in educating their children.

Charlotte Waring was a remarkable woman. She was a child prodigy; a fiercely independent, well-educated teacher; an early feminist; a loving mother with progressive views on girls' education, who brought her daughters up to be some of the finest scholars, artists and writers in the colony; a pioneer in the fight for women's legal rights; and a naturalist— as well as being the first Australian children's author.

Charlotte's career inspired her own daughters. Her eldest daughter, Charlotte Elizabeth, became an artist, writer and teacher, running her own school. Her youngest daughter, Louisa, became a celebrated naturalist, artist and the first Australian-born female novelist and journalist. The history of women writers in our family has continued all the way through to the current generation of our own children.

Charlotte Waring led an extraordinary life. Yet many of her experiences were mirrored in the lives of other colonial women whose stories have also been lost and ignored. The more Kate and I researched her life, the more we realised that there were many gaps and contradictions between the factual records and the family stories we were told. There were so many mysteries. What inspired her to leave England and seek her fortune as a governess on the other side of the world? Why did she marry George Barton, a violent alcoholic? What happened that fateful day in the bush when Charlotte was accosted by one of Australia's most notorious bushrangers?

The family stories of Charlotte have been a recurring theme through our childhood and into our own lives as writers, teachers, mothers and daughters. Over the years both of us have spoken many times at literary events about Charlotte's life, as well as writing articles and, in my case, a novel inspired by her family, called *The River Charm*. Yet there was still so much we didn't know.

There have been many occasions when, while experiencing tough times, I have thought of Charlotte and taken inspiration from her courage and determination. Kate and I hope that by sharing Charlotte's story we can shed light on her life and the experiences of other brave colonial women. The achievements of these invisible women deserve to be remembered and celebrated.

✍

What will we learn as we set off on our own voyage of discovery—searching for Charlotte? Our journey together as sisters will take us from trawling dusty archive boxes to drinking tea with far-flung relatives, four-wheel-driving through remote forests and river crossings, and discussing nineteenth-century etiquette with historians.

It will consume our lives, taking more than two years of intense research and writing. It will be incredibly frustrating and incredibly rewarding. As two strong-willed sisters we will disagree and debate and argue, but most of all we will be ecstatic with our discoveries.

The highlight is travelling together to England, with my 21-year-old daughter Emily and Kate's 15-year-old daughter Ella, to follow in the footsteps of Charlotte's early life, before she came to Australia in 1826. We explore the crowded laneways of London, hike the rolling green downs of Kent and wander the wild heathery moors of North Yorkshire. We can feel Charlotte's spirit touching us. We discover and learn so much about Charlotte, but also about ourselves and what it means to be sisters, mothers, daughters and writers. Our search for Charlotte becomes a family obsession and an inspirational journey.

Chapter 1

ALMOST AN ORPHAN

Written by Belinda

I was a tender-hearted child

Charlotte Waring Atkinson

———◆———

The story of Charlotte Waring's childhood reads like something out of a Jane Austen novel. Perhaps because Charlotte was born 21 years later than Jane, which meant her childhood was spent during the Georgian and Regency periods that we know so vividly from Austen's books. Charlotte's birthdate was halfway between those of two of my literary heroines—Jane Austen in 1775 and Charlotte Brontë in 1816.

Charlotte Waring was born in Marylebone, during a period of violent winter storms, on 13 February 1796. It may have been because of the wild weather that she was not christened until a month later, on 13 March, at St Marylebone Church.

Fittingly, it is wild and inclement weather when Kate and I set off to explore the streets of Marylebone, where Charlotte grew up, with our daughters Emily and Ella. The radio has announced a severe weather warning. Roads are flooded, traffic is in chaos and trains are cancelled.

It is not winter, though. It is early June, and we packed for summer sunshine, so we are stylishly dressed in thin denim jackets, and light shirts and pants. That morning, when I rang home, my husband had been delighted to tell me that it was 25 degrees in Sydney and my boys had been swimming at Manly beach. In London, we battle the commuter crowds in pouring rain with just one flimsy umbrella between us. We are soon soaked through and freezing. The girls are blue with cold but determined not to complain.

In the late eighteenth century when the Waring family lived here, Marylebone was a fashionable, semi-rural retreat for London's wealthy families, bounded by Oxford Street to the south and Marylebone Park (later The Regent's Park) to the north. The area was owned by the Duke of Portland, who transformed his farmland into a residential development called Portland Estate, with wide boulevards, elegant tree-lined streets, grand Georgian terrace houses and garden squares set in a grid pattern around Cavendish Square. Marylebone Park was the extensive parkland of the old manor house, which had been demolished in 1795.

To the south was the small village, jumbled on the banks of the Tyburn, around the medieval church of St Marylebone. The name was originally St Mary le Bourne, from the days when all self-respecting English aristocrats spoke French, while 'bourne' or 'burn' was an old word for stream. Further south again was the residential estate. This new, highly fashionable suburb ended at Marylebone Road. A few streets away, to the north of the Waring home in Upper Charlton Street, were sheep and cows grazing in green meadows, rustic farm cottages, and geese wandering the laneways. It was an idyllic escape from the crowded, stinking slums and city streets of London just a couple of miles away.

Surprisingly, there is still a remnant of this rural history. At lunchtime we take shelter at the Barley Mow, one of London's oldest pubs, just off Baker Street. The inn was built in 1790, to cater for local farmers bringing their produce to the London markets. The interior of the pub is quaint and charming, with wooden panelling, private inglenooks, fireplaces and steep narrow stairs, almost just as it was when the locals came here to spend their market profits in the eighteenth century. We are soaked, and frozen to the cockles of our hearts. As we dry off, over our homemade chicken-and-wild-mushroom pie, we laugh about how amazing it is that we are sitting in a pub built before Charlotte was even born, and that in those days it was surrounded by hay fields.

Unfortunately, we can't stay all afternoon in the warmth, so we head out again into the torrential rain, battling the crowds and jostling umbrellas. Half an hour later, I'm leading the way, head down as we plough through the squalls. We've walked more than ten kilometres in the rain. As we cross Cavendish Square, Kate calls out to me.

'Binny, I think we should stop now and get out of this miserable weather.'

'It's not far now. Just a few blocks,' I protest. 'We've so little time and so much still to see.' There is still a long list of places we'd hoped to visit today.

'I think we should go into a department store, get a cup of tea, get dry and buy some clothes more suitable for an English summer—like warm jumpers and raincoats!' jokes Kate.

Emily and Ella look hopefully at me. They are soaked to the skin and shivering with cold.

I sigh, admitting defeat. 'Okay.'

'We can try again tomorrow,' Kate suggests.

'But if we come back, we won't get everything done that we need to do tomorrow.'

Much to the girls' delight, we do some shopping for winter woollies, then retreat to our cousin Clare's terrace house in Wandsworth, feeling dejected and damp. Clare is the daughter of my beloved godmother, Rosalind, my mother's younger sister who died way too young.

Clare and her husband Fred cheer us up with French champagne and an Ottolenghi feast of grilled chicken accompanied by a delicious salad of barbecued corn, mint, parsley and coriander with lime and chilli. Clare asks us dozens of questions about our research, and it is lovely to share stories with someone who is also descended from Charlotte.

It is so wonderful to be here, with our extended family, around the kitchen table, warmed by the Aga stove. They have a gorgeous garden filled with roses and a huge cherry tree, with squirrels scampering in the trees and a fox who lives behind the garden shed, right in the middle of London. We are all delighted with the local wildlife, squealing every time a squirrel dashes across the lawn and desperately hoping to catch a glimpse of the urban fox.

We don't see Clare, Fred and their children Minnie and Ollie very often, but we immediately feel at home. Ignoring our jet lag, we stay up way too late, talking and laughing and sharing memories of our childhood growing up on Sydney's North Shore.

Fred promises us the weather will be better tomorrow. He is right. The rain stops and we try again, hoping to find the places where Charlotte and her extended family lived.

Our first stop is St Marylebone, the elegant church that the family attended in the early nineteenth century, with its ornate green, white and gilt interior and crystal chandeliers. We wander the church and I imagine what Charlotte's christening might have been like in 1796— filled with her proud family and their friends. Charlotte's beautiful mother Elizabeth, with her dark hair and dark eyes, wearing a high-waisted empire dress with feathers in her bonnet. Her father Thomas Albert clad in tight breeches tucked into boots, a high-necked cravat, a waistcoat and tails, standing proudly by the font, clutching his top hat and gloves. Charlotte's ten-year-old brother James would be dressed just like his father, while her sisters—Elizabeth, seven, and Letitia, three—would be in their best long white frocks with satin slippers. I imagine the extended Waring family would all be there, the tightly knit group of aunts and uncles, celebrating the birth of a much-loved child.

Charlotte was the fourth child of Thomas Albert, always known as Albert, and Elizabeth Turner Waring.

According to the stories that Charlotte told her own children, Elizabeth Turner *was 17 the day she married, of exquisite beauty & small stature. Her hair & eyes black.* She was so small as a child that her father, the Reverend Turner, had a pocket made in his greatcoat and *was able to carry her about with him while riding around the parish up to her third year.*

Albert Waring was born in Shoreham, Kent, where his family had lived for many generations. He was 20 when he and Elizabeth married in 1782 and *was remarkable for his handsome appearance. His hair according to the custom of the times flowed down his shoulders in natural curls. He was a good height & slender stature.*

Albert was a barrister but *was a man of fortune* so sufficiently wealthy that he didn't practise his profession. He *lived in London amusing himself with many pet birds & animals, and drawing, for which accomplishment he had great talent. His manners were gentle & disposition affectionate.*

According to stories told by my grandfather, Albert Waring's private zoo was one of the largest in London. During my childhood, I imagined this menagerie to be full of tame tigers and lions, who wandered around the garden like gentle house cats.

This is not as fanciful as it may seem. The sound of lions roaring was quite common in the wealthier suburbs of Georgian London. During the late eighteenth century, collecting exotic birds and animals was all the rage among wealthy aristocrats. Queen Charlotte, wife of 'mad' King George III, kept two zebras and an elephant in the stables at Buckingham House and started a craze for owning pet kangaroos.

In the 1780s and 1790s, there were numerous 'menagerists' selling everything from monkeys and peacocks, to antelopes, orangutans, giraffes, wolves, lions, tigers, leopards and camels.

In my family, we loved the idea of Albert having a private zoo, as we had our very own menagerie at home. Both my parents adored animals, and my father was a veterinary surgeon, so we always had plenty of pets. At various times we had four dogs, four cats, a lamb, calves, piglets, ducks, turtles, two ponies, a baby possum and even an orphan wallaby called Christabel—all wandering in the back garden or curled up in a corner of our family room.

Charlotte inherited her fine looks from her mother, particularly her small stature, black hair and dark eyes. From her father, she inherited an affectionate nature, her talent for drawing, a love of animals and a keen intellect. Charlotte was a child prodigy, reading fluently from the age of two.

Her early childhood sounds idyllic, adored by a loving and close family, living in a gorgeous and grand home filled with books, art, music and animals. Yet it was not to last.

Beautiful Elizabeth Waring gave birth to her fourth daughter, Jane, on 7 October 1798, and died soon after. Elizabeth was 33. Charlotte was just two years and eight months old. I can imagine the overwhelming shock and grief the family felt at so suddenly losing their beloved mother.

In eighteenth-century England, childbirth was a dangerous business. Many women made out their will as soon as they discovered they were pregnant. Nearly half the women who died had puerperal fever, an infection often spread by doctors who had not washed their hands or instruments between patients—so it was particularly common among the upper classes, who could afford a doctor to attend the birth. The infection usually set in two or three days after the birth.

Albert Waring was grief-stricken at the loss of his young wife. Shortly after Elizabeth's death, *when driving in a fog on Hounslow Heath—[he] met with an accident which rendered him an invalid for life. His companion was killed.*

At the age of 36, Albert was left a disabled single father with five young children.

When mothers died, it was common for the children to be sent away to be raised by a relative, just like Frank Churchill and Jane Fairfax in Jane Austen's *Emma*.

In the Waring children's case, three of the daughters—Elizabeth, aged nine, Charlotte, aged two, and baby Jane—were sent to live with their aunt Charlotte Waring Fisher.

We don't know what happened to twelve-year-old James or five-year-old Letitia. Perhaps they stayed with their father or were sent to live with other relatives, such as Aunt Letitia, who lived close by. In fact, the Waring papers don't mention James at all. For many years, we thought Charlotte's family had just four girls. It wasn't until I read Thomas Albert Waring's 1829 will that I realised there was an older son. Strangely for the time, James is named as a beneficiary but not as a witness or executor of his father's will. Charlotte's daughter Louisa doesn't mention James in her Waring family notes, yet she named all her cousins and many far-flung relatives whom she'd never met.

Was it just that James was ten years older and they were brought up in different households, so Charlotte didn't really know him? Or did Charlotte not get on with him? It seems strange that Charlotte's own children didn't know she had a brother.

This is one of the many mysteries that we will probably never solve.

Albert's sister Charlotte had married a merchant called John Fisher in 1792, when she was 32 years old. In 1795, she had a son called Robert, who died at birth. Three years later, Charlotte Fisher took in her three nieces and raised them as her own children.

According to Charlotte's stories, Aunt Fisher was a *handsome & stately woman* and her husband was *serious & remarkable for his great abilities & high principles.*

John Fisher is such a common name that it is hard to discover exactly where they lived. I spent weeks of research tracking Charlotte down to this point. Hours of getting lost down rabbit holes, only to find that I'd been following the wrong lead. For example, I followed another John Fisher, of Cossington, perhaps a cousin, who also married a Charlotte and had an only son who died. They moved to a beautiful estate called Brockhall, where he was the minister. I found gorgeous photos of the old rectory and imagined Charlotte and her sisters playing in the gardens. Yet further research revealed this was the wrong John and Charlotte Fisher, and that our Fisher family lived in London. This was just one of many, many frustrating wrong turns over many months.

Hours digging through London land tax records and archives revealed more clues. The extended Waring family were very close, with several aunts and uncles living within a few streets of Cavendish Square, including Albert's brother Ericus Waring and his sister Letitia Robinson.

A John Fisher esquire lived right in the heart of Marylebone during the early 1800s, in Henrietta Place. His neighbours included the Countess

Dowager of Guilford and the Countess of Mornington. I'd like to think that the girls lived there, just a few streets from their father's house.

In London, we set off on a walking tour to visit the streets where the various members of the family lived. We start with Henrietta Place, just off Cavendish Square, where we think the Fishers lived. Just on the other side of Cavendish Square is Margaret Street, where Albert's younger brother Ericus lived with his wife Mary.

When we look around us, we see taxis, cars and buses, puddles and crowds of commuters. When we look up, we see grand Georgian mansions, turrets and elegant six-storey townhouses, much as they were in the eighteenth century.

About half a mile away was Upper Charlton Street (now called Hanson Street), where Charlotte's father was living in 1805. He later moved a couple of streets away to Cirencester Place (now Great Titchfield Street), and his sister Letitia Robinson lived just around the corner. While the homes where Albert Waring lived are no longer there, having been replaced by modern buildings, we get a strong sense of the opulence of nineteenth-century Marylebone from the neighbouring terraced townhouses that survive. Seeing the grandeur and size of these mansions we get an insight into just how wealthy Charlotte's family was.

The extended Waring family all lived so close to one another that I can imagine them getting together regularly for dinners, musical evenings, picnics in the park and afternoon tea, as well as socialising at St Marylebone Church every Sunday.

It was so exhilarating to stand on old Upper Charlton Street, knowing that Charlotte would have walked the same street, seen the same buildings and felt the rain on her face, just like us. Charlotte's London would have been just as charming, chaotic and noisy as modern-day Marylebone, and it made me wonder how she felt about leaving busy, exciting, stimulating London for quiet, provincial, colonial Sydney. Even more removed was the wilderness of Oldbury, with its exotic Aboriginal people, strange flora and fauna, violent bushrangers and unruly convicts.

From gentry to governess

Buried deep in the archives at Sydney's Mitchell Library is a folder containing a sheaf of loose pages, inscribed in elegant nineteenth-century calligraphy. Kate and I have come to read these fragile, difficult-to-decipher pages as our first act of research together. The first page is headed by the words *Warrenne Waring*, beautifully drawn and coloured.

The opening lines read: *The Warings are descended from the Norman family of de Warenne. William de Warenne came to England with William the Conqueror. The name has been corrupted into Waring within the last two hundred years.* A brief family history follows, written in 1872 by our great-great-great-great aunt, Louisa Atkinson, the first Australian-born female novelist, for a baby daughter she would never see grow up.

Louisa's family history is fascinating, but incomplete, so we must do many months of research to fill in the gaps.

According to correspondence in *The Gentleman's Magazine* of 1793, the Warings were *an ancient family*. Like most members of the privileged English upper classes, Charlotte had been brought up with proud stories of her family history and a knowledge of her family tree, going back for hundreds of years. Charlotte shared stories of her family history with her own children, stretching all the way back to William de Warenne from Normandy. I can remember my own grandmother and mother telling me stories about Charlotte de Waring's aristocratic ancestors, who came from France to fight at the Battle of Hastings in 1066.

The de Warenne family flourished in England as earls of Surrey, with vast landholdings covering many counties, from Sussex to Yorkshire.

Charlotte Waring's family descended from one of the junior branches, who, during the fourteenth, fifteenth and sixteenth centuries, held substantial estates north and south of Wolverhampton, in Staffordshire— including Lea Hall, a half-timbered manor house with a defensive moat and a dovecote, which was the family seat for many generations.

The family were then known as the Warynges de la Lea. The Norman surname de Warenne had become de Warynge by 1309, and was then anglicised to Warynge, or Waringe, about 1330. The Warynges de la Lea were members of the landed gentry, knights and armigers with the right to carry a coat of arms.

During the seventeenth and eighteenth centuries, the Warings moved south to Kent, owning large estates near Shoreham. The quaint village of Shoreham is set on the banks of the River Darent, around the twelfth-century stone church of St Peter and St Paul.

Kate and I rent a farm cottage near Shoreham, in the middle of the Kent Downs Area of Outstanding Natural Beauty, so we can explore the region where our ancestors lived for so many years. The countryside is gorgeous—rolling wheat fields sprinkled with scarlet poppies and blue cornflowers, hedgerows of wild pink roses, banks of lavender and thick woodland. Mossy stone bridges cross the River Darent, beside ancient fords. The country laneways are narrow and winding, with high hedgerows and leafy beech-tree tunnels, designed for horse and cart, not for cars.

As we explore this beautiful countryside, Kate and I discuss how we can feel a strong ancestral pull. On one of our long walks, we pass the ruins of an ancient Roman villa, as well as Lullingstone Castle and Preston—the extensive estate where our own ancestors once lived.

Charlotte's great-great-grandfather Richard Waring and his wife Catherine lived at Preston manor house, north of Shoreham, with their

17 children. They owned multiple tenanted farms and cottages around the area, which, after their death, were divided between their eight sons.

Charlotte's grandfather, Thomas, was *a man of property and style driving in London a carriage and four grey horses.* Only the very wealthy could afford their own carriages in London. In Georgian times, one quality carriage horse cost about £100 and about £120 per annum to keep in London, while a carriage cost about £400. At this time, the average farmer earned between £15 and £20 per year, and more than 90 per cent of families earned less than £100 per year.

Thomas and Jane Waring built a large house at number 1 High Street, Shoreham. They also owned smaller Lilac Cottage up the road, and Oxbourne Farm on the Darent. Thomas and Jane had six surviving children, with Thomas Albert being the second youngest. Only the eldest son, Robert, stayed in Shoreham, with the others moving to Marylebone.

The four of us love discovering the countryside about Shoreham. We explore on foot and by car, loudly singing old classics as we drive along—'Marianne' by Leonard Cohen, 'These Boots Are Made for Walking' by Nancy Sinatra and 'Sisters Are Doin' It for Themselves' by the Eurythmics, as well as modern favourites by Ed Sheeran, Imagine Dragons and Passenger. We hunt through churchyards, discovering ancient gravestones, wander down impossibly green country lanes looking for old family landholdings and hike through meadows brimming with wildflowers. I am so excited when we find Woodlands House, a large manor house once owned by William Waring, Charlotte's second cousin. We feel like detectives on a treasure hunt, finding the places that are part of Charlotte's family history. Each new discovery fills us with euphoria, as our months of research finally pay off.

Emily and Ella collect English wildflowers—cornflowers, purple heather, buttercups, pink valerian and wild hedge roses—which they artfully press between the pages of their journals. Kate buys the girls a flower press to preserve their treasures properly, just as Charlotte used to do with her own daughters. Just as Kate and I used to do when we were children.

In the evenings we cook beautiful meals on the tricky English Aga stove—hearty pasta dishes, chicken Provençal, ratatouille and spicy lamb ragout. The four of us sit around the kitchen table, sipping wine, discussing our discoveries and planning our itinerary for the next day.

On Thursday, we spend the day with our mother's second cousin, Jan Gow, a professional genealogist from New Zealand, who has come to Kent to visit some of the important Waring and Atkinson sites with us. Jan has spent many years researching our family tree. She confirms many of our genealogical findings, which is very reassuring.

We all love hearing her stories. Jan tells us that the women of our family, for many generations—from Charlotte Waring, to her daughter Charlotte Elizabeth Atkinson, to *her* daughter Flora McNeilly—all had a reputation for being clever, tough, resilient and strong. They were women who knew what they wanted and were determined to achieve it. Jan's stories are inspiring, and Kate and I are thrilled that our daughters Emily and Ella are hearing them first-hand from an older relative.

Jan also delights in telling us about some of our other famous distant relatives, including Winston Churchill, Charles Darwin and Diana, Princess of Wales, who like us were all descended from Thomas Warynge de la Lea, born in 1530. Apparently, Princess Diana was his 12 x great-granddaughter.

Jan takes us to meet local historian Brenda Copus, who, together with her late husband Geoffrey, spent decades researching the history of local families such as the Warings of Woodlands House. Brenda had told her neighbour, a local BBC Radio journalist, about our visit, and we are surprised to hear that our story of searching for Charlotte has been discussed on Sevenoaks local radio.

One of the questions that we are keen to answer is why Charlotte was reduced to earning her living as a governess from such a young age, when her family was once so wealthy.

The history books tell us that Charlotte's childhood was a time of social and political unrest in Europe. The French Revolution spanned the years 1789 to 1799, toppling the monarchy of King Louis XVI and Queen Marie Antoinette and throwing France into a period of violent upheaval. Thousands of French emigrants fled to England, and many of the wealthier aristocratic refugees settled in Marylebone, close to where the Warings lived. Charlotte probably learned her fluent French from an aristocratic émigré.

Britain was at war with France almost continuously from 1793, after the execution of King Louis XVI, until the Battle of Waterloo in 1815, when the Duke of Wellington defeated Napoleon Bonaparte. Throughout the wars, the English feared the very real threat of invasion. France attempted to invade Britain via Ireland in 1796, the year Charlotte was born, and again in 1798, the year her mother died.

The long periods of war caused severe economic distress in Britain, resulting in loss of trade, increased taxes, raging inflation and mass unemployment. Many small businesses went bankrupt and families were starving. The exorbitant cost of grain led to violent food riots, which the aristocracy feared would turn to revolution, as had happened in France.

A series of bank failures left many wealthy families penniless. This economic upheaval also impacted the Waring family fortunes. Charlotte's father Albert inherited substantial wealth, but some time during the Napoleonic Wars he lost his fortune.

Chapter 2

A KENTISH MAN

Written by Kate

In the midst of their boyish pursuits, [the brothers] exhibited
marks of what they would ... be in after years

'Peter Prattle'

Oldbury Hill

In 1805, when Charlotte Waring was living in London, the boy who
would one day be her husband was growing up in Kent, only 30-odd
miles away as the crow flies. She was nine, and he was ten-and-a-half.

James' father—also called James—had been born in Soho, London,
on 29 September 1756, and married a Derbyshire woman named
Elizabeth Stuart Fox in February 1786. They set up their home in Butt
Lane, Deptford, where James senior worked as a shipwright.

Founded by Henry VIII in 1513, Deptford Dockyard was the most
significant royal dockyard of the Tudor period, Neil McCormack, our
mother's second cousin, tells us. Neil has a long interest in naval history
and is the guardian of an extraordinary collection of private family
papers that he has kindly shared with us. It was at Deptford that Francis
Drake was knighted by Queen Elizabeth I on board his ship the *Golden*

Hind, and it was here that Walter Raleigh flung down his cloak so that the Queen would not muddy her shoes. Christopher Marlowe was stabbed to death in a tavern nearby, and Russian Tsar Peter the Great came to Deptford in 1698 to learn from the English master shipwrights.

In the summer of 1768, HMS *Endeavour* was refitted at Deptford for James Cook's famous voyage of discovery. It cost £2,294, almost the price of the ship itself. Almost two years later—on 29 April 1770— HMS *Endeavour* was the first European vessel to land on the east coast of *Terra Australis*, in the country of the Gweagal and Bidjigal peoples of the Dharawal Eora nation. Its landing place is now known as Botany Bay, New South Wales, Australia.

It is possible that James senior—who was then 12 years old—saw the *Endeavour* set sail from the dockyards, and was inspired by its many white sails and fluttering flags to learn how to build such a beautiful ship. Or perhaps he was the son of a shipwright. An apprentice paid every penny he earned during the seven years of his training to his master, so it was usually a craft passed from father to son, Neil tells us.

At that time, the dockyard at Deptford employed 400 or more shipwrights. They built and repaired ships, but also dismantled old vessels, salvaging timber. James Atkinson senior would have worked from daylight to dusk, handling heavy tools like adzes, axes, mallets and hacksaws, for around three shillings per day.

Three daughters, Jane, Elizabeth and Mary Ann, were born to James senior and Elizabeth between 1787 and 1790. Two years later, at the age of 36, James suddenly gave up his job at the docks to buy a farm in Kent.

We do not know what prompted this abrupt change. It is possible James senior inherited money. A man named Samuel Atkinson had made his fortune in the naval services in the early eighteenth century, and—dying childless in 1718—left everything to his grand-nephew, also named Samuel Atkinson. James senior's father Samuel was born around that time, and so may have been the lucky beneficiary of this bequest, passing it down in turn to his son.

Or the Atkinsons may have been concerned about the health of their daughters. Their youngest, Mary Ann, was clearly delicate, for she died less than two years after the move to Kent, aged only three.

James Atkinson was born a few months later, on 31 July 1794, at Oldbury, a small settlement in the Weald, the undulating green valley that lies between the embracing arms of the North and South Downs. It sits at the foot of Oldbury Hill, where people have lived for more than 50,000 years, leaving behind hand-hewn flint tools as the earliest evidence of their existence. In the first century BC, a local Celtic tribe built a massive fort on the summit of the hill. Made from a ring-shaped bank of earth, wooden gates barred its entrances. One of these gates was burned to ashes, perhaps at the time of Julius Caesar's invasion of Britain in 55 BC. It is this fort that gives Oldbury Hill its name: from the Saxon 'eald' meaning 'old', and 'byrig' meaning 'fortified place'.

As Kent is only 50 kilometres from France, the Romans were just one of many invading armies. Indeed, our ancestor William de Warenne would have passed Oldbury Hill as William the Conqueror's troops travelled the old pilgrims' way to Winchester after the Battle of Hastings.

The Norman invasion of 1066 is the source of long rivalry between those born on opposing sides of the Medway River, which divides the county in half. Anyone born on the eastern shore is called a man of Kent. Anyone born to the west is called a Kentish man.

According to legend, when William the Conqueror travelled through the county, the men of Kent prevented him from passing into their lands, offering him a choice of a branch of greenery (which meant a treaty) or a sword (which meant war). William chose the branch, and so agreed the people of East Kent could keep certain rights and customs if they would accept him as their king.

Being born on the western side of the river, James was a Kentish man—or, rather, a Kentish lad, as boys of the time were called.

When Elizabeth Atkinson went into labour in the summer of 1794, the world was convulsed with the terror of the French Revolution. King Louis XVI had lost his head the year before, and England was at war with France. Three days before James Atkinson was born, Maximilien Robespierre—the architect of the Terror—was denounced and guillotined, along with 21 of his followers.

Revolutionary ideals had spread across the Channel. Thomas Paine published *The Rights of Man* in 1791–1792, selling more than a million copies. Ordinary working people began to call for reform, but the government responded with harsh repression that led to riots. James was therefore born at a time of immense change and uncertainty. Charles Dickens famously called it *the best of times … the worst of times … the age of wisdom … the age of foolishness … the season of Light … the season of Darkness … the spring of hope … the winter of despair.*

Elizabeth Atkinson, still grieving the death of her little girl a few months earlier, must have held her baby son close, fearing for his future and her own.

She could never have imagined how far he would travel in pursuit of his fortune.

When I first travelled to England with my husband and kiddies in March 2006, researching a series of children's novels set during the English Civil War, I made a pilgrimage to Oldbury Hill, looking for my ancestor's birthplace. I remember the electric thrill of excitement I felt at the first sight of Kent's green skeins of hills and meadows and forests, punctuated with tall church spires and the square crenellations of castles.

I felt a profound connection to the landscape, even though I had never been there before. Was it because of all the British books that I read as a child, full of nightingales and snow, the works of Edith Nesbit and C.S. Lewis and Enid Blyton and Frances Hodgson Burnett? Was it because I knew my ancestors had once walked these roads and gazed across these mist-wreathed meadows? Or did my blood and bones carry my ancestors' memories, an epigenetic inheritance of belonging and yearning and loss?

I do not know. I only know I recognised my country, the land of my ancestors, the cradle of my story.

To be rooted is perhaps the most important and least recognised need of the human soul, the French philosopher Simone Weil wrote in 1942, while living in exile in London. I have always longed to be deeply rooted into a landscape. I dream of a river like a ribbon of quicksilver winding past an old house with a long story, an orchard of gnarled apple trees growing among wildflowers, a secret garden of roses and foxgloves and forget-me-nots, an iron gateway that leads into a dark enchanted wood where the trees whisper secrets, and, far away, my blue remembered hills.

I always say I am searching for Narnia.

In my first pilgrimage to Kent in 2006, I knew only that James Atkinson had been born at Oldbury. Our grandmother used to say their home had been called Oldbury Manor, and so as a child I liked to imagine a stately castle with turrets and crenellations like Moonacre Manor in one of my favourite books, *The Little White Horse*, by Elizabeth Goudge.

I found Oldbury Hill on the huge fold-out paper map, and then the narrow line below it that read Oldbury Lane. 'That's where it'll be!' I cried, and directed my husband as best I could through the narrow, winding streets of little villages with charming names like Cotman's Ash and Ivy Hatch. At last we found the turnoff to Oldbury Lane and drove along it, gazing about us with interest. There was no grand stately house, only a few small cottages, and my heart sank with disappointment.

Then we drove past a beautiful fifteenth-century timber-framed farmhouse named Oldbury Hall. 'This must be it!' I cried to my husband, and we stopped the car and scrambled out and took some photos. It made sense that the name of the house could have been changed as it was passed down through the family. Although it was nowhere near as grand as I had imagined, Oldbury Hall was still utterly picturesque. I was delighted to think that my great-great-great-great-grandfather had once lived there.

Fourteen years later, I show Binny a photograph I have found on the internet (the one I had taken was lost long ago).

'Isn't it gorgeous?' I exclaim.

'It's too grand,' Binny replies. 'James Atkinson's father wasn't rich, you know. It was only a small landholding.' She reminds me that there had been 14 freeholders at Oldbury in the 1790s, and five of them had paid more land tax than the Atkinsons. And she doesn't remember Nonnie telling us about Oldbury Manor. She thinks I'm glamorising.

'Oldbury Hall is not grand,' I answer rebelliously. 'They could have lived there.'

It is a medieval Kentish hall house, which meant it was originally built as one long room with a high ceiling of vaulted oak beams, blackened with smoke from the hearth in the centre of the floor. The walls were whitewashed wattle-and-daub, and the steep pitched roof would have been thatched. There might have been a small parlour at one end and a pantry at the other, or even perhaps the piggery. By the 1790s, a second floor would have dissected the great hall, creating a series of small attic rooms up in the rafters, and fireplaces would have been installed, with tall brick chimneys.

'It wouldn't have been very luxurious in James' day,' I tell Binny. 'Hall houses were built for the common people, not the rich.'

She is not convinced.

I badly wanted Oldbury Hall to be the place where James had been born, partly because of its old-world charm and partly because I had been so excited to find it on my first-ever visit to England.

So I set out to prove it. I studied old parish records online until my eyes felt like holes burned in paper by a poker. I emailed the local history societies and libraries, and scoured old books and newspapers. I asked my mother and her cousins if they remembered any old oral stories about James' birthplace. I even hired a local historian to do some digging for me. She was able to confirm that the Atkinsons had lived in the Oldbury part of Ightham from 1792, but was unable to find the exact address. It's very disappointing.

Months later, digging around in the archives at the National Library of Australia in Canberra, I find a letter written to Janet Cosh, Louisa Atkinson's granddaughter, in March 1967, by another remote cousin, called Lucy. She writes that *the aunts always said the family lived at Oldbury Manor.*

This makes me laugh out loud. I show it to Binny. 'See, I wasn't making it up!'

We both grin, thinking of the many ways oral history is garbled as it is passed down through the generations.

My daughter Ella was not yet two years old during that first pilgrimage to Oldbury. She had her second birthday a few days after we got back to Sydney.

I wrote in my diary:

it really is the most delightful age. She's such a gorgeous little thing ... lots of fine, silky curls, big blue eyes, a dimple, a cheeky grin and wicked laugh, and very taking ways. She insists on dragging her tattered little elephant round with her more than ever—it gets filthy every day and then she cannot bear to wait until it gets washed.

I write a list of how many words she can speak: 'play, Mumma!'; 'where Dada gone?'; 'what's dat?' 'Ow-ees' means shoes. 'Where baby mine?' means 'where's my elephant?'

In that long-ago trip to Oldbury, I had to tie her baby elephant to her with a ribbon, in fear of it being lost forever. When I washed the raggedy old thing, I would peg it low on the drying rack so she could sit and hold its trunk, sucking her thumb while it dried.

Now my daughter has turned 15 and is as tall as me. Ella is just the age Charlotte was when she first began work as a governess. I cannot imagine sending my girl off to live with strangers. Expecting her to care for other people's children, responsible for teaching and disciplining them, lying awake at night listening to the strange noises of a house that was not her home. I imagine how lonely and unhappy she would be. Fifteen is such a vulnerable age.

I think of one of Sappho's verses:

I have a fair daughter
with a form like golden flowers,
Cleïs the belovedest
whom I cherish more than all Lydia.

Sappho wrote that poem in Greece two-and-a-half thousand years ago, but I know exactly the tender love she felt for her daughter.

I am so enjoying having our daughters along with us on our trip to England. My daughter Ella and Binny's daughter Emily are six years apart in age, but they have grown up together and are very close. Our families live only ten minutes away from each other, and it is rare for a week to go by without a visit between our houses.

The two girls are sharing a room at the quaint old farmhouse where we are staying. At night, as I lie in my bed writing in my journal, I can hear them talking and laughing through the thick walls. It makes me smile. I remember when Binny and I shared a room as little girls. I was scared of the dark, and Binny used to come and curl up on the end of the bed and tell me stories until I fell asleep. Sometimes we'd whisper and giggle long into the night, just like our daughters now.

The next day we are up early to explore. We walk for kilometres through the enchantingly misty but muddy landscape, searching for any traces of Charlotte, then plod back to our car, tired out and damp to the skin. Part of us yearns for a glass of wine and a bowl of hot soup by the fire, but we have come so far and have so much to see.

'Shall we go to Oldbury?' I ask eagerly. Binny agrees. We turn the heater and the music up, and drive through long green cathedrals of beech trees, down winding roads hidden deep between tangled hedgerows, through tiny villages set about tiny churches, and past quaint oast-houses with conical roofs that make me squeal with excitement.

By the time we reach Oldbury Hill, it is absolutely pelting down. We pass a charming gatehouse that guards a formal entrance to a manor hidden behind tall hedges and trees. The name plaque reads 'Oldbury Place'.

'Maybe?' I say.

'Far too grand,' Binny says, and I have to agree.

I take a photograph through the rain-smeared windscreen, nonetheless.

Down a narrow steep road, past some brash new builds, and then swooping up to Oldbury Lane and a row of workers' cottages named Oldbury Cotts, tiny gardens brimming with delphiniums and columbines.

'Too small,' I say firmly, and—laughing—Binny concurs.

We turn right, and find Oldbury Hall, just as ancient and romantic as I remember.

'Don't you think …?' I venture.

'It's too big,' Binny says gently. She knows how much I love it.

I nod reluctantly, but gaze back at it longingly as Binny turns our car around in the narrow lane. We edge past a recently converted barn named—of course—Oldbury Barn.

'No, too new,' we agree.

At the end of the lane, the road turns abruptly to the right. I do not remember driving so far last time I came. On the corner there is a beautiful old house, built of red brick and stone, with a mossy tiled roof. Smoke drifts from a tall chimney into the misty air. Water drips from every leaf. A small green sign says, 'Oldbury House'.

'This is much more likely,' Binny says.

'It's very pretty,' I say, and take a multitude of photos from the laneway just in case.

Binny drives down the lane, and we see an old oast-house that has been converted into a house. We know, from the notes left by Louisa Atkinson's granddaughter Janet Cosh, that James senior was a hop-grower as well as a farmer.

'Perhaps this was their oast-house?' Binny wonders.

Across the road is an old shed. It is almost hidden behind ferns and lacy wildflowers. Its tiled roof is thick with moss, and its rough brick-and-stone walls are overgrown with ivy. The roofline is level with my hip. A weatherbeaten wooden sign reads 'Oldbury Farmhouse'.

'Could this be it?' I ask, with a thrill of excitement.

'It could be,' Binny says, with just as much excitement.

A narrow brick path leads down beside the shed to a house hidden behind thick trees and shrubbery. All we can see are glimpses. Stone rubble walls. Steeply pitched tiles. Cream-hatched windows set in mellow red brick. All framed in dark leaves, dripping with rain and wreathed with mist.

I do not know if this is the house where my great-great-great-great-grandfather was born. It occurs to me that we can only ever see the past in such brief, misty glimpses. As I climb back into the car I am both cold and damp, but also flushed with excitement and joy.

Somewhere along this muddy lane, my ancestor was born. He would have toddled along, hand-in-hand with his mother, perhaps clutching a beloved toy in his chubby hand. He would have learned to say 'Mumma' and 'Dada' and 'what you doing?' and 'more!' Perhaps he sat on his mother's knee by the fire, as she told him stories of his ancestors, just as Charlotte told her children, and Binny and I tell ours.

As we drive back over rain-swept Oldbury Hill to that glass of wine and that bowl of hot soup by the fire, I feel very close to my ancestors, as if they walked beside me, showing us the way.

Back in Sydney, I write to the owners of the houses we thought most likely. The week the manuscript for our book is due—when I thought all our astonishing discoveries had been made—I receive an answer from Meg, one of the owners of Oldbury Farmhouse.

She tells me that their beautiful home used to be called Oldbury Manor Farmhouse, until her parents shortened it some 50 years ago. It had once been part of the estate of Ightham Court, which lies about two-and-a-half kilometres from the farmhouse and from Oldbury Hill. It is a glorious Grade II listed manor house with crenellations and a tower, set in formal gardens and woodland, much as I had always imagined James' birthplace to be.

The history of Oldbury Manor Farmhouse has been researched by a friend of the family. It mentions a Mr Adkinson who had once lived next door, in Oldbury House, the beautiful old stone-and-red-brick house set right at the foot of Oldbury Hill.

I read her email at six o'clock in the morning, and have to restrain myself from ringing Binny right away. I send her an email: *Ring me when you're awake!*

At last she rings, and I can tell her that we've found the place where James was born at last.

Laughing, I say: 'you were right!'

'I knew it!' she cries, just as excited as I am.

Mereworth

In 1796, when James was two years old, his family moved seven miles away to the richer pastures of Mereworth, a fertile valley to the south, through which the Medway River winds.

His younger brother John was born there in 1797.

It is clear from his later career that James learned a great deal about farming and brewing during these formative years in the hop gardens and orchards of Mereworth. I imagine the four children helping their mother churn butter, gathering eggs from the chickens, hoeing the vegetable patch, feeding the orphaned lambs in spring.

In September, the lanes and roads would have been choked with wandering travellers come to harvest the hops. All day they worked in the hot sun, picking the hop blossoms. As the sun went down, horse-drawn wagons clopped along the sunken lanes to the oast-houses, where the flower cones were spread to dry in the heat of a fire laid in a hearth below. The hop-scented air rose through the cowl in the roof, which swung with the wind. At the end of the season there would be a great feast, and a king and queen of the hop fields would be chosen to lead the dance.

I imagine James and his brother and sisters gathering apples from the orchard for their mother to make apple tarts. They would head out with baskets to gather hazelnuts and blackberries from the hedgerows, and bore holes in chestnuts to make shining conkers. Perhaps, like the family in Edith Nesbit's classic novel *Five Children & It*, they decided *to dig a hole through … to Australia. These children, you see, believed that the world was round, and that on the other side the little Australian boys and girls were really walking wrong way up, like flies on the ceiling, with their heads hanging down into the air.*

In winter, the four children would have sat cross-legged before the fire, roasting withered apples on sticks, while their mother Elizabeth sewed and their father puffed on his pipe and read out accounts of the war from *The Times*. I can see James heating a penny in a candle flame so he could melt a peephole in the frost-flowers that grew over the windows. Perhaps he skated on the pond, or had snowball fights with his brother.

As James grew from a Kentish lad to a Kentish man, his life would not have been all fun and games. It is clear from his later writings that he was well-educated, which was unusual for the son of a farmer. Brian Fletcher, his biographer, believes he may have attended Counter Hill Academy in Deptford, located at the site where Goldsmiths College now stands.

Wherever it was that James received his education, by the time he was 16 years old he was employed as an under-clerk at the shipbuilding yard at Deptford, where his father had once worked. In those years, Napoleon Bonaparte crowned himself emperor of France and set out to conquer the world.

In her novel *Persuasion*, Jane Austen wrote: *Many a noble fortune has been made during the war.* Perhaps James was hoping to win such prosperity for himself when he left his father's farm and moved to Deptford?

He was still so young, not much older than Charlotte—and, like her, expected to make his own way in the world.

The day we plan to explore Mereworth, it is once again cold and rainy and windy. I think sadly of my suitcase, full of pretty summer dresses and sandals that have not yet been worn, and pull on my muddy jeans and boots once more.

Our mother's second cousin, Jan Gow, has come to join us for the day. She is the former president of the New Zealand Society of Genealogists, and our family tree owes a great deal to her tireless digging. We show her around our little farmhouse, then head out on the next stage of our adventure, talking all the way.

'I often think of how strong Charlotte was,' Jan says. 'Whenever I need to do anything hard, I think of Charlotte and what she went through. It gives me courage.'

Mereworth is not as old and quaint as some Kentish villages, because the local lord—the Honourable John Fane, the seventh earl of Westmorland—had the old church and village knocked down when he built a grand Palladian manor house in the 1720s. The Earl built a new church and village just over half a mile away, out of sight. Stables were erected over the site of the old church and its graveyard.

St Lawrence is a beautiful church, with a dramatic soaring spire and a neoclassical portico. James senior and his wife Elizabeth are buried in its churchyard. Jan remembers visiting their grave many years earlier, and we hope to find it again. We wander through the headstones, huddled into our coats against the rain, but cannot find any mention of the Atkinsons. The church is all locked up and the street is empty, so we cannot ask for advice.

Jan says, 'I seem to remember their headstone was flat.'

That narrows the field, as most of the headstones are upright. She finds one that lies horizontally, and bends over to read the engraving. 'It's not this one,' she says.

Binny calls out. 'Here's a flat one.'

I go over to join her. The gravestone is level with the ground, and so overgrown with moss and weeds that the inscription can hardly be seen. It's too rainy to put my glasses on, so I kneel down in the mud and peer more closely.

'I think that's an A … and that could be a T.' I find a sharp-pointed stick and scratch away the moss. 'I think it says ATKINSON!'

Jan and the girls hurry to join us. Emily and Ella together slowly excavate the inscription, using broken sticks and twigs. Gradually the words emerge from under centuries of moss and lichen. It reads:

Elizabeth, wife of

JAMES ATKINSON

Of this parish

Departed this life

Aged 71 years

Also in memory of the above named

James Atkinson

Who departed this life

January 5th 1828

Aged 72

It is such a powerful moment of discovery and connection. We pick wildflowers and lay them on our great-great-great-great-great-grandparents' grave, feeling closer to them than ever before.

I wake the next morning to blackbirds singing, and the sun shining in long rays through the mist. It is so wonderful to see blue sky, though the air is crisp as a new apple. We get on the road early, eager to take advantage of the sunshine to continue exploring Mereworth, as the rainstorm had cut our expedition short (again!) the previous day.

We have one or two small clues about where James might have lived as a lad, found for us by Gillian, the local historian who had dug through the archives on our behalf.

We know the Mereworth property was larger and richer than that at Oldbury, and that in his will James Atkinson senior had given his children first refusal on his land. His daughter Jane and her husband Charles Goodwin took up the offer. The 1851 census (taken 23 years after James senior's death) shows them living at a property called Swayhorne. Gillian has sent me a small heritage map that shows its location.

Unfortunately, it was emailed to me after I'd left home, and so I was only able to download it on my phone. It shows a small golden star marked on the B2016, which was once called Seven Mile Lane. We park our car at the pub and walk down the verge of the road, but trucks and buses and cars zoom past at frightening speed, spraying us with dirty water and sharp-edged pebbles. We take refuge in a small lane, the hedgerows embroidered with wild roses and blackberry flowers. It seems to curve to the south, where we want to go, and it is much more pleasant walking through the countryside than along the highway, so we set off with a pleasurable sensation of derring-do. Stands of oak and beech and flowering elder hang over the road, and to the south the land falls away in gentle layers of vibrant green.

As we had hoped, the land curved round and led us down the hill. A green pond lies before us, dappled with waterlilies. A sign reads: 'Swanton Cottage'.

A thrill runs through us. This is the name of the cottage that James had built in 1827 on the Oldbury estate in New South Wales.

'James must have lived near here!' Binny exclaims. 'He's named everything at Oldbury after places that were special to him in Kent.'

It's exhilarating confirmation that we are on the right track. We follow the muddy road through the trees, imagining James and John coming here to fish as boys. It leads to a little house amid blazing meadows of buttercups, where we take a multitude of photographs with the girls. I hold one under Ella's chin and tell her she must like butter.

'What?' she asks, confused.

I explain that in old English folklore, if yellow is reflected onto your skin from the shiny petals of the buttercup it means you like eating butter.

She thinks this is hilarious. 'The things you know!' she cries.

I've given my phone over to Ella, who has been our navigator since we arrived on English soil. After a lot of scouting round and comparing the heritage map on my phone with the electronic map on hers, we find a big Georgian mansion in a huge garden, just where Swayhorne is marked on the map. It is now named Graythwaite Lodge, and has a flight of stairs leading up to a white portico, with two big sashed windows on either side and three above. There's an enormous copper beech in the garden, and clipped hedges, and sweet-scented lavender by the steps.

'It looks like Oldbury,' I say, and pull up an image on my phone to compare.

'Maybe James' father built it?' Binny says. 'And then, when James moved to Australia, he was inspired to build his new house in the same style.'

We do not know. I push open the gate and rather timidly go to knock on the front door, but no one is home. So we walk back through the pretty country lanes to the eighteenth-century pub where we'd left our car. It's now called 'The Moody Mare', but inside it looks exactly how I imagine it might have when James was a boy living just down the road. I order sausages and mash with gravy, and a tankard of cider, the closest thing to traditional Kentish food on the menu, and we raise a toast to our ancestor, whose footsteps we'd been following all day.

Chapter 3

THE GOVERNESS TRADE

Written by Belinda

I was very fond of rambling about in the woods, or forests
Charlotte Waring Atkinson

———◆———

When Albert Waring lost his fortune, Charlotte's privileged life changed dramatically. The first clue is that in 1806, at the age of ten, Charlotte was sent away to school. In the early nineteenth century, girls of Charlotte's class did not go to school. They were educated at home by a governess, with the help of specialist masters, who would teach them all the accomplishments expected of a genteel young lady.

Instead, Charlotte was sent to a 'superior' boarding school, run by Mrs Brown in Bromley in Kent, not far from Shoreham. Before we visit Bromley, I have imagined it as it was when Charlotte lived here—a small, rural market town of thatched cottages, with a village green and a couple of posting inns, about ten miles from London. One of these, the Bell Inn, was mentioned by Lady Catherine de Bourgh in Jane Austen's *Pride and Prejudice*: '*Where shall you change horses?—Oh! Bromley, of*

course.—If you mention my name at the Bell, you will be attended to.'
Jane Austen wrote this about the time Charlotte was living there.

In those days, Bromley was nearly three hours away from Marylebone
by horse and carriage, on the main coaching route from London to
Hastings on the south coast. It was considered to have a very healthy
climate, with its fresh country air, so several private schools were
established here. About three of these were small boarding schools for
young ladies, run in private homes by respectable women.

Bromley was surrounded by meadows and woodland, which in
spring were filled with wildflowers—swathes of bluebells, primroses,
pink valerian, red campion, dog violets and wood anemones. Charlotte
and the other young ladies would have walked out every day into the
surrounding countryside to gather wildflowers, chatter and observe
nature. To the south was Bromley Common, which in summer
was a haze of yellow broom blossoms, giving Bromley its name
(broom meadow).

Thursday was market day, when the town was bustling with shoppers
and pedlars. At dawn, the streets were filled with the sound of clanking
carts and horses whinnying, as farmers from miles around brought
their produce to the market square to sell. Women carried baskets filled
with fresh vegetables, fruit, eggs, wheels of cheese, pats of butter and
fragrant herbs. Stalls sold everything from fresh eels, sheep trotters,
pickled whelks and slabs of beef, to ribbons and boiled sweets. Hawkers
cried out their wares, selling meat pies, sweet-smelling gingerbread
and pea soup.

Bromley is no longer the quaint country village it once was. Now it
has been engulfed by the sprawling city of London. I'm driving as we
arrive, and it is a stressful crawl on high alert through peak hour traffic
in the pouring rain.

It is not until we leave the town and enter the gorgeous Kentish countryside that I get a real feel for how beautiful it was when Charlotte lived here. In the gathering dusk, we drive through narrow winding laneways lined with hedgerows, thick dark woods, overarching avenues of beech trees like leafy cathedrals, rolling green fields and tiny ancient villages.

Bromley's rural location, surrounded by woodlands, farms and moors, was an ideal place for Charlotte to develop her love of natural history and botany.

An anecdote in Charlotte's book *A Mother's Offering to Her Children* gives an insight into her sensitivity as a 12-year-old.

When I was a little girl about your age, I had the measles severely. I was a little better; and was sitting in an easy chair, propped up by pillows; when the servant threw some coals from a skuttle on the fire; and with them a poor brown beetle: which endeavouring to escape from the ... heat, ran into the fire. I was a tender-hearted child; and tried to tell the servant to take it out; but was too weak ... and I fainted: much to the alarm of my kind friends.

She relates several similar instances of saving beetles and other insects from harm.

Bromley was close to Chelsfield and Shoreham, where the Warings still had family. As children, Charlotte and her sisters would have visited their various Waring relatives.

Albert's older brother Robert inherited his father's estates at Shoreham and married a local woman called Ann Venner. Charlotte's younger sister Jane was later to marry Richard Venner and settle in Kent, at Bexley.

Other Waring children also attended boarding schools in Bromley. Charlotte's second cousin William Waring, of Chelsfield, attended Rawes' Academy at about the same time. William Waring inherited his father Thomas' many estates in Kent, including Woodlands House. In later life, William Waring was a regular correspondent with distant cousin Charles Darwin, who lived just a few miles away at Down House. They compared notes on selective breeding in greyhounds, on litter sizes and the sex of pups.

Charlotte later wrote about her five years at boarding school, where she was *instructed not only in the general branches of polite female education but was also instructed in Music … Drawing … in the use of the Globes, writing, ciphering … and French*, and later Italian. Charlotte noted that *she attained considerable celebrity at … school for diligence and talent in her various studies.*

It seems Charlotte's father was keen for his daughters to have an outstanding education, learning more than the usual 'polite female accomplishments' of needlework, music, dancing, deportment and decorum taught to genteel ladies. This was at a time when 60 per cent of women could not sign their name at their marriage.

Albert Waring arranged for Charlotte to have lessons with the celebrated landscape artist John Glover. Glover moved to London in 1805, and under the patronage of Countess Harrington established a practice at Marylebone as an art instructor. He became famous as an Italianate landscape painter and was called the 'English Claude', a reference to his romantic style, similar to that of the seventeenth-century French painter Claude Lorrain. In 1831, Glover emigrated to Van Diemen's Land, and today he is known as 'the father of Australian landscape painting'. Charlotte Waring developed a similar style in her paintings, which in turn was passed down to her daughters.

In later years, Charlotte Waring wrote scathingly of boarding schools and refused to allow her own children to be sent away to school.

Sending Charlotte and her sisters away to the country may have been motivated by another change in the Waring family's circumstances. The following year, in 1807, Albert fathered a fifth daughter, Mary Waring, with a woman called Maria Roberts. Two years later, they had a son, called Thomas Albert Waring (also known as Albert) after his father.

While we knew that Albert had a second family, what we didn't realise was that he didn't marry Maria Roberts until 1821, when their daughter Mary was 14 years old and their son was 12. Interestingly, they chose to marry at St Mary's Church, Newington, in Surrey, rather than at the local family church at St Marylebone, where all the children had been christened. This was almost certainly done to avoid provoking scandal in the local community, highlighting that their two children were illegitimate. We don't know if Maria Roberts was a servant or housekeeper, or perhaps a distant poor relative—Albert's mother was Jane Roberts before her marriage.

Instead of being the straitlaced wealthy English gentleman that we'd imagined, Albert was far more bohemian and unconventional than we'd realised. His address at Cirencester Place was in the heart of an artistic hub, frequented by artists, sculptors and poets, including John Linnell, William Blake, John Glover and the artistic brotherhood of the Shoreham Ancients, who coincidentally also based themselves in Albert's birthplace.

The theory we'd always heard from family stories over the years was that Charlotte had to earn her own living as a governess because her father remarried and had a young son, who was to inherit everything. In fact, Albert's 1829 will bequeathed the household goods to Maria Waring, with the rest of the estate to be divided equally among the children of his first marriage—James, Elizabeth, Letitia, Charlotte and Jane. Mary and Albert junior were not mentioned in his will.

Whatever the reason, Albert could no longer afford to support his daughters in the upper-class manner to which they had been born. They had to make their own way in the world.

In 1811, at the age of 15, Charlotte Waring finished school to begin her career as a governess. For a girl of Charlotte's background, this was an absolute last resort—yet instead of bemoaning her fate, Charlotte seems to have embraced the opportunity for independence, further education and discovering her vocation.

Charlotte's first post as governess was with the family of Mary and John Christopher Lochner esquire, for the salary of £50 per year. The Lochner family lived in Caroline Place, Mecklenburg Square, just over a mile from where Charlotte's father lived in Marylebone.

It is a beautiful sunny Sunday when Kate, Emily, Ella and I explore Bloomsbury. I feel butterflies in my stomach as we round the corner into Mecklenburg Square, where Charlotte lived for four years with the Lochner family. It seems especially poignant when we consider that Ella is 15 years old, the same age that Charlotte was when she had to leave school and start earning her own living.

The Lochners were one of the first families to live here, when the square was built in 1810. The house where Charlotte lived was destroyed by a bomb during World War II, but we get a clear sense of the opulence of the remaining buildings. The square has grand Georgian townhouses built on three sides around a fenced garden. Most of the terraces are painted white, with black wrought-iron railings, and have balconies, basement kitchens, and window boxes filled with geraniums and violets. Several have blue heritage plaques commemorating famous residents such as Virginia Woolf.

The central landscaped garden is about two acres, planted with formal lawns, flowers and trees such as beech, oak, almond, sweet briar, jasmine and laburnum, and accessible only to residents with keys. The square had been named after Charlotte of Mecklenburgh-Strelitz, wife of King George III.

I feel a strong sense of serendipity. The private gardens are usually locked, hidden behind high hedges. On the summer's day that we visit, the main gate is open, and we confidently wander in. The gardens are gorgeous—wide green lawns sprinkled with daisies and buttercups, bordered with ancient plane trees. Wide flowerbeds bloom with white and pink roses, foxgloves, feverfew and purple hebe.

I can almost see Charlotte running across the lawns in her long skirts, her black curls flying in the wind, playing chasings or hide-and-seek with the children. She was only small, *five feet 1½ inches in height*. I can see her bending over a tiny creature, her black eyes sparkling with enthusiasm, as she taught the children about butterflies, earthworms or caterpillars. Perhaps she chose to teach them their lessons in the sunshine on a day like today, on a blanket spread on the grass. In her free time, I imagine her quietly sketching under a tree or reading a book on one of the garden benches. I am sure she stopped to breathe in the divine scent of an overblown cabbage rose, just as I do.

Ella turns cartwheels on the grass, her long legs tumbling over and over. We spend well over an hour wandering in the summer sunshine and soaking up the atmosphere. It is only later that we sheepishly discover that we shouldn't be here. The gate was open for a private function, and we see a mother with her pram being firmly told the garden is definitely not open to the public. Kate and I decide that luck, or perhaps the spirit of Charlotte herself, is smiling down on us.

By Charlotte's account, she taught three Lochner children, the eldest being eight years old when she started. According to the birth records, the Lochners' first child, Mary Ann Rawson Lochner, was born in 1808, so would only have been three years old in 1811, with the next child not born until 1812. It may be that John had two other children from a previous relationship, or that they were other relatives, such as nieces or nephews, whom Charlotte also taught.

When researching the Lochner family, I was thrilled to discover details of Captain Lochner's swashbuckling career. He served with the Honourable East India Company, commanding a series of East Indiamen that traded between Britain, India and China. Every year, these ships traded in goods worth millions of pounds, such as tea, porcelain, cotton, silk, indigo dye, saltpetre for gunpowder, and opium. He must have been a fascinating, well-travelled and wealthy employer.

These voyages could take up to two years. Captains could then have two years leave before heading back to sea. Over the four years that Charlotte was employed with the family, it is likely that John Lochner was away in the Far East for half the time.

With its fields and gardens, Mecklenburgh Square was a pleasing combination of urban elegance and semi-rural space. It was considered a healthy place to bring up children. Charlotte, with her love of nature and open spaces, would have enjoyed the opportunity for walks and fresh air, and the chance to observe wildlife and draw.

Charlotte's role as governess would have been to teach her charges the basics of writing, reading and ciphering (as arithmetic was called), as well as manners, morals, and accomplishments such as music, drawing, French and Italian. She also accompanied them when the family visited their country estate at Forty Hill in Enfield, 12 miles north of London.

Her employment with the Lochner family gave her the opportunity to further her own education with specialised masters. Charlotte wrote that:

> *during that period [she] perfected herself in various accomplishments ... She studied music both theoretically and practically under the tuition of Monsieur Logier, a German professor of Music of great eminence in London, and perspective drawing ... also the Italian language under the tuition of Signor Villa, who could not speak any language but Italian and French, and all instruction was conveyed ... in the latter language.*

In 1811, when Charlotte joined the household, Mary Lochner was just 20.

Charlotte Waring was only five years younger than her mistress, and with John away for two years at a time they developed a close friendship. They were to continue to write to each other for decades after Charlotte left the Lochners' employment, and Charlotte was to ask one of the daughters to be godmother to her own baby, Louisa.

After visiting Mecklenburg Square, we make a pilgrimage to St Pancras Old Church, less than 1.5 kilometres away, where Charlotte would have attended church every Sunday. Mary and John Lochner were married here, and their children christened. In those days it was surrounded by fields. It still has a beautiful churchyard filled with ancient trees, and emerald-green lawns sprinkled with white daisies and yellow buttercups.

This was also the local church for radical writers and philosophers Mary Wollstonecraft and her husband William Godwin. They caused a scandal when they were married here in 1797, as Mary signed herself as a spinster, admitting that her first child, Fanny Imlay, had been born out of wedlock. Mary Wollstonecraft died just five months later, of puerperal fever, after giving birth to her daughter Mary Wollstonecraft Godwin.

The four of us set off on a treasure hunt to find Mary Wollstonecraft's grave marker. Emily and Ella race off, checking grave after grave until they find it. The mossy old stone is covered in leaves and looks neglected and forlorn. We pick a bouquet of white pansies and buttercups to leave in homage to Mary—early feminist, philosopher and writer.

It was also here in the churchyard, at her mother's grave, that 16-year-old Mary Wollstonecraft Godwin secretly met her lover, the 21-year-old Romantic poet Percy Bysshe Shelley, and planned their elopement. Unfortunately, he was already married—his wife Harriet was pregnant, and Percy had been cut off by his aristocratic father, who disapproved of Harriet. In 1814, while Charlotte was living with the Lochners, Mary and Percy ran away to France, together with Mary's stepsister Claire Clairmont, causing a huge scandal.

We wonder if Charlotte met young Mary and Percy wandering in the churchyard. We wonder if Charlotte sat under a tree here and read *A Vindication of the Rights of Woman*. Or perhaps she read Wollstonecraft's children's book *Original Stories from Real Life* to her charges? This book, like Charlotte's *A Mother's Offering to Her Children*, is in the style of a conversation, with an older woman teaching children about life by answering their questions. Perhaps this was an inspiration for Charlotte's own writing? Mary Wollstonecraft, like Charlotte, was a gentlewoman who had earned her own living as a governess.

Living so close, Charlotte was certain to have heard of the scandals and adventures of the Wollstonecraft family, who were to become an important part of her future.

Kate and I have enrolled in a course at London University—*Writing the Memoir*—to learn more about writing narrative non-fiction. It is run by highly respected journalist and author Jane Shilling.

Like Charlotte, Kate and I both love learning, and we feel honoured to have the opportunity to study at London University. Most of the students are aspiring writers who are working on stories about their own lives. Some are writing to heal themselves, some are writing to help others. It is an intensely emotional workshop, as students tell their harrowing stories of childhood sexual abuse, rape and grief. One mother reveals the tragic story of losing both husband and daughter to suicide. I am sick with sorrow and anger at some of their experiences.

I feel like an intruder when we are asked to share details of our own project. Kate and I talk about the joys and difficulties of writing about Charlotte.

One of the students, Nicola Crichton-Brown, looks surprised. Nicola is the only other student in the course who has previously been published. During the break, she comes over to us.

'Are you writing about Louisa Atkinson's mother?' she asks.

'Yes!' says Kate. We are both shocked, not expecting anyone in London to know anything about our ancestors.

'I've written about Louisa in one of my books,' Nicola replies.

Nicola is English and lives in London, but she and her family spent several years in rural Australia, where she wrote two history books. One of these is *Cavan Station*, about an iconic sheep station near Yass in New South Wales. This is where Charlotte's youngest daughter Louisa lived when she was first married.

The three of us are delighted with the impossible coincidence that, in a small class of 12 students in England, there would be three authors who had all written about the same almost unknown Australian woman writer.

'I adore Louisa,' says Nicola. 'She was an amazing woman. And her family was fascinating.'

We have no time to talk more during class, but Nicola invites us to morning tea on Tuesday. Kate and I debate what to do, because it means spending an extra day in London, so less time for our research in Kent. However, it is too special an opportunity to miss—it is as though Charlotte is guiding our footsteps. Something else will have to go.

Tuesday is a stunning English summer's day. Kate and I catch the Tube to Notting Hill Gate, arranging to meet the girls later in Baker Street. We walk to Nicola's house near Kensington Church Road, soaking up the elegant terraces, wrought-iron railings, quaint pubs and shops, and the gardens brimming with blooms and topiary.

Nicola lives in the most beautiful, grand Victorian terrace, filled with antiques, paintings, books, marble fireplaces, Persian rugs and objets d'art, with a leafy view over the neighbouring gardens. If I were to live in London again, I would love a terrace just like it. The three of us have tea and cake while we chat about Nicola's writing process, researching her book on Cavan and her life in Australia. We talk about our own books and writing life, and bond over our shared passions.

Louisa Atkinson married James Calvert in 1869 and lived at his property, Cavan, for about 15 months. Nicola tells us that during her research for her book she was shown a beautiful watercolour landscape of Cavan. The painting was unsigned, but Nicola recognised it as the work of Louisa. Nicola took the painting to the Mitchell Library, where the identity of the artist was confirmed. She shows us a photograph of the painting and we can clearly see the similarity to Charlotte's style.

We are just as excited as Nicola with this fabulous discovery. We talk about how addictive it is—the many hours of painstaking research, but then the thrill of discovering these long-lost treasures from the past. We show Nicola photos of some of our own finds.

At last we have to say our goodbyes, as we have stayed far longer than we planned. Kate and I are buzzing with exhilaration as we hurry off to meet Emily and Ella to continue our research. We chatter all the way on the Tube about the book and how to write it. We are loving stepping back in time and following in young Charlotte's footsteps.

After four years with the Lochner family, Charlotte left and moved to Trafford Hall in Lancashire, about three miles from central Manchester, to work for Laura and Thomas Trafford. Her move to the north coincided with the end of the Napoleonic Wars, following the Battle of Waterloo in June 1815.

Being a governess for the Trafford family was a step up in terms of salary, responsibility and cachet. For Charlotte, this position was indicative of the gradually changing role of the governess, the first truly professional vocation open to women, as teachers and educators. It was a reward for Charlotte's efforts to educate herself to the highest possible standard and reflected her own passion for girls' higher education.

The Traffords were one of the most ancient aristocratic families in England and had owned this estate since about 1200.

Trafford Hall was an Elizabethan mansion, filled with fine art, which had been extended significantly during the eighteenth century. The stately home was on a huge estate comprising nearly 1,200 acres of lightly timbered deer park, meadows, woodland and three farms, with a long tree-lined drive leading from the gatehouse. The grounds included a sunken rose garden, a lake with its own boathouse and island, and formal gardens of rare and exotic plants.

Charlotte Waring later wrote about how much she enjoyed exploring the countryside in her free time, examining and drawing insects and plants. *I was very fond of rambling about in the woods, or forests ... [where] there is also an endless variety of beautiful little plants ... Some of these curiosities I delighted to draw; others I dried, and thus made a pleasing addition to my herbal.*

In 1815 the Trafford family had eight children. Charlotte later wrote that she taught five children when she started, without the help of specialist masters, and was paid a salary of £70 per annum, which was a high salary for a governess at this time, reflecting her excellent qualifications and teaching skills. For example, although well-educated and clever, Charlotte Brontë was only paid £20 per annum as a governess in 1841.

The Trafford children were Laura, aged ten, Jemima, eight, Humphrey, seven, Jane, six and Maria, five. In the nursery were the younger children: Caroline, three, Thomas, two and baby Sybilla. A year later, the Traffords had another daughter, called Belinda. When I discovered this, I was thrilled by the coincidence that not only did this baby share my name, but my maiden name, Belinda Jane Humphrey, was made up from the names of three of the Trafford children!

Being governess for the aristocratic Trafford family may have been very different from life with the Lochners.

A governess often held a very lonely and isolated position, as she was not part of the family and not one of the servants. She was expected to be refined and well-educated, with a variety of genteel accomplishments. However, upper-class ladies did not participate in paid employment, so a working governess was automatically excluded from her own socio-economic class. Nor was she was welcomed by the working-class servants below stairs.

As an employee, it would have been difficult for her to meet eligible men.

The hours were long, as she was expected to supervise and teach the children for most of their waking hours. At night, she probably took her meals with the children or alone in the schoolroom, whereas with the Lochners she was more likely to take her meals with the family.

At Trafford Park, although Charlotte was living in a grand house and earning an excellent salary, she was over 200 miles away from her family and friends. The journey from Manchester to London would take about 36 hours, or three days if she stopped overnight along the way.

Many nineteenth-century writers illuminated the difficulty of working as a governess. For example, Charlotte Brontë described the life of a governess as one of *inexpressible misery* and drew on her own unhappy experiences to create Jane Eyre. Jane Austen depicted her character Jane Fairfax in *Emma* as an object of pity. Jane Fairfax was an orphan—although beautiful, clever, well-educated and exceptionally talented, her poverty meant her only option was to become a governess, a career choice that filled her with despair.

Charlotte Waring stayed with the Trafford family for two years, and then in 1817 she *was obliged to retire from her duties on account of ill health … she was then about twenty-one years of age.* The same age as my daughter Emily.

Nothing is known of her life over the next few years—however, it seems likely that she continued working as a governess. She later wrote rather acidly *that having spent nearly the whole of her life in educating young ladies she conceives that she is perfectly qualified to educate her own children.* By 1826, Charlotte was considered to be a *highly recommended* teacher. It was her experience and qualifications as a governess that would create an outstanding opportunity for adventure and romance.

Chapter 4

SEEKING ADVENTURES ABROAD

Written by Belinda

It required much perseverance and courage I should imagine
Charlotte Waring Atkinson

———◦———

In August 1826, when she was 30 years old, Charlotte Waring applied for a job as a governess for the very high salary of £100 per year. Twenty-four governesses applied for the position, but withdrew their applications in horror when they realised that it meant travelling halfway around the world to the colony of New South Wales. But not intrepid Charlotte. She accepted the job, but only on condition that she travelled first class.

It is hardly surprising that almost all the governesses refused to contemplate travelling to Australia. At that time, it was considered a colony of thieves and cutthroats. The women would have heard terrifying stories of storms and shipwrecks, murderous bushrangers and savage natives, hardship and peculiar wild animals. So, it is a testament to Charlotte's courage and curiosity that she decided to travel alone to a country where she knew no one.

From reading Charlotte's shipboard journal, it seems that she was keen to experience a more adventurous and independent life. Her writing and many of her sketches show a fascination with exotic places and people.

Her new position was to teach the daughters of one of the leading pastoral families in the colony—the children of Maria and Hannibal Hawkins Macarthur. Maria King, the eldest daughter of the former governor of New South Wales, Philip Gidley King, had married Hannibal Macarthur, nephew of Captain John Macarthur. Maria charged her sister-in-law, Harriet Lethbridge King, with the task of finding a highly qualified governess in England and bringing her out to the colony.

The foremost families of the colony of New South Wales were very closely entwined. None more so than the Macarthur, King and Lethbridge families.

Harriet Lethbridge was born in Launceston in Cornwall in 1796, the same year as Charlotte Waring. Her father, Christopher Lethbridge, was a lawyer, three times Mayor of Launceston and Under Sheriff of Cornwall. He was an old friend of Governor Philip Gidley King, and the two men had discussed that one day the King and Lethbridge children might marry. In the summer of 1816, this prophecy came true when Governor King's son Phillip visited Launceston and met 21-year-old Harriet Lethbridge outside the church of St Mary Magdalene. They were married at that very church some months later and sailed for New South Wales. Phillip spent the next few years exploring and surveying the coast of Australia, while Harriet ran their extensive properties and raised their children on her own.

In 1826, Phillip Parker King set sail for South America, on a mission to chart the west coast, taking their eight-year-old son Philip Gidley King with him. He wouldn't see his wife and his other children for a further six years. Harriet wrote many letters to Phillip during his absence, describing everyday activities, the exploits of their other sons and her financial worries, and lamenting the length of their separation.

On 25 July 1826, Harriet's younger brother, Robert Copland Lethbridge, married Phillip Parker King's youngest sister, Mary, at Marylebone, binding the two families even closer.

Harriet wrote to her husband describing the wedding in London and telling him about the arrangements she had made to return to the colony. She also wrote to him with good news about another business transaction. *I believe we have procured a Governess, a Lady about 30, a Miss Waring, she has been highly recommended to us and agrees to go to the Colony; so there is no time to be lost in making preparations for her.*

There was indeed little time to prepare, as the combined Lethbridge, King and Macarthur families had already chartered a small ship, the *Cumberland*, to bring them back to the colony. Three Macarthur family members were to be on the return trip: Hannibal's brother Charles; 17-year-old John Francis Macarthur, their second cousin; and Charles' 12-year-old nephew James, who had been at school in Plymouth, in Devon. Most of the travelling party was to join the *Cumberland* at Plymouth, as Charles was staying with his sisters there and the others were visiting King and Lethbridge relatives in nearby Launceston.

The *Cumberland* began its journey in Gravesend, on the Thames, under the command of its owner, Captain Robert Carns.

On 2 September 1826, Charlotte Waring caught a steamer from London to Gravesend in the company of her younger sister Jane and her cousin Ericus, who came down to see her safely on board. Her luggage included her scientific collection of fossils, shells and geological samples. Charlotte didn't record how she felt about leaving her family and homeland behind forever. It must have been heartbreaking saying goodbye to her beloved sister Jane, not knowing if she would ever see her again. I imagine her clinging to Jane, never wanting to let her go. But trying so hard not to cry, not to show her fear or her dread—trying to show a brave, carefree face.

Her journal focuses on recording interesting details of shipboard life and imparting a sense of adventure. The *Cumberland* had suffered some damage the night before, which delayed its departure for several days, giving the passengers time to go shopping, visiting and walking onshore.

Charlotte found the *Cumberland* in chaos:

Came on board the Cumberland lying at Gravesend between one and two. The ship was all in confusion and cabins in darkness which gave a dreary appearance. Pens containing one and forty sheep of the Saxon (Mareno) kind were in the middle of the quarter deck and trusses of hay and luggage of all kinds heaped on the deck and outside the ship.

There was also a stallion, purebred horses, a bull, dairy cows, several sheep dogs, 23 dozen poultry and various plants. The owner of all these animals and plants was James Atkinson.

According to an account written many years later by Charlotte's eldest daughter, Charlotte Atkinson McNeilly:

a pen was made for the sheep on the deck; the stallion and bull were below. Ships were small in those days. My father also brought sheep dogs, poultry, etc., cuttings of hops, fruit trees, wallflowers, white lilies, etc., in boxes with glass tops, that could be opened on fine days.

As I was growing up, we were often told the story of how Charlotte Waring met the love of her life on board the ship. The kind, charming and gentle James Atkinson, one of the most eligible bachelors in the colony, came on board and tipped his hat to her. It was love at first sight.

James Atkinson had originally left England on 25 December 1819, on the private merchant ship the *Saracen*, when he was 24 years old. He arrived in Port Jackson on 19 May 1820 with £1,000 of capital, provided from his father's estate in money and farming tools. He worked for two years for Governor Lachlan Macquarie as principal clerk in the Colonial Secretary's office at a salary of £60. During this time, James was given several grants of land in the newly settled Bong Bong district, where he established Oldbury in 1821, naming the property for his birthplace in Kent. In just a few years, James became a highly respected and successful farmer, who moved in colonial high society.

James returned to England in February 1825 on board the *Mangles*, travelling with his friend Charles Macarthur. His friend John Bingle wrote that James was suffering with a broken leg at the time. James had visited his family in Mereworth and written a book called *An Account of the State of Agriculture & Grazing in New South Wales*, which was published in London in 1826. The book was a 'how-to manual'—a practical guide, based on James' own experiences, to help new settlers prepare for life in a strange and faraway land. James and Charles Macarthur had spent the summer of 1826 travelling over 1,500 miles, from England to Hamburg, then through Hanover, Brunswick, Leipzig, Dresden, Prussia, Saxony, Cologne and back, studying methods for farming the Saxon (merino) breed of sheep.

Charlotte kept a journal of her voyage to send back to her family in London. In 2012, I transcribed a copy of this journal, which is kept in the National Library of Australia. It was terribly difficult to read, with her old-fashioned calligraphy, and many abbreviations to save paper. Its tone is lively, enthusiastic and optimistic, giving a real sense of her personality. I remember my jolt of excitement, reading her account of her first meeting with my great-great-great-great-grandfather.

Saturday September 2, 1826 ... what with the noise of ... [the anchor chain] and the 'yo ho' of the sailors little sleep could be procured that night however I made myself as contented as possible in so novel a situation and felt no alarm tho' none of our party were on board except a gentleman of the name of Atkinson of whom I had before heard from various quarters tho' I was not personally acquainted with him.

He is an English gentleman and has been a settler in New South Wales about 7 Years and has a good estate of 2000 acres in Sutton Forest Argyleshire NSW, called by himself Oldbury, by the natives Tillynambulla ... Mr A received me with politeness on my entering the ship.

Her language is formal, but you can sense that Charlotte's interest is piqued. I imagine it was her way of gently introducing James to her family back home.

I was intrigued that Charlotte recorded the name Tillynambulla, the local Wodi Wodi people's name for the area that included Mount Gingenbullen, and to me this revealed the first inkling of her fascination with the traditional owners. Later she would sketch Aboriginal people and their artefacts, and be invited to watch their sacred ceremonies, as well as writing about their customs and beliefs.

James Atkinson had four passengers under his protection, including 13-year-old Henry Sayer Lewes (son of Samuel Lewes esquire, of the British Admiralty), who was to live at Oldbury to learn farming; 21-year-old John Woodger, from a neighbouring village in Kent, who was to be the estate overseer; and 23-year-old Mary Throsby.

Mary and Charlotte became friends, sharing a cabin, working together on their needlework in the 'cuddy'—or communal saloon— shopping and going for walks onshore. Mary was travelling to Australia to live with her brother Charles and their uncle Dr Charles Throsby senior, who was a close neighbour of James Atkinson in Sutton Forest.

Sunday 3. Fine day. Miss T [Miss Throsby] the young lady under Mr Atkinson's care during the voyage came on board about 12 am. She is my cabin companion. Her aunt and an uncle whom I had seen a few minutes the evening before came with her. He was a Mr Cox and had called on Ericus [Charlotte's cousin] in London the week before. Miss T was in great grief at leaving her friends more particularly as she was averse to leaving England and had the great dislike to the voyage. She is much out of health and has two years ago met with an accident and greatly injured her head. I did what I could to comfort her and after her friends were gone took her down to her cabin. I did not sleep there for a few days but occupied a longer one.

It was hardly surprising that poor Mary Throsby was devastated at leaving her friends, family and England behind forever. With her family history, it was no wonder she was frightened of the sea journey to come.

James and Mary would undoubtedly have told Charlotte the fascinating story of Mary's famous sister-in-law Betsey Broughton Throsby, married to Mary's brother Charles. In 1809, two-year-old Betsey was one of only four people who survived a Maori massacre. She and her mother were travelling back to England on the *Boyd*, which called into Whangaroa in New Zealand.

Local Maoris attacked the ship in retaliation for the mistreatment of crew member Te Ara, a Whangaroa chief's son, who had been flogged for an alleged theft. About 70 people, including Betsey's mother, were murdered and eaten, and the ship was ransacked and destroyed. Betsey, severely emaciated, was rescued three weeks later by James' close friend Alexander Berry, who was sailing nearby on his ship. Betsey was eventually returned to her overjoyed father in New South Wales, via Lima in Peru, and married Charles Throsby when she was 16.

Monday September 4, 1826 ... Mr A escorted us on a pleasant walk over the hills at Gravesend from whence we had a delightful view of the opposite coast (Essex) ... we walked about the Milton Church. In the morning sent a letter to town by Mrs Wynn to my Aunt.

Kate, Ella, Emily and I set out to recreate this romantic first stroll taken by our great-great-great-great-grandparents, James and Charlotte, with Mary Throsby as their chaperone. We drove from Shoreham to the old stone church at Milton, with its ancient trees, buttercups and mossy gravestones.

In 1826, the church was surrounded by meadows running down to the River Thames, scattered with the odd farmhouse, barn or cottage. The view would have encompassed sailing ships, pilot boats and fishing craft plying back and forth.

The surrounding neighbourhood is now a jumble of crowded streets, multicultural businesses and rundown terraces. We cannot see the Thames nor the *opposite coast* of Essex. The church itself has a grim reminder carved onto the clock face: *Trifle not. Your time's but short.*

As we push open the old wrought-iron gate, I wonder if James and Charlotte pushed open this very same gate to stroll around the church. Did Mary dawdle behind so Charlotte and James could converse alone?

I wander in the churchyard, imagining the scene. Charlotte with her dark curls under her broad straw sun hat decorated with ribbons and roses. Her walking dress, with its puffed sleeves, high waist and full, ruffled skirts. James in his cravat, narrow-waisted jacket and top hat. I imagine him leaning in to point out something or taking Charlotte's gloved hand to help her over a patch of uneven ground. They laugh with the joy of walking in the beautiful English countryside on a warm, autumn day.

In Gravesend itself, we stroll along the riverside, admiring the historic buildings, piers and cobbled laneways. I can imagine the Thames bustling with sailing ships, the noise of sailors yelling, timber creaking and boys scrambling up masts. The air would have smelled of salt, tar and a stink of sewage, unwashed bodies and horse manure. It must have been an exciting, exotic scene. I feel a clench of nerves, envisioning Charlotte about to leave her family, her friends, her homeland behind forever. I can see Charlotte walking these streets with Jane and Ericus, and later with James and Mary, her tummy fluttering with anticipation and fear. This is where Charlotte said goodbye to her beloved family forever. This is where Charlotte met the love of her life.

I'm jolted back to the present by the modern shops, the workers patching the road and our daughters running on ahead. It is such a gift to walk in Charlotte's footsteps. It makes her more real, more alive, as though giving me a glimpse into her innermost thoughts and feelings.

Did she feel a flicker of romantic interest as she walked along with James and Mary Throsby, while they chatted and laughed? Was James doing his best to charm and beguile her? Did they talk of ships and journeys and foreign lands?

Three days later, James' fascination with Charlotte Waring had not gone unnoticed.

Tuesday September 5, 1826 ... Mrs W had joked me on Sunday about Mr Atkinson's attention to me and Mrs Carns also remarked ... but I would not listen to it ...

Wednesday September 6, 1826 ... At 5 in the afternoon having got all the damages repaired we set sail with a fresh breeze from the w and at 7 anchored for the night at Sea beach ... Blowing in strongly now and all night the ship lay down to Starboard very much and we were much shook about yet I did not feel at all ill or fearful—not so with Miss T [Mary Throsby] she was very unwell from the time the ship began to sail and kept in bed. I sat on the poop wrapped in Mr Atkinson's plaid cloak.

In an era when a gentleman couldn't speak to a lady, or even tip his hat, without being formally introduced, it is clear that Charlotte Waring and James Atkinson were already on very friendly terms for her to be wrapped up in his cloak only a few days after meeting him on board the ship. Charlotte sitting on the poop deck, wrapped in James' warm plaid cloak when she was cold, would be an important detail of their courtship ritual that would be passed down in family stories for generations.

James Atkinson was a lively, sociable gentleman with a wide circle of friends. With many hours to be filled on board ship, I imagine that James charmed Charlotte with tales of his adventures travelling through Europe, of colonial life and the exotic animals of Australia. He may have told Charlotte about his many exploring expeditions on horseback, with Errombee, his Aboriginal friend and guide.

In 1822, James and Errombee had spent several weeks exploring from Sutton Forest to the coast, looking for grazing land and red cedar. On their return they became hopelessly lost in the impenetrable Shoalhaven gorges. When their provisions ran out, Errombee found bush tucker, roasting a goanna and harvesting honeycomb, but refused to eat anything himself for many days, saving the food for James. Errombee eventually managed to find the way back to Oldbury. James credited Errombee with saving his life.

Charlotte and James found they had much in common—their spirit of adventure, intelligence, lively curiosity, and shared passion for plants, animals and natural sciences. They both had the experience of growing up in Kent. Oldbury and Mereworth, where James grew up, were only a few miles from the Waring estates at Shoreham, so they shared several acquaintances. Charlotte had been asked to meet James at a dinner the week before, but *the time of my embarkation being so near to hand I could not accept the invitation.*

On 7 September, the ship anchored off Deal on the east coast of Kent, and John Francis Macarthur joined the ship.

Charlotte wrote several times that she was not frightened, even when they experienced extreme weather: *our passage hitherto had been so rough it was impossible to stand. I got several bad falls. Once I was thrown off a large case in the cabin whence I slept for a time and hurt my collarbone and sprained my wrist a good deal.*

She records a conversation with the pilot, Mr Wynn, when he was leaving the ship at Deal. He shook her heartily by the hand and congratulated her on her bravery. *You are the best sailor ever. It is perfectly astonishing to me such rough weather as we have had and never to have been on the sea before. Tis surprising that you are not alarmed.*

The weather continued to be extremely rough as the *Cumberland* continued its journey west along the *coast of Devon … bold and beautiful … Stood in for Plymouth Sound … and tacked to Berry Head … many fishing vessels with their red sails in sight.*

On 15 September, the *Cumberland* anchored in Plymouth to pick up the rest of the party: Harriet King and her four young sons; Robert and

Mary Lethbridge, who had only been married a few weeks; and Lieutenant Charles Macarthur and his nephew James. The next few days were a whirl of shopping in Devonport, visiting St Aubyn's Church, attending luncheons and dinners, and being hosted by Charles Macarthur's sisters at their home, as well as joining an extended Lethbridge family gathering at the Royal Hotel.

Charles Macarthur refused to allow Charlotte and Miss Throsby to sleep in their cabin on the *Cumberland*, insisting that they stay onshore at his sisters' home.

Strong elements of Charlotte's character are revealed through her journal, particularly her determination and independence. She found Charles Macarthur's manner to be *very arbitrary*.

They insisted on our staying til the ship was ready to sail and as I thought this was ridiculous made up my mind to go if I could ... Mr C McA said indeed we should not go on such a night. I said I was not afraid of the rain ... I made a joke of it [but] was quite determined to go ... We then came down with our parcels in our hands. On the stairs we met the gentlemen. I burst out laughing. Mr McA said 'No, surely you are not so mad.' I said 'Yes really. We're going. We should have much rougher weather than the present to contend with therefore it is of no use to mind a little rain.'

Another side of her personality was her liveliness, her strong sense of humour and fun. She several times refers to herself bursting out laughing at something funny or ridiculous. In the heavy rain and darkness, Charlotte made a mistake, climbing into the wrong carriage parked outside the Royal Hotel. Looking around for her companions, she realised they were in a different coach some distance away. *We caught a sight of each other then [they] began calling me with such eagerness and it altogether appeared so ridiculous that I was taken with such a laughing fit I could scarcely apologise to the man.*

On Tuesday 19 September, Charlotte wrote that *the captain wished to sail in the morning as the wind was fair and all the passengers ready and willing but Mr C McA who seemed determined to quarrel with everything.*

Charles Macarthur found fault with the ship, the captain, the number of poultry and with the health of the sheep, insisting that they had 'the rot'. One was killed, but was found to be healthy. Charles refused to embark. Letters flew back and forth until Captain Carns sent a letter with his attorney, telling Charles that the ship would sail at 5 pm, with or without him. John Francis Macarthur went ashore to reason with him, then the captain tried again. Charlotte wrote that *we paced the deck anxiously awaiting his return.*

Captain Carns waited until midnight, but Charles refused to come, so the *Cumberland* set sail without Charles and James Macarthur, even though all their luggage and cargo were on board. This event caused an irreparable rift in the friendship between Charles Macarthur and James Atkinson.

Harriet King's letters reveal more about the argument. In June, she wrote: *Charles is returned from Saxony ... he is looking very ill and obliged to blister himself continually ... he has a continual pain in his chest and coughs ... and was much out of spirits.* His illness made his behaviour difficult and irrational.

Charles was suffering from consumption, or pulmonary tuberculosis, a wasting disease of the lungs, which caused up to 30 per cent of deaths in nineteenth-century Europe and was romanticised by Victorian artists and writers. Those with tuberculosis slowly wasted away, and were characterised by pale skin, rosy cheeks and sparkling eyes, influencing the nineteenth-century concept of ideal beauty. Tuberculosis caused the early death of all six Brontë siblings—Maria aged 11, Elizabeth aged 10, Branwell aged 31 (exacerbated by alcoholism and laudanum), Emily aged 30, Anne aged 29 and Charlotte aged 38.

The King, Lethbridge and Macarthur families had originally been booked to return to the colony on the *Admiral Cockburn*—however, Charles Macarthur didn't want to share the ship with other passengers.

Charles also quarrelled with James Atkinson about how much cargo would go out on the *Cumberland* and who would pay for it. Charles had negotiated to take 100 tons including sheep, animals, personal belongings and trade goods such as iron, port wine and cloth. He wanted James to pay for one-third of this, but James only committed to one-sixth. Charles then insisted that Harriet should make up the tonnage.

Harriet King was a strong-willed and competent woman, but the long separation from her husband and eldest son, the trials of raising five young sons on her own, and dealing with unexpected expenses—as well as organising the voyage—proved extremely demanding. Another concern was the health of her two-year-old son Charles, who Harriet feared might not survive the voyage. She was also upset at leaving her second son, six-year-old John, behind in England to be educated.

Perhaps the strongest reason for Harriet's trepidation at the delay was that she was expecting her seventh child. She was only 29. In her letters to her husband she dwells on her fear of giving birth on the journey.

Charles was furious at being left behind, and later tried to sue Captain Carns, although Harriet wrote to her husband that <u>We</u> *think Captn C behaved very temperately ... he does all in his power to accommodate us ... [and] is very kind to the children.*

Charles and his nephew James found passage to New South Wales on a convict ship, the *Midas*, a few weeks later.

Chapter 5

COURTSHIP

Written by Belinda

I must be mistress of my own actions
Charlotte Waring

———◆———

Charlotte soon settled into her shipboard routine—writing letters or recording in her journal, sitting on the poop deck, sewing, exchanging stories and laughs with James Atkinson, reading books, walking on the deck, taking tea and dining in the cuddy. James wrote the draft of a paper based on his journey through Germany with Charles Macarthur, 'Remarks on the Saxon Sheep Farming', which was later published in *The Australian Quarterly Journal* of 1828.

I imagine Charlotte and James in the cuddy, their quills scratching across the paper as they wrote. Perhaps they read excerpts from their writing to each other, or Charlotte read James one of her poems.

For the first stage of the journey, from Gravesend to Plymouth, their rations were basic—old ship's biscuits which were *left of a former voyage which were stale and hard and we had not many other things such as milk in our tea and coffee.* Once they left Plymouth,

Captain Carns ensured the first-class passengers ate well—soup, fish, poultry, hot meat, vegetables, puddings and desserts, served with wine and tea. The nine steerage passengers ate the same basic food as the sailors.

The *Cumberland* then entered the Bay of Biscay, the weather continuing to be rough and squally. All the passengers were suffering from seasickness.

Monday September 25: Very sick dressing. It is so dreadfully fatiguing. Quite impossible to stand or kneel or sit and almost to lie. The water is so dreadfully putrid with being kept up close they say it will get better. It is much to be hoped it will or I think there will be nothing left of me.

Friday September 29: Michaelmas Day being squally ... I was very poorly and was obliged to go and sit on the Hen coops of which one made little garden seats ... 'twas blowing so tremendously. The ship was completely thrown on its side ... Mr J.F. MacA, Mr Atkinson and myself were on deck at the time. The former ran up the poop ladder. Mr A took me by the hand and put me a little way up also and then stood a step or two below me—just as the ship had passed a tremendous sea, mountain high came rolling toward us. The ship was so down on its side there was no means of escape ... The Captn called out 'hold on there' and Mr A had just time to say 'hold on, have courage' when it came with desperate force against my face. I held on with all my strength tho' struggled for breath and was completely wet through—I had on at the time my bonnet, black shawl, and my black and white gown ... 'twas as much as our lives were worth to get down below ... the Hatches were down however with Mr A's assistance who was very little wet compared to me the Captn and First Mate I managed to get down and with great difficulty got dressed again in my Holland trimmed with red—I was in a fright lest I should not be able to get up again but I did at last I only laughed at this ducking tho' I felt very sore and exhausted from the violent motion of the vessel.

I love that in the middle of describing a frightening storm, Charlotte took the time to include details of what she was wearing.

The storm increased in intensity. Having made their way down below, the party were sitting in the cuddy, trying to eat, when *such a sea as is seldom seen took the ship, knocked in her bulwarks and rushed into the cuddy. Unfortunately Mr A had put me in the lowest corner for safety and the sea came there and kept for some time dashing against my mouth. I was almost strangled. I struggled but could not get up. Mr A dragged me away and gives me credit for behaving very courageously. We all were quite sick and sadly frightened ... The cuddy was filling with water—we knew not where to go everything was ... uncleated and dashing about. Mr A brought me his warm plaid cloak.*

Charlotte had just changed for the third time into a dry holland (linen) gown *when we heard the captain calling through his trumpet 'Hold on there boys' 'Cheerily now. Cheerily lads'. We thought something bad was happening and so it proved. Such a sea! struck the ship and threw us all on the floor and dashed everything about. Broke the neck of one of our stock sheep, cleaned the deck of a good deal of hay—washed Mr Mitchel our first mate from one side to the other and he had nearly gone overboard. I got up and held by the Captain's Table in silent horror of what was to follow. The stern windows were broken and the sea foaming and washing up with awful grandeur … I viewed it all with fortitude … Mr A was the only gentleman who exerted himself … helping to bail the water out of the cuddy … I must leave off here—I have no time to say more—than God bless you all—CW.*

Charlotte's journal ends here after the dramatic account of the terrifying storm in the Bay of Biscay. She later wrote that she lost her precious collection of fossils, shells and geological samples during the storm. What she failed to include in this journal, which she sent home to her family, is what happened next.

James Atkinson had saved Charlotte's life by dragging her from under the water when she was trapped by her heavy skirts, then tenderly wrapping her in his warm plaid cloak. The next day, James asked Charlotte to marry him.

Lines Written During a Storm in the Bay of Biscay.

Almighty God, by whose command,
The winds and tempests rise;
Whose pow'r can still the raging sea,
And clear the low'ring skies.

We, thine enfeebled creatures bend,
Prostrate in humble pray'r,
Pity and save us Lord we cry,
Our lives O! Father spare.

Lo trembling on the verge of fate,
What horrors meet our ear;
Is it the thunder's awful sound,
Or angry waves we hear?

Unaided by thy pow'r O Lord!
Our barque we cannot save;
Thou only can the tempest hush,
And check each rising wave.

Thy mercy Lord we would implore,
Oh! hear us when we cry;
Speak comfort to our drooping souls,
Lord cheer us, or we die!

Not for our *merits Lord we pray,*
To have our sins forgiv'n;
But through the merits of thy son,
Our advocate in Heav'n.

Charlotte Waring

On a spring morning in Sydney it is pouring with rain as Kate and I huddle under my flimsy umbrella and hurry across the city, dodging puddles and damp pedestrians. It is Year 12 muck-up day for our two 18-year-old sons. My younger son, Lachie, and Kate's middle child, Tim, are at the same school studying hard for their final exams, and it has been an emotional time of nostalgia, celebrations and HSC stress.

The wild weather seems perfect for a day trawling through the archives of the Mitchell Library. The Atkinson Papers are a collection of miscellaneous material attributed to different members of the family, particularly Charlotte's daughter Louisa, donated to the State Library of New South Wales by Louisa's granddaughter Janet Cosh. There are boxes of papers, letters, sketches, specimens and newspaper cuttings, which have been locked up in storage for decades. There is so much material that I only order a few boxes to be brought up.

On a whim, I've ordered a sketchbook, dated 28 December 1848, which is dedicated to Charlotte's daughter Emily Atkinson and attributed to Emily's brother, James. It is one of the last things we look at, because James would only have been 16 in 1848—so we don't expect it to be very helpful. As soon as we open the long-forgotten sketchbook, we realise its significance.

The sketchbook is filled with exquisite watercolours and pencil drawings, and we instantly know it is not the work of James junior. It is instead the work of Charlotte herself.

We immediately recognise her sketching style and handwriting. Kate and I have both seen Charlotte's 1843 sketchbook, which was auctioned several years ago and bought by a private collector for $70,000. It too was dedicated to Emily Atkinson, on her thirteenth birthday. Kate and I inspected it prior to the auction with our mother Gilly, and our daughters Emily and Ella. At the time, I was thrilled by the coincidence that it was dedicated to Emily on her thirteenth birthday, because my daughter, Emily Charlotte Jane, had just turned 13 when we went to see it.

Our belief is confirmed by the handwritten attribution of the donor Janet Cosh, which clearly says: *A gift to Emily. Not her work. Almost certainly her mother.* However, we can see how it might mistakenly be read as brother.

This discovery is exhilarating, especially as we soon realise that the sketchbook has several family portraits which we didn't know existed.

'She's wearing a plaid cloak,' I shriek with excitement, as I turn the page. 'It's Charlotte.'

Everyone turns to glare at us in the silent reading room of the Mitchell Library, and I hurriedly apologise, my heart pounding and hands shaking. The portrait is of a beautiful young woman, wrapped in her cloak, with flowers in her hair. It is surely *handsome and brilliant* Charlotte, with her *full black eyes, black hair which curled naturally, and fine features*, illustrating the family story of her shipboard romance with the love of her life, James Atkinson, and their swift engagement.

This portrait is the first image I've ever seen of Charlotte, except for a rough sketch done by her teenage daughter Charlotte Elizabeth. To me this sketch of Charlotte in a plaid cloak, glowing with love and happiness, is an unbelievable discovery.

I remember my mother's cousin, Kaye McBride, telling me a story many years ago about how Charlotte wore James' plaid cloak on board the ship. I was so excited when the story was confirmed by Charlotte's journal. I later checked, but Kaye had never read the journal, she had just heard the tale from the family.

The sketchbook includes several other portraits and we can immediately see the strong family resemblances. There is an older Charlotte, looking matronly but still handsome in her early fifties. There are portraits that match descriptions of 18-year-old Emily and 14-year-old Louisa, as well as an exquisite sketch of our great-great-great-grandmother Charlotte Elizabeth on her nineteenth birthday, which was also her wedding day. Charlotte Elizabeth looks so much like her mama—black hair, black eyes and very beautiful.

❧

Charlotte's sudden engagement to James Atkinson caused great dismay to Harriet King.

Harriet wrote to her husband Philip about the engagement on 3 October 1826, when they were 300 miles from Madeira on their way to the Cape Verde islands.

I am very much disappointed in Miss Waring the Governess. She is very different from what she ought to be, or we expected. We had not been 2 hours on board, before I saw she was flirting with Mr Atkinson, and ere 10 days were over she was engaged to him: she came round in the ship from London but altogether, it was about 3 weeks acquaintance. Her conduct is far from what I could wish otherwise, as she does not act with propriety. I have spoken to her, and represented how vexed Hannibal and Maria will be, but she told me, it should not interfere with her engagement with them, but she must be mistress of her own actions; It is well Charles is not on board, as I am sure there would have been a war with him and Mr Atkinson and further interference would do no good.

Harriet was extremely annoyed at having her plans thwarted. A few months later her nanny also resigned to get married—however, Harriet refused to accept her resignation and talked Nanny out of the marriage.

Charlotte had written that Mrs King initially received her very kindly and included her in the family dinners. However, Harriet King had a strong sense of her own social superiority to a mere governess like Charlotte, even though Charlotte came from an old, genteel family. Charlotte would not be bullied, and stood up for herself by agreeing to fulfil her one-year contract with the Macarthur family but not backing down on the engagement. She may well have echoed Elizabeth Bennet's sentiment expressed to Lady Catherine de Bourgh: *He is a gentleman; I am a gentleman's daughter; so far we are equal.*

Ten days of pleasant sailing later, the *Cumberland* came into anchor at the slaving port of Port Praya in St Jago, one of the Cape Verde islands, 412 miles off the west coast of Africa. The joy of coming into port after weeks at sea was offset by sad news. Mary Lethbridge suffered a miscarriage on the morning they anchored.

On 15 October, Charlotte, along with the rest of the party except for the Lethbridges, went ashore to dine with the British Consul General, Joseph Pitman Clarke, and his wife Sarah. Harriet wrote that *the children were delighted with the monkey*. I'm sure Charlotte was too.

According to Harriet's letters, the *Cumberland* also planned to stop at the Cape of Good Hope for water and supplies. Charlotte's 1848 sketchbook includes several illustrations of hunting scenes from South Africa, which may have been inspired by experiences she witnessed during their stopover.

I particularly love the sketch of a lion hunt in South Africa. This may sound odd, because I hate hunting generally, and of course lions are endangered, but what I love is the dogs. Our family grew up owning Rhodesian ridgebacks, which were originally bred for lion hunting in Africa. They are brave, bold, nimble and fiercely loyal—and just like the dogs that Charlotte sketched 170 years ago.

Her drawings also remind me of my own travels in Africa, riding horses on safari in Zimbabwe, hunting giraffes not with rifles but with my camera. In Kenya, my husband Rob and I walked in the footsteps of Karen Blixen in the Ngong Hills and imagined life as it was when she lived here. In Tanzania, Rob and I stalked leopard, buffalo and elephants in the Serengeti and the Ngorongoro Crater. We tried to sleep in our tiny tent, in the bush, but were kept awake by lions and hyenas prowling around our camp. A massive lion lay against our tent and purred and rumbled next to us all night. I could feel the heat of his body through the thin fabric. It seemed impossible that he didn't shred the tent with one swipe of his powerful paw and find us shivering there.

The *Cumberland* arrived safely in Sydney Harbour on 24 January 1827. Harriet noted that:

> *It is impossible we could have had a more favourable voyage, with respect to our weather, provisions etc etc, but we had a great deal of sickness to contend with ... Miss Throsby we gave over ... several times and supposing death approaching, took leave of her; But she rallied and we landed her in comparative health. Copland [Harriet's brother Robert] had an attack of Febry fever, which kept him below four weeks.*

As soon as they arrived in Sydney, the first-class passengers wrote a letter to *The Sydney Gazette*, all of them praising Captain Robert Carns for his kindness.

The 1826 voyage of the *Cumberland* may have been successful, but it had a very tragic postscript. Harriet wrote that:

> *Charles and James arrived about a fortnight after us and [Charles] has entered proceedings against Captain Carns ... angry at the letter written to thank [him]. Charles has quarrelled with Mr Atkinson. He says he was at the bottom of the whole, and instigated Capt C to sailing without him.*

Macarthur's attempt to sue Captain Carns was unsuccessful, as his health worsened. Charles Macarthur died just a few weeks after reaching Sydney, at Vineyard Cottage, on 14 April 1827. He was 34 years old.

Captain Robert Carns set sail on the return journey to London with his son and daughter on board, leaving Hobart on 26 May 1827.

The ship never made it to London. The *Cumberland* was captured by pirates off the Falkland Islands. According to an account written many years later by Charlotte Elizabeth: *A plank was placed, and he was ordered to walk along it into the sea. He caught his daughter by the waist, and jumped over with her, and the son jumped after them, and all three were drowned.*

Chapter 6

BETROTHED

Written by Belinda

*enjoying the blessings which a bountiful Providence
has showered upon us*

Charlotte Waring Atkinson

———⊰◆⊱———

Charlotte Waring's new home was The Vineyard, on the northern banks of the Parramatta River, about 12 miles from Sydney, the household of Maria and Hannibal Macarthur.

At that time Parramatta was the centre of colonial society, with many of the wealthiest families living there. Governor Sir Thomas Brisbane, like Governor Macquarie before him, had preferred to live here at the Georgian country residence of Government House, rather than in Sydney itself.

Charlotte's charges were the three elder daughters—Elizabeth, eleven, Annie, nine and Kate, eight.

Maria Macarthur had given birth to her eighth child, John, just ten days before and was still laid up in bed. The other children were James, aged twelve, Charles, six, Mary, four and George, one. Maria Macarthur was just four years older than Charlotte.

It is mind-boggling to think of the workload of colonial women like Maria Macarthur and Harriet King, with such large families— even when their household included servants and nannies. Despite her recurring bouts of ill health, Maria fostered a warm and loving family life, and encouraged her children to paint and draw.

The Kings and Lethbridges went to stay with the Macarthurs when they arrived in Sydney. Harriet King had managed the journey without giving birth at sea. Her seventh son, Arthur Septimus King, was born at The Vineyard two weeks later.

Harriet wrote to Philip:

You would be astonished were you to see this House, it is so altered, so nicely furnished, and such high rooms ... Elizabeth, Anna and Kate are much grown, they are now very busy with their governess, Miss Waring; it will be a great relief to Maria if she goes on steadily with them. Her engagement still continues with Mr Atkinson but they both say it will not interfere with her engagement to Maria, indeed the Gent has cooled so much, I very much doubt whether it will not cease altogether.

James Atkinson stayed in Sydney for several weeks while he sent to Oldbury for bullock drays to transport his sheep, plants and stock. On 15 February 1827, he was awarded a large gold medal from the Agricultural and Horticultural Society for *An Account of the State of Agriculture & Grazing.*

His return also resulted in several extracts from the book being published in *The Australian* and *The Sydney Gazette*, together with glowing reviews: *Those who would avoid many evils, and secure future happiness, will find an excellent instructor in Mr. Atkinson's book. It is written with great clearness and elegance.* Although the reviewer criticised

James for having written *disrespectfully of a class which is the honour and prop of the community*. These were the poor (mostly emancipist) *dungaree* settlers, who, James lamented, were indolent and had little knowledge of farming—their agricultural practices were *rude and miserable in the extreme.*

Charlotte was only to remain with the Macarthur family for seven months, but during this time she encouraged her students to draw and paint, took them out collecting plants and specimens, and imbued them with a love of nature. This early and ongoing encouragement resulted in both Annie and her younger sister Emmeline becoming accomplished artists and naturalists.

Charlotte continued to write to her students for many years after she left to be married. *A ... governess who had come from a noble house in England cared for us. She ... never lost her interest in us*, wrote Emmeline many years later, although Emmeline was not born until a year after Charlotte Waring was married.

In early April 1827, James Atkinson came to The Vineyard to take Charlotte to stay at his friend Edward Wollstonecraft's Crows Nest cottage on Sydney's North Shore. Edward Wollstonecraft and Alexander Berry, merchants and business partners, had encouraged James Atkinson to emigrate to the colony. Berry and Wollstonecraft had arrived just a few months before him, and James had stayed at the cottage when he first came to Sydney.

In 1822, the partners had been granted 10,000 acres at Coolangatta, at the mouth of the Shoalhaven River, south of Wollongong. Here, with 100 convicts, they established the first European settlement on the south coast of New South Wales. Wollstonecraft mostly managed their merchant business at Sydney Cove, while Berry spent much of his time running the Coolangatta estate—although they sometimes swapped roles.

Wollstonecraft's charming sister, Elizabeth, had recently emigrated, and later the same year married Alexander Berry. Edward and Elizabeth Wollstonecraft were the nephew and niece of Mary Wollstonecraft, author of one of the earliest works of feminist philosophy, *A Vindication of the Rights of Woman*. Their cousin, Mary Shelley, was author of several novels, including *Frankenstein*.

Charlotte stayed at Crows Nest for more than ten days. It is likely that she and Elizabeth discussed Elizabeth's fascinating relatives and their feminist ideology.

Charlotte agreed with many of Mary Wollstonecraft's philosophies, including a woman's right to a quality education and to live an independent life. Charlotte's own vivacity and independent spirit proved distasteful to conservative Scotsman Alexander Berry. He was a strict Calvinist with old-fashioned views on a woman's place.

Alexander wrote about Charlotte to Edward Wollstonecraft, who was away at Coolangatta at the time: *I must say I never saw a lady whose manners were less to my taste, nor do I think less fitted for our plain and plodding friend—the grossest levity!*

Charlotte was always ready for a laugh.

Alexander warmed to Charlotte over the visit, writing a week later: <u>*Our Jim*</u> *... his intended has been living with your sister for the last ten days—No doubt according to the doctrine of contrasts and contraries it will be an excellent match.*

During her stay, James would have taken Charlotte on excursions by boat across the harbour to Sydney, to shop for their coming marriage and to see the sights. The couple would have bought necessities and luxuries for their future home, including books, furniture, china and household items. Sydney in 1827 was less a penal colony and more a growing town of free settlers, with a strong sense of confidence and civic pride as a result of Governor Macquarie's reforms. The city had a thriving commercial sector, and paved streets on a grid plan, with several grand Georgian buildings, particularly along Macquarie Street. This holiday gave Charlotte and James the chance to reconnect and discuss their future.

Charlotte returned to the Macarthurs and stayed until September, when her one-year contract was up. I imagine her growing anticipation as she stitched her wedding dress in the quiet evenings when the children were in bed. In line with the changing fashions of the late 1820s, it would have had puffed 'leg-of-mutton' sleeves and a full skirt, with corseting at the waist, as opposed to the high-waisted empire dresses popular earlier in the decade. In contrast with later Victorian wedding dresses, it was unlikely to have been white—rather, it was probably made from a coloured fabric. Her wedding dress would have been beautiful, but practical enough to be worn again.

Charlotte Waring married James Atkinson by special licence on 29 September 1827 at Denbigh, in Cobbitty, about 37 miles south-west of Sydney. Denbigh was the homestead of the Anglican minister, Reverend Thomas Hassall, who had recently been appointed as the rector of the new parish of Cowpastures. He was known as the 'galloping parson' because he covered such a huge parish, from Cobbitty to Goulburn, while also farming sheep and acting as the local magistrate. Witnesses to the wedding were James' younger brother John and his wife Jane, of Mereworth Farm.

John Atkinson had followed his brother to the colony in 1821 and was granted 2,000 acres adjoining Oldbury to the north, which they called Mereworth after their local village in Kent. John returned to England to marry his sweetheart, Jane Martin. The couple arrived in the colony on the *Mariner*, on 18 October 1823. The two brothers were very close and worked in partnership, with John and Jane living at Oldbury for the first few years.

Harriet King of course had something to say about Charlotte's marriage: *Miss Waring has left them, and is now Mrs Atkinson, she behaved very ill, and gave herself many airs.*

Historian of children's literature, Marcie Muir, noted:

One can understand Mrs King's chagrin in having found and engaged a suitable governess for her sister-in-law, to be thwarted so early … But over and above this natural annoyance there is more than a little malice in Mrs King's tone, inspired by her disapproval of the governess … daring to become betrothed to a gentleman of their acquaintance … One cannot believe from Charlotte Waring's background, or from her character, strongly religious, sensitive and upright, that she would ever have behaved like the giddy or vulgar girl Mrs King suggests.

According to family lore, the Macarthur family never forgave Charlotte for leaving their employ so soon and marrying James. Elaine Johns, a distant relative, told me: *The Macarthurs were not happy with Charlotte because they had paid her handsomely and paid her passage and they expected her to be governess to the children until they had all grown up.*

The Atkinson party would have spent the night before the wedding at Denbigh with Thomas Hassall and his family. After the service, the Atkinsons would have enjoyed a festive wedding breakfast before heading off on the long journey south to Oldbury.

Oldbury was located between Berrima and Sutton Forest, about 80 miles south-west of Sydney. The 56-mile trip from Cobbitty would have been a dangerous, two-day journey, with an overnight stay at one of the early roadside inns.

James probably drove Charlotte in his curricle—a light, two-wheeled carriage, drawn by two matched horses. Completed in 1821, the southern road was a rutted dirt cart-track, which had been cleared by convict gangs under Dr Charles Throsby's supervision, following the old tracks of the Dharawal people. When it rained, the road became boggy and impassable, sometimes for weeks at a time. There were many steep sections over the Mittagong Ranges, where passengers had to walk to save the horses, as well as several rocky and flooded river crossings. The Bargo Brush, 13 miles north-west of Oldbury, was an area of thick bushland, notorious for bushranger attacks.

They passed through Bong Bong, the first settlement in the Southern Highlands, described as *A few miserable huts.* Close to Oldbury was Sutton Forest, an *English village in miniature ... [with] neat cottages, the snug little church, the light timber with its umbrageous foliage, and the refreshing lagoons on the road-side, which invite the weary horse or bullock to slake his thirst on a sultry summer's day.*

✌

On a sunny spring day, Kate and I drive the old way to Sutton Forest, following the route that Charlotte, James, Jane and John Atkinson would have taken in 1827. Fittingly, it is late September, almost 192 years to the day since their wedding. We drive from the historic Hassall farmstead at Denbigh through the rolling green farmland of Cobbitty, past the Macarthur estate at Camden Park, and up and over Razorback Mountain. The road here is a narrow, corrugated dirt track, steep and treacherous even now.

Along the way we spy sandstone churches, tumbledown pioneer cottages, and colonial homesteads. Golden wattle blooms beside the

One of the highlights of our research was discovering this beautiful portrait of our great-great-great grandmother, Charlotte Elizabeth Atkinson, on her nineteenth birthday—and wedding day—in Charlotte Waring Atkinson's 1848 sketchbook, Mitchell Library.

Portrait of Jane Emily Atkinson, who turned 18 on 6 June 1848, perhaps dressed for her first ball, from Charlotte's 1848 sketchbook.

Portrait of Caroline Louisa Atkinson, aged about 14, from Charlotte's
1848 sketchbook.

Butterflies and flowers, from Charlotte's 1843 sketchbook, owned by our mother's second cousin, Neil McCormack.

The 1843 sketchbook features an exquisite dedication from Charlotte to her daughter Emily, on her thirteenth birthday.

Charlotte loved her garden and often drew favourite flowers, such as these roses from her 1843 sketchbook.

Charlotte painted many portraits of beloved family pets, including this curious ginger cat and a cheeky possum, from her 1843 sketchbook.

'Robin, thou art a welcome guest,
When winter comes with chilling gale,
Then in thy ruby corset drest,
Thee as a winter friend we hail.'

'Robin, thou art a welcome guest' is an extract from a poem by her distant kin, Samuel Waring of Alton, featured in his collection of nature poems titled *The Minstrelsy of the Woods* (1832).

The Oldbury garden was filled with birds of all kinds, and Charlotte delighted in sketching them. These examples are from her 1843 sketchbook.

Meticulous studies of various bugs, moths and insects from Charlotte's 1843 sketchbook.

Sailing ships—perhaps including the *Cumberland*—from Charlotte's 1848 sketchbook.

road, along with scarlet Christmas bells and honey-sweet gum blossom. Further south, the thick dark 'brush' around Bargo still looks like it could be the haunt of desperate bushrangers. As we head south towards Berrima, the countryside changes, becoming lush and fertile.

From the west, the road to Oldbury is a dirt track, as it has always been, which crosses a flooded ford of the Medway Rivulet, named for the Medway River in Kent, near James' childhood home at Mereworth. I get out to check the depth, making sure it is safe for us to cross in the Land Cruiser. The water is half a metre at its deepest. My husband Rob has reminded me to check for a tree on the riverbank, in case I need to winch us out! Luckily we get through safely.

Weeping willows line the creek. The elm trees planted by James have a haze of green foliage contrasted against the deep blue sky. The bare hawthorn hedges give us a glimpse through their thorny branches to the golden stone house at the foot of Mount Gingenbullen. Indigo hyacinths cluster on the bank, while past the gate is a swathe of nodding bluebells. Most spectacular are the fruit trees: pear, cherry, peach and apple, with a profusion of sweet-smelling blossoms, from white to hottest pink.

Spring was the perfect season for Charlotte to see Oldbury for the first time.

James brought Charlotte home to *a rustic little white cottage, whose pillars overgrown and shaded by sweetbriar, [with swallows who] chaunted many a merry lay, as they skimmed to and fro.* Charlotte's image of the simple cottage, overgrown with old-fashioned pink roses, sounds charming and homely.

James included a plan of this original cottage in *An Account of the State of Agriculture.* The white-washed timber cottage was built of slabs, with a shingle roof, and finished with lathe and plaster. It included a central sitting room, a kitchen with fireplaces, and the main bedroom, with extra bedrooms on each side. A shady verandah ran across the front and back.

The first simple cottage was built on the side of Mount Gingenbullen, a flat-topped volcanic mountain rising approximately 150 metres above Oldbury. The outbuildings were close by: the stables, dairy and carriage house, a smokehouse for preserving meat and a windmill for grinding grain—the first in the district.

I wonder if the first sight of her new home was a spiral of smoke coming from the campsite of the Wodi Wodi people down by Medway Rivulet.

In *A Mother's Offering*, Charlotte wrote about an old Aboriginal burial mound on the side of Mount Gingenbullen, which hadn't been used since before the Europeans arrived. *The grave on the side of our hill, must have been made at least 23 years ago; and yet the carving in many of the trees is quite visible.* The carving of the trees symbolised that persons of importance were buried there.

From the stories written by Charlotte and later her daughter Louisa, it seems the Atkinson family enjoyed a strong friendship with both the local Sutton Forest and Budgong mobs. The Atkinson family were invited to attend sacred corroborees and ceremonies. Likewise, 'old friends' from the Wodi Wodi people were welcome at Oldbury whenever they came by.

To us, as modern-day readers, their observations of the Aboriginal people seem racist and patronising. However, by the standards of colonial society, their attitudes were unusually sympathetic, concerned and affectionate. They recognised that the Indigenous Australians had been dispossessed of their land, and that colonisation had brought widespread death, disease and destruction of Aboriginal culture.

In 1828, the Oldbury estate covered 2,000 acres, of which 260 acres were cleared for grazing and 86 acres were cultivated with wheat, potatoes, grapes, rye, hops, maize, turnips, barley, flax, oats, grass and peas. The fields were separated by prickly hawthorn hedges, and James had planted windbreaks of conifers and poplars. I don't know if it is true, but I remember my grandparents telling me that Governor Macquarie advised James he could have as much land as he was able to ride around in a day. With the first grant being 1,500 acres, his perimeter would have been about 24 miles, which was a good day's ride in the bush. Later grants brought the Oldbury estate to nearly 3,000 acres.

In addition to the farm at Oldbury, James had permission to graze stock on 4,000 acres of Crown land at Dittalie on the right bank of the Wollondilly River, about one day's ride away, and a cattle outstation at Budgong in the Shoalhaven.

Charlotte's new life must have been very different for her. Now that she was living in the bush, far from civilisation, there were very few other women nearby—and none with her education or background. Most of the population of Oldbury was made up of convicts or labourers, and hardly any of them were female. It didn't take long for her to realise that the bush was a harsh and dangerous place. Two weeks after her marriage, a nest of highly venomous brown snakes was discovered in a hollow tree at Oldbury by one of the workers chopping wood. He counted 35 snakes and killed 15 of them. A child, perhaps four-year-old John Atkinson junior or his brother, two-year-old James, narrowly escaped being bitten. The adults must have been petrified.

On 22 July 1828, ten months after her wedding, Charlotte gave birth to a daughter. She was called Charlotte Elizabeth, after her mother and two grandmothers. Charlotte Elizabeth was our great-great-great-grandmother. Like her mother, Charlotte Elizabeth had black eyes, black hair, a sharp intelligence and a feisty disposition. I often wonder what it must have been like for pioneering women such as Charlotte to give birth in those days, on the edge of civilisation, with no medical assistance. The only women in attendance would have been Jane Atkinson, and perhaps one of the convict's wives who lived nearby. Charlotte's fear of dying must have been very real, especially as her own mother had died in childbirth.

From Charlotte's writing, she seemed to be extremely happy in her new home. Charlotte wrote a story in *A Mother's Offering* about the 'History of the Swallows', inspired by her early time at Oldbury.

> *It was one of those lovely days so frequent in spring, when the sun shines forth in all its splendour; and all nature seems enjoying the blessings which a bountiful Providence has showered upon us ... the lady who inhabited the white cottage (the parlour of which opened into the verandah) sat busying herself with her needle; while her darling baby lay wrapt in soft slumber, in her little cot. All seemed peace and serenity; and the little swallows ... flew into the parlour.*

Charlotte's early married life in the simple cottage would have been a busy whirl—waking at sunrise, tending to her baby, cooking pies and puddings, overseeing the housekeeping, mending and darning, sewing clothes, supervising servants, making tallow candles and soap, visiting the Oldbury families in their rude bark huts, ministering to the sick, cooking meals for harvest and sheep-wash days, and tending to the beehives, henhouse and kitchen garden.

There would not have been much time to enjoy her hobbies of drawing, painting, reading, writing and 'botanising'. Free time would be spent riding on horseback over the estate with James, walking and enjoying the gardens. Charlotte loved to gather wildflowers and observe the native animals and birds in the bush. Birds such as kookaburras, lorikeets, yellow-tailed black cockatoos, rosellas, king parrots, bellbirds, superb fairy wrens, magpies and swallows could be spied in the trees around Oldbury.

In these first years of marriage, Charlotte would have had to learn many new skills that were not part of her English background as a gentlewoman or her profession as a governess. These included gardening, cooking, preparing preserves and jams, baking, and making household goods like candles and soap from scratch.

James would often have been away—travelling to Sydney for business or meetings of the Agricultural Society, visiting the stations at Budgong and Wollondilly to check on the stockmen and cattle, and visiting his *dear friends* Berry and Wollstonecraft at their Coolangatta estate in the Shoalhaven. He had also recently been appointed a magistrate and, together with his neighbour Charles Throsby, regularly sat on the Sutton Forest Court of Petty Sessions, primarily dealing with local convict offenders. James had a reputation for being fair and humane with his judgements.

Essential supplies, such as sugar, tea, coffee, rum, tobacco and tools had to come from Sydney on bullock drays. In bad weather, the drays could be held up for six weeks at a time by flooded rivers or impassable tracks. Oldbury farm was largely self-sufficient, producing its own vegetables, fruit, meat, bread, flour, soap, candles, honey, cheese, poultry, eggs, potatoes, apple and peach cider, leather and cloth.

Oldbury had a store, which distributed rations to all the workers and convicts on the estate. Each worker received a weekly allocation of sugar, tea, wheat, tobacco and meat—beef, mutton or pork. Animals would be slaughtered about once a week to provide fresh meat. With no refrigeration, the leftover meat would be either smoked or salted to preserve it. The store also sold other goods, including pickles, vinegar, jam, currants and rice.

Oldbury was cleared and built with the labour of assigned convicts, as well as that of paid employees and craftsmen. The convicts assigned to Charlotte and James at Oldbury were better off than if they had remained in England, laboured in the colonial work gangs or worked for many of the other settlers in the colony. James had a reputation for being liberal but firm with his assigned convicts, rarely having to resort to the local magistrate to resolve disputes. He really cared about their welfare and actively worked to help them live a better life.

In his book, James urged settlers that in dealing with convicts *Kindness will generally be found more effective than severity*. He encouraged masters to allow convicts to grow their own vegetables, to reward them with cash or animals, to supply them with plentiful rations, to provide comfortable huts and to foster good behaviour rather than resorting to flogging.

James' background made him particularly suitable for life in the colony. The experience of growing up and working on his family's farm in Kent had given him practical farming skills. Additionally, his experience of working with the Royal Navy at Deptford had provided him with excellent people management skills, which proved invaluable when supervising the convict and free workforce. James was intelligent, energetic, generous, practical and thorough.

James employed many skilled tradesmen among his convict workers, including weavers, shoemakers and tailors—who worked for other neighbouring properties for additional wages. Building work on the property was done by skilled free tradesmen.

In November 1828, the colony of New South Wales held its first census, which found the total European population was 36,598 people, including both convicts (15,728) and free settlers (20,870). Of these, 23.8 per cent of the population were born in the colony and only 24.5 per cent were women.

The Aboriginal population was counted in a separate return. In 1828, James wrote to the Colonial Secretary expressing his concern about the welfare of the Indigenous people and their future:

The Black Tribes in this district have greatly decreased in number within the last few years, and it is probable in a short time, will be nearly extinct;—When I was first acquainted with this country about 8 years since, the Sutton Forest Tribe consisted of at least 50 Men, Women and Children. They are now reduced to 18.

James' concern for the Indigenous people was unusual for its time, and he believed it was possible for colonists to develop *what was before a Wild and Worthless wilderness into a cultivated and highly improved farm* while living in harmony with the traditional owners.

James wrote that the Aboriginal people *are a mild, cheerful and inoffensive race; passionately fond of their wandering life, and averse to labour of every kind … and live among the Settlers on terms of perfect amity and confidence.*

This report by James clearly reflected his own warm relationships with Wodi Wodi communities. Not all colonists cultivated such friendly relations, and there were several instances of clashes between the Indigenous people and Europeans in the region. James laid the blame for most intercultural hostilities at the door of the Europeans. The Aboriginal people *have seldom been the original aggressors; unable to bear the continual ill treatment of the unprincipled herdsmen and shepherds in the interior, who … have taken away their women by force, and otherwise wronged them, they have at length been roused to revenge.*

James reported on the Aboriginal people of Sutton Forest and Budgong and requested that the government provide blankets and clothes.

This Tribe, although one of the most docile and peaceable possible have never had any Slops given to them. The principal person among them is Thomas Errombee an elderly man of the most quiet inoffensive disposition, and greatly respected by his countrymen. I beg to recommend that a plate should be presented to him inscribed 'Errombee Chief of the Budjong tribe'.

It was this Errombee who had saved James' life when they became lost in the gorges of the Shoalhaven. His community was described as living at Sutton Forest, Kangaroo Ground and both sides of the Shoalhaven River.

At Oldbury, James, Charlotte and baby Charlotte Elizabeth lived in the main cottage with 15-year-old Henry Sayer Lewes, who had come out with them on the *Cumberland* to learn farming. James employed 17 people, mostly convicts, including overseer John Woodger, two ploughmen, four labourers, one dairyman, three shepherds, one miller, one female servant and one male servant, and two stockmen at the outstation at Budgong. Their livestock included 17 horses, 184 cattle, 974 sheep and 32 pigs as well as hens, ducks, geese and peafowl.

James reported that the improvements to the property included the main cottage, costing £150, a dairy, £100, a barn, £100, a stable, £50, plus a cow-yard, piggery, workers' huts and 14 miles of fencing, together costing £300.

Oldbury itself was like a private hamlet. As well as the main residence, and the usual farm buildings, there were several smaller timber slab huts, for farm workers and convicts. These were simple dwellings with bark roofs and rough wooden shutters instead of glazed windows. In one of these lived a constable, Phillip Dunahoe, with his wife and three children, supporting James' work as a magistrate.

There were also two families whose presence there gives a real insight into James Atkinson's kindness, compassion and concern for people.

Some of the first convicts who were assigned to James Atkinson were Robert Ritchie, John Jenkins and John Hollands. Robert Ritchie, a labourer from Norfolk, stole eleven geese, nine ducks and six turkeys and was sentenced to seven years transportation, leaving behind a pregnant wife and four children. In 1822, James successfully petitioned for Robert's family to be brought to New South Wales. Ann Ritchie and three young children arrived at Oldbury in 1825, with two daughters having died back in England.

John Jenkins and John Hollands were illiterate labourers from East Malling in Kent. James requested convicts who came from his home county.

Jenkins and Hollands had *feloniously and burglariously* broken into the house of a widow, stealing four beds, seventeen blankets, six counterpanes, eight pillows, four bolsters, one pair of snuffers and a pin cushion. They were originally given a death sentence, but were later sentenced to transportation for life, arriving in Port Jackson in 1821. John Jenkins left behind his wife Charlotte and five children under the age of nine, while John Hollands left his pregnant wife Mary and four children under the age of eight. Without their husbands, the families were left destitute and were consigned to a workhouse in Halling.

Workhouses were the last resort of paupers. Living conditions were appalling, designed to discourage the poor from seeking charity. People worked long hours for no pay, doing menial work such as breaking rocks, cooking, scrubbing floors and making clothes. Families were split up and slept in overcrowded dormitories, with four or five to a bed. When illness such as smallpox or typhoid swept through the workhouse, the death rate was high.

Over several years, James Atkinson lobbied for the Jenkins and Hollands families to be brought to the colony. Eventually permission was granted, but the wives themselves were reticent about coming halfway around the world to an unknown future. James wrote several letters to the wives encouraging them to come to Australia. It is indicative of the reputation of New South Wales that both women preferred the known squalor of the workhouse to the unknown terror of the new world.

When James Atkinson was in England, he went to visit both Charlotte Jenkins and Mary Hollands to convince them of the merits of the plan. Mary Hollands' case was complicated by the fact that she had given birth to twin girls, to a different father. James assured her that the twins would be welcome. It took some time for the women to agree, and then several petitions from James Atkinson and a visit to the Home Secretary, but eventually permission was granted. One of Mary Hollands' twin girls died in the poorhouse before they left.

The two families came out to New South Wales on the *Grenada*, in September 1826, just before the *Cumberland* sailed. James Atkinson stayed in Deptford to see them safely onto the ship. The *Grenada* surgeon noted how malnourished the Hollands children were and believed seven-year-old John would die. However, the whole family survived the rigours of the journey and arrived in the colony the day before James and Charlotte.

As free settlers, the two women were given land grants close to Oldbury, and then James organised for their husbands to be assigned to their care. James found jobs for the children, including 11-year-old Elizabeth Jenkins, who worked as a serving girl, helping Charlotte in the house.

The Jenkins became one of the most successful farming families in the district, buying Berrima House, where their family lived for generations—a far cry from the poorhouse in Halling.

There is another lovely twist to the story of the Hollands family. Many, many years later, Jen Paterson, our fourth cousin, a descendant not only of Charlotte and James Atkinson, but also of the Macarthur family, married Martin Paterson, a descendant of Mary and John Hollands. Jen tells us that the Hollands family descendants are still eternally grateful to James Atkinson for their good fortune.

These stories give a fascinating insight, not only into James Atkinson's character, but also into the opportunities available to convicts who worked hard in the colony. Working-class families like the Hollands, Jenkins and Ritchies could never have afforded to own land in England.

Life at Oldbury was going well for Charlotte, James and baby Charlotte Elizabeth. Charlotte's contentment shines through in her anecdotes of those days.

Chapter 7

OLDBURY

Written by Belinda

All seemed peace and serenity

Charlotte Waring Atkinson

―――●◆●―――

Building a home

For Charlotte's wedding gift, James built her a beautiful eight-bedroom, three-storey house, surrounded by extensive gardens, to recreate a small piece of England in the harsh Australian bush. The homestead was built of golden sandstone, in the Georgian style, and today is one of the oldest surviving houses in the Southern Highlands.

The ground level has an entry hallway with a grand carved cedar staircase leading upstairs. To the left is an elegant drawing room with a cedar fireplace, to the right a large dining room. Both have multipaned windows overlooking the garden and the circular carriageway. The craftsmen's work on the cedar joinery is particularly fine, especially considering how inaccessible Oldbury was from Sydney at the time. James wrote that it was exorbitantly expensive to entice skilled craftsmen so far from town. The red cedar probably came from Budgong, while the sandstone was quarried from nearby Black Bobs Creek by Ambrose Brian, the stonemason who built the house.

Towards the back of the house, in Charlotte's day, there was a breakfast room, an office, a storeroom and a schoolroom. Upstairs were three large bedrooms facing the front garden and five smaller bedrooms across the back. The bottom level comprised four stone-paved cellars. Separate stone buildings housed the dairy to the left and the kitchen to the right. Behind the house were other farm buildings, including stables and a barn.

A large orchard of quince, apple, pear, peach, plum, cherry, crabapple and citrus trees was planted to the right of the house, running down towards the string of deep waterholes along Medway Rivulet. The peaches were so plentiful that James fed his pigs on them for months at a time.

In front was a rambling cottage garden of old-fashioned 'China' and cabbage roses, lilacs, the rare white *Camellia japonica* 'Planipetala', lilies, bluebells, scented geraniums and violets, with shrubberies on either side. The garden was protected by clipped hawthorn and conifer hedges, and framed by plantings of English oak, Monterey pine, Himalayan cedar and Mediterranean cypress. A circular carriageway, surrounded by rolling lawns, marked the formal entry to the homestead. Many of these trees and shrubs survive to this day.

Over the years, I have visited Oldbury many times. There were the very first visits with my grandparents when we were children, when the house was run-down and neglected. I can remember fervently assuring Nonnie and Papa that when I grew up I would buy the old house and return it to our family, where it belonged. In my early twenties, I took my boyfriend, Rob, to see the house, long before he became my husband. Later, I took my own three children, Nick, Emily and Lachie, to show them the house built by their great-great-great-great-great-grandparents, sharing with them the stories that I had grown up with.

Each time, it would be a bumpy drive down a dirt road, lined with ancient elms. Somewhere near the locked gates or the flooded creek crossing, we would pull over and park, then wander along the boundary, peering through the prickly, overgrown hedges, trying to get a glimpse of the sandstone house. Over the years, I rejoiced as the house was renovated and the gardens slowly brought back to their former glory.

I badgered my grandmother so often for stories about Charlotte de Waring and Oldbury that when Nonnie died in 2001 she left me a pile of her treasures, including a painting she had done of Oldbury, which hangs in my study, and her handwritten account of the Atkinson family. She also left me copies of Charlotte's book *A Mother's Offering to Her Children* and James' *Account of the State of Agriculture*, as well Patricia Clarke's biography of Louisa Atkinson.

In 2012, when I was writing *The River Charm*, my novel based on the Atkinson family, I approached the owner of Oldbury, asking if I could come to visit the house. At first, keen to preserve his privacy, he said no, but a few weeks later he invited me to bring Kate, my mother Gilly and my stepfather Glyn to a fundraising spring cocktail party that he was hosting at Oldbury.

Kate and I arrived together, dressed in our best silk cocktail dresses, and I parked in the creek paddock. As we walked up to Oldbury over the lawns I burst into sobbing tears, completely overwhelmed by finally visiting the house that had played such a huge part in my imagination and dreams since I was a child. I felt in a strange way like I was coming home. Visiting Oldbury properly for the first time was an intensely emotional experience.

We had the most magical spring evening, with our mother and Glyn, wandering around the formal gardens, parterre and orchard in the golden evening light, sipping champagne. The gardens were glorious—filled with spotted foxgloves, blue lupins, pink and white old-fashioned roses, forget-me-nots, lavender and shasta daisies. We chatted with the owners and members of the local historical society, smelling the heavenly roses and seeing the house that I'd only ever glimpsed from afar. In many ways, the house is just as it was when it was built in 1828, although a couple of upstairs bedrooms have been converted to bathrooms. The kitchen is still in a separate stone wing, while the dairy has been converted to a separate study and living room.

It was easy to imagine what it might have been like when Charlotte and James first built it, nearly two hundred years ago.

A long straight driveway, lined with English poplars and elms, led north-west from Oldbury across to James' brother John's property, Mereworth, a mile away. John and Jane replaced their simple timber cottage with a two-storey, nine-bedroom brick house, also surrounded by beautiful gardens. John bred horses and ran cattle, but didn't cultivate his property like James did. John loved horseracing and had a racing track near the house. In the 1828 census, John and Jane also had a growing family, with John Oldbury, aged five, James Oldbury, three, and baby Jane Elizabeth, who was five months older than Charlotte Elizabeth.

The two Atkinson families would have been constant visitors, travelling back and forth between Mereworth and Oldbury, enjoying dinners, picnics by the creek, fishing, horse-riding expeditions and musical entertainment. Charlotte played the pianoforte and sang, while John Atkinson played the bass viol (a mini cello) and oboe. Extended family dinners would have been merry affairs, with much laughter and joking as they enjoyed Sunday feasts of roast pork or chicken, baked potatoes and vegetables, peach and apple pies, strawberry tarts and plum cake.

Over the coming years, both families were blessed with more children. At Oldbury, Jane Emily was born on 6 June 1830, named after Charlotte's beloved sister but always called Emily. Emily was everyone's favourite—she was a gentle peacemaker, with brown hair and grey eyes. Her sister Louisa later described her as *pious, clever, amiable, her gentle face & peaceful form rendered her at once an object of admiration & love.* James John Oldbury, the son and heir, was born on 7 April 1832.

At Mereworth, John and Jane Atkinson would go on to have another four children.

Oldbury was a magical place to grow up. The children ran and played in the orchard with their dogs, went yabbying in the waterholes and rode their ponies. I was told that Charlotte Elizabeth was prone to escaping out the schoolroom window to go exploring. Charlotte began their education early, teaching them to read and write, to draw and paint, to play musical instruments and to embody the Christian morals that she espoused—generosity, kindness, humility and charity. Most importantly, Charlotte nurtured their creativity and curiosity, and kindled an avid passion for learning and the natural world.

The back schoolroom held a museum of curiosities, with shelves of shells, fossils and rock samples, as well as collections of plant specimens, and the latest pet wildlife—perhaps an orphan possum, curled in an old shawl, or a tame joey. However, Charlotte believed the best place to learn was outdoors, rambling through the bush, drawing butterflies and birds or poking in the waterholes. Her philosophy was always to observe, draw and learn, but not to take life unnecessarily.

Like her father before her, Charlotte loved animals. The family had numerous dogs, including working sheepdogs and James' hunting dogs, who would all race from the house barking and wagging their tails when visitors arrived. Charlotte drew tender sketches of several family cats.

The children raised orphan lambs and calves, as well as taming wildlife such as possums, kangaroos, echidnas and koalas. All the children rode horses almost from the time they could walk. I can imagine James, with his patience and gentle humour, teaching the children to ride their ponies just as my father taught me to ride when I was young.

Charlotte had servants to help her in the house, including a cook, a nurse to help with the children, a housemaid to do the cleaning and washing, and a dairyman to make cheese and butter and milk the cows. Even with this domestic help, her work day would have been busy.

In June 1829, a young English emigrant called Randolph Want arrived at Oldbury with a letter of introduction from Sir John Jamison, one of New South Wales' wealthiest pastoralists. According to Randolph's diary, *Mr Atkinson was considered to be one of the most advanced agriculturalists in the colony.* James welcomed him warmly but confessed to being *a little embarrassed* as the family were in the *midst of arrangements for a ploughing competition.* Oldbury was a *hive of activity*, with guests bunked on the verandah or sleeping on their drays under tarpaulins. Charlotte would have been busy feeding and looking after all these guests. *In the kitchen … a large fire burned continuously. A bullock had been slaughtered for the occasion and there was no shortage of meat for the guests.*

Randolph stayed for several days, recording the details of the ploughing competition and James' rationale behind it—to encourage better agricultural practices in the colony. It sounded like a fun and festive affair, with participants travelling from far and wide to attend.

James continued to implement his agricultural reforms—running ploughing competitions, erecting a windmill and later a steam mill to grind grain for local farmers, and experimenting with stock breeding, cheese making and cultivation practices. He introduced grape growing to the area, and was the first farmer to distill spirit from his own grain, grow hops, and build a malthouse and brewery to provide beer for the district. Several contemporary sources compliment James for being an outstanding, innovative and model farmer.

In 1829, a small wooden chapel was erected at Sutton Forest. At first, Reverend Thomas Hassall, the 'galloping parson', would visit every few weeks to conduct a service. In 1831, John Vincent was appointed as the first minister for All Saints, arriving with his wife Eliza and four young daughters. This gave the leading families of the district, including Charlotte and James, and Jane and John Atkinson, a new opportunity to socialise after services and create a strong sense of community. The first christening conducted at the new church was for James John Oldbury Atkinson.

James continued with his writing career. He frequently sent letters to the newspaper about issues of the day and wrote several short essays, including 'Remarks on the Saxon Sheep Farming', which was published in 1828. In 1829, he published *On the Expediency and Necessity of Encouraging Distilling and Brewing from Grain in New South Wales*, proposing that settlers owning over 100 acres be allowed to operate their own stills, rather than having to send grain to the distilleries in Sydney. It was so popular that a second, expanded edition was published later the same year.

I'm sure Charlotte was involved in discussing James' literary work with him and proofreading his articles and papers, just as my husband Rob and daughter Emily help me by proofing my writing. It was James' success as an author that inspired Charlotte to publish her own book and encouraged their daughters Charlotte Elizabeth and Louisa with their writing as adults.

Charlotte and James moved in the highest society of New South Wales. They frequently entertained visitors from England and elsewhere in the colony, as well as hosting the 'landed gentry' from the district. A highlight of their success was a visit by the popular new governor, Major General Sir Richard Bourke (accompanied by his son and private secretary Richard, as well as Surveyor General Sir Thomas Mitchell and surgeon Dr Alexander Imlay), on Tuesday 26 June 1832, as part of his tour of the Southern Highlands. The party had lunch at Oldbury and the Governor inspected the estate, *with which he expressed himself most pleased.*

Governor Bourke had planned to attend the annual Sutton Forest Ploughing Match and dinner hosted at Oldbury two weeks earlier, but the Governor's tour had been delayed when his horse fell and rolled on him. Instead, Sir Richard offered to present the winning ploughman with a silver medal. This was won by Patrick Smith, one of James' assigned servants. *The Sydney Gazette* of 19 June 1832 recorded that *in the evening a large party dined at Oldbury, and spent the evening with the utmost cordiality.* The party would have included all the leading families of the district.

While Charlotte and James had good relationships with most of their assigned convicts, the Oldbury estate was often the target of thieves and bushrangers. Sometimes it would be the odd stolen horse, cow or sheep. At other times, it was far more serious.

On 17 August 1829, the store at Oldbury was robbed, the thieves making off with 40 pounds of soap, half a chest of tea and 30 pounds of sugar, as well as leather, tobacco and other items. James suspected one of his assigned convicts, Patrick Brady, who eventually confessed and named three accomplices—another Oldbury convict, Joseph Shelvey, and John Yates and John Champly from Bong Bong.

On Brady's detailed testimony, the three men were charged, found guilty and sentenced to death. The coffins had already been made when the sentence was commuted by Governor Bourke to hard labour and transportation for life to Norfolk Island. The incident was complicated by a confession two years later, made by notorious bushranger William Webber, prior to his execution, claiming that he had committed the robbery alone. James Atkinson refuted this, as Webber did not seem to have an intimate knowledge of the robbery. However, sufficient doubt was raised and the original prisoners were set free.

In 1830, Charles Peak was indicted for stealing sheep from Oldbury, then, in 1832, John Johnson was indicted for breaking into the Oldbury dairy and stealing a horse, hens and butter. He was sentenced to death.

A horrific crime was committed at Oldbury just before Christmas, when Charlotte was heavily pregnant with her fourth child. On 23 December 1833, Frances Cunningham, the wife of the new Oldbury overseer, was raped in her cottage by John Elliott, who worked on a neighbouring farm. He found her at home alone with her child, tricked his way inside the house and then threatened to kill her. The Cunninghams had arrived in the colony in November, and Frances' husband had only started work at Oldbury four days before. At the time of the attack he was out reaping the harvest with the other workers in a field a mile away.

At first Frances did not admit that she had been raped, but her husband suspected so from her agitated manner. John Elliott was indicted in February and hanged in March 1834. This violent crime, conducted in Frances' own home, must have caused great distress to all the Oldbury residents, especially the women. Charlotte, who usually administered medical aid to the Oldbury workers and their families, may have had to care for Frances after her ordeal.

On 25 February 1834, Charlotte gave birth to a daughter, Caroline Louisa Waring. The baby was delicate and was later diagnosed with a heart defect. Charlotte must have worried about whether her daughter, who was always known as Louisa, would survive.

However, Charlotte had something much worse to worry about. In January 1834, James fell sick and was severely ill for many weeks, his condition gradually declining. On 5 February, Scotsman George Bell wrote in his journal that he tried to call at Oldbury *to enquire after James Atkinson whom I understood to be very ill* but Charlotte was too upset to see him. James was being treated by his close friend, Berrima surgeon Dr John Godden Colyer, who was James junior's godfather.

It has been conjectured that James contracted typhoid fever after drinking contaminated water on Razorback Mountain, when returning from a trip to Sydney. Typhoid fever is a bacterial infection, which causes prolonged high fever and sweating, delirium, severe headaches, abdominal pain and diarrhoea, lack of appetite, dehydration and weight loss. Over a few weeks, the patient becomes exhausted and emaciated. In the days before antibiotics, the disease caused many deaths.

Charlotte, still weak from childbirth, would have nursed James through his final illness, bathing him, feeding him and trying to alleviate his pain and fever.

Louisa later wrote:

James Atkinson was a handsome, clever man much respected. He died in the prime of life when only 39 years of age from inflammation brought on by drinking impure water on the top of Razorback when heated. It was during his last illness that I was born & probably he never saw me as when carried into his room I cried & he ordered me to be removed.

James Atkinson died on 30 April 1834, *after a painful and lingering illness*, leaving Charlotte and the children bereft. He was buried in the graveyard of All Saints Church at Sutton Forest in a sandstone vault. The inscription read:

Sacred to the Memory of

James Atkinson of Oldbury, Esq. J.P.

Who departed this life April 30th 1834

in the 40th year of his age

after a long and severe illness, which he

bore with exemplary patience and Christian

resignation, leaving a widow and four infant

children to lament their mournful bereavement.

To them his loss is irreparable.

He lived universally beloved and respected

and died regretted by all who knew him.

He was a sincere friend and benevolent neighbour

and an impartial and upright magistrate.

MAY HIS SPIRIT REST IN PEACE

For he remembered the poor when they cried

the needy also and him that had no helper.

Charlotte was devastated. She was left a single mother, with four children under the age of six and vast estates to run. As well as the 2,760 acres at Oldbury, James and Charlotte had a small sheep station at Galgan, about four miles from Berrima, sheep out-stations at Belanglo, the right to run stock on 4,000 acres of crown land at Dittalie on the Wollondilly River, and a cattle station at Budgong in the Shoalhaven.

I can only imagine how grief-stricken Charlotte was at James' tragic death and how difficult it must have been to deal with the multiple estates, numerous servants, unruly convicts and four small children, one of whom was sickly. How all-encompassing the grief must have been and how hard to carry on, day after day, battling against overwhelming odds. How it was only her love for her four young children that kept her going.

I have such huge admiration for Charlotte for her courage, sheer grit and determination. Due to the turmoil following James' death, baby Louisa wasn't christened until 15 October 1834, when she was eight months old.

As a child, I had an inkling of what it was like to lose a father. My own father, whom I adored, left us when I was a teenager and moved away to Queensland. Like all children in this situation, we struggled with the implosion of our family when my parents divorced. Of course, we still saw my dad for holiday visits, when he whisked us away for adventurous sailing trips or journeys to remote cattle stations. There was the occasional dinner when he came to Sydney. We loved spending time with him as he always shared fascinating travel tales, or funny stories of life as a vet. I missed him terribly.

It was only later, when I was an adult, that I realised how hard it must have been for my mum to be a single working parent—the one making us clean our teeth and do our homework, the one juggling the finances and tackling the tricky teenage years. The one to inspire us to do our best, to make sure we had an outstanding education, to cultivate our talents.

It was my mother Gilly who taught Kate and me to be strong and independent women. It is our mum who encourages all three of us to write and to follow our dreams, to fight for what we believe in and to value our family above all else. My mother is also a fabulous cook, who creates amazing meals where you can taste the love. She taught us to cook as children, and we have always treasured the joy of eating together as a family. It is my mother who binds us all together.

It is around the time that I am writing about James' death that I feel like I lose my way with our *Searching for Charlotte* book. It has been months of research, much of it resulting in dead ends or getting lost down rabbit holes that lead nowhere. The book seems to me like a many-headed monster, which I am unable to control. There is so much information and I am struggling to know what to include and what to leave out.

One Sunday, Kate and I drive down to Exeter to interview historian Linda Emery, Archivist of the Berrima District Historical and Family History Society. She lives in a beautiful country house, not far from Oldbury, surrounded by cottage gardens. She welcomes us with tea served in delicate fine bone china, accompanied by homemade scones, cream and strawberry jam. We chat about the Atkinsons. Linda has spent years researching the family and knows its history intimately.

At first, she is rather reserved, asking us questions to see what we have researched and what we know about the history. We talk to her about our findings and the difference between the historical facts and the family stories we were told as children. Linda laughs.

'One of the problems with oral history is that people don't want their family to be ordinary—they want them to be extraordinary,' she says.

We have the most delightful afternoon, discussing Charlotte and James, and their fascinating stories. Linda has great admiration and affection for them both.

'I think Charlotte was a romantic,' says Linda. 'She was tiny—a feisty pocket-rocket, who knew what she wanted. She wasn't cowed. I don't think many young women of that time would have stood up to the combined disapproval of the Kings and Macarthurs.'

Linda feels that some of the local gentry would not have warmed to Charlotte because she was so outspoken and opinionated. 'She was a difficult woman for her time and too strong to be bullied. She fought for her children and her inheritance. She loved her children, educated them well and they adored her.'

She tells us that Charlotte was a superb horsewoman and a great walker. As Linda talks about Charlotte and James, I feel so proud of them both. She tells us stories about James' compassion and humanity, as evidenced by the trouble he took to bring out the Jenkins and Hollands families.

'James was a shrewd businessman … a man of integrity. He was a great humanist, who understood people, which is why he was able to run such a successful enterprise. He managed the men so well and rarely brought his convicts to court. After he died, Charlotte and George Barton were less able to manage their convicts and had to bring them in front of the magistrate to discipline them more regularly.'

We chat about etiquette, morals and what life was like for colonial women.

Linda shocks us when she suddenly changes the subject. 'Have you heard about the rumour of the alleged Aboriginal massacre at Oldbury?' she asks.

'*No*,' we both chorus.

'There was a rumour that James Atkinson might have massacred members of the local Aboriginal community at Oldbury.'

Kate and I look at each other in horror. I feel sick in the stomach. Could our ancestors be responsible for murdering innocent people? Of course, I know that many shameful atrocities were committed against the Aboriginal people all over Australia. I know that James Atkinson and other European settlers were responsible for dispossessing the Wodi Wodi of their land, but I'd always believed that the Atkinson family were unusually fascinated by Aboriginal culture and concerned for the welfare of Indigenous Australians.

'Really?' I ask, my throat dry. 'I can't imagine that.'

'No, neither can I,' said Linda, firmly. 'James was highly respectful of the Aboriginal people and admired their intellect.'

She explained that someone had published an article claiming that James Atkinson 'had died young of sheer obesity—but not before poisoning and disposing of an entire tribe of Aborigines' and buried them in a mass grave on Mount Gingenbullen. The concept is horrible.

Linda shows us a book called *The Aborigines of the Southern Highlands*, which extensively examines the evidence. Thankfully, the author, local historian Narelle Bowern, concludes that there is no evidence to support the allegation. She writes: *The most compelling evidence against the occurrence of a massacre relates to the chronology of events.*

Charlotte's own written account from 1841 states: *The grave on the side of our hill must have been made at least 23 years ago; and yet the carving in many of the trees is quite visible: though we can only from that circumstance, conjecture where the grave was.* Later, Louisa recorded it was *forty-four years since an old man was buried there.*

This dates the last interment at about 1818, three years before James Atkinson arrived. Louisa's sketches also show the trees carved with totem patterns. Bowern writes that *the presence of carved trees is important, since it indicates that the grave site was a traditional Aboriginal burial ground reserved for important people, rather than a common mass burial.*

Bowern examines the population of local Aboriginal people and concludes the numbers did not vary greatly between 1820 and James' death in 1834. She notes that James, unlike many colonists, always welcomed the Aboriginal community at Oldbury, and that local corroborees, attended by hundreds of Indigenous people, were regularly held there.

It is clear that they trusted him and he treated them well. Atkinson was mourned by the Aboriginal people for years after his death. Bowern concludes that the rumour of a massacre is *plainly untenable* and that it *detracts from the real value of the history of the site ... as a traditional Aboriginal burial ground.*

Kate and I feel hugely relieved.

I confide to Linda my struggles with writing Charlotte's story. What to include. What to leave out. How to stop myself from spending months getting lost in the research.

Linda is sympathetic and gives us a mantra to try to keep us focused. 'It's interesting but is it relevant?'

I find myself asking this question over and over as I plough through my research notes and try to decide what should be included and what must inevitably be left out. There are hundreds of details that I find fascinating, but that I suspect only a close family member might want to know. I waste days trying to determine minor details and then realise that perhaps no one really cares.

Day after day, Kate and I walk up and down Manly beach with our faithful Rhodesian ridgebacks, Rosie and Lola, discussing what should be included and what should be cut out. The manuscript is getting too long and we disagree on minor issues. We are both frustrated, hampered by questions we can't possibly answer or by conflicting opinions. Once or twice we argue heatedly.

It all seems too hard. Will we ever finish writing this book?

Chapter 8

GRIEF

Written by Belinda

This my loves, should teach us never to despond;
however painfully we may be situated

Charlotte Waring Atkinson

———⟫⬥⟪———

My frustration with the book at this time is exacerbated by stress in our everyday lives. Our father, Gerry, who has always been as strong and fit as a country vet, is suddenly struck by a series of illnesses, which he does his best to hide from us. In February he comes to stay with me as we celebrate his eightieth birthday. Dad has been unwell but assures us it is nothing.

We celebrate his birthday at my house with a loud and noisy extended family dinner, a Mediterranean feast of baba ganoush, roast lamb with lemon, garlic and rosemary, baked vegetables, eggplant, mint and pomegranate salad, and tzatziki. There are 18 of us including the nine grandchildren, and Dad's brother John and his wife Mardi up from Melbourne. We share stories, laugh and tease each other. Over ten days, we have many family celebrations, a trip to my brother's farm, and quiet chats over cups of tea. Dad seems much better when he flies home.

Two weeks later, he drops a bombshell. Dad rings to tell me that he has been hiding a secret from us for 37 years.

We have a secret half-sister. Her name is Emma Jane. Coincidentally, her name is made up of Kate's and my middle names. She grew up a few kilometres from where we lived on the North Shore and is now married with two little girls. Dad tells me that I have already met her very briefly, when I dropped him off to meet some of his old friends in February. At that meeting, Emma knew who I was, but I didn't know who she was. Emma was conceived after my parents divorced, when Dad met Annie, an adventurous, bubbly and well-travelled Scottish woman, in Hobart. Dad has only met his other daughter a handful of times, but he tells me that Emma is clever like us.

My whole world view shifts. My whole concept of the family I knew changes. At first, Dad struggles to talk about it, but then he is so relieved to have the secret out in the open. It is as though a huge burden has been lifted. The first thing I do is ring my sister Kate, then my brother Nick. I talk about it with my own family, trying to get my head around it. My children are so accepting. They feel sad for Emma, growing up with no siblings and no father. They think it would be wonderful if Emma becomes part of our crazy family! I text Emma and ask her if she would like to meet us. She would.

On a Saturday morning in late March, Kate, Nick, Emma and I meet at my house. Emma arrives looking nervous but excited. She looks a little like Kate—with dark hair and pale Scottish skin with a smattering of freckles. My husband Rob makes us all coffee. We sit around my kitchen table, talking, laughing, sipping flat whites and eating croissants with raspberry jam. My kids wander in and out on their way to various jobs or to go for a swim. Our dog Rosie sniffs around. The four of us talk for nearly six hours, sharing stories of our childhood, our family history and our shared father. Emma is keen to know everything. She is keen to discover familial similarities. There are many. When she leaves, we all hug and promise to keep in touch.

I visit Dad in Queensland a few weeks later. He is still not well but has been seeing various doctors and heart specialists. The day before we fly to England, Dad collapses. I speak to him hours before we get on the plane and he assures me he is fine, that there is nothing to worry about.

Shortly after we return from England, we realise just how ill Dad has been. He collapses again, rings the ambulance and is rushed to Sunshine Coast University Hospital. He is so sick that he cannot tell the staff who his next of kin are or where we live. It is 48 hours before the doctors can get enough information to track me down. I am devastated when I receive the call on Friday afternoon telling me that my father is in intensive care, with a dissected aorta, and he may not survive the weekend. I am asked if I think Dad would wish to be resuscitated in a critical situation. I can't answer for crying.

I go into hyperdrive, phoning first Kate, then Nick, then the many members of our extended family. There are endless calls with doctors, social workers, specialists and nurses, explaining how critically ill he is. The dissected aorta is like a time bomb and could burst at any time.

My brother and I cancel everything, book the first available flight and spend the journey writing lists, making plans and trying not to cry.

Nick and I are hugely relieved when we walk into the ICU ward and find Dad, weak and delirious, but conscious that we are there. He looks like a shrunken version of his usual self, and is so relieved to see us. As though he never expected to see us again. Nick and I have the worst three days, making decisions, keeping the family informed and discussing with Dad what his resuscitation wishes are. He is adamant that in a life and death situation he does not wish to be resuscitated.

Little do we know that as we fly home our mother Gilly is being rushed to hospital by ambulance, with a life-threatening kidney infection and septicaemia. Both our parents are delirious, in intensive care, with critical illnesses, in different hospitals in different states, not expected to live. I can't sleep. I have intense migraines. I focus on ticking my way through my list of jobs to stop myself from falling into a quivering heap.

My stress levels are through the roof, yet I have so much to do for work. Not only am I writing *Searching for Charlotte*, but I am in the final editing stage of two separate junior fiction stories, plus the early stages of a middle grade novel. My beautiful publisher and editor tell me to take the time I need.

It is also the beginning of Book Week term, and I have 38 speaking presentations at schools in Sydney, Melbourne and country New South Wales over the coming month. Most have been booked for months. For one of these I am parked at the school, talking to the doctor on the phone, and desperately crying, then I need to wipe my face, summon a dazzling smile and walk into the room to run creative writing workshops with 200 students.

Two weeks later both Mum and Dad are discharged from their different hospitals. They are out of immediate danger, but weak. Mum goes home to recuperate, looked after by my stepfather Glyn. Dad has no one at home, so I set off with my husband Rob and two of my children, 21-year-old Emily and 19-year-old Lachie, to drive a 2,300-kilometre round trip to Eumundi. We have four days to drive 13 hours to Queensland, pack up his life, prepare his home for sale and drive him back to our house in Manly. Dad is too sick to fly.

It is emotionally traumatic for all of us. Dad is very weak, and the doctors have told us to make sure he stays calm and avoids stress, to keep his blood pressure low at all costs. His aorta could still burst at any moment. Dad doesn't know what to bring, or what to do, and we must make tough decisions for him. We pack up his life—photos, books and exotic carvings from his many travels around the world. And of course, Toby, his beloved, huge and rambunctious Rhodesian ridgeback.

Before we go, my friend Sarah gives me some words of wisdom. 'I know it will be a really tough time, Binny. But remember, among all the sadness and stress, there will be moments of joy and celebration. Try to make the most of the happy times.'

She is so right. My kids love the chance to revisit the farm at Eumundi that holds so many vivid holiday memories. My son Lachie rescues a large carpet python that we discover entwined in one of Dad's dining room chairs. Dad's friends have been a huge help, minding Toby the dog, doing odd jobs and visiting Dad in hospital. On his last night in his old home, we invite them over for a farewell dinner.

It is a gorgeous golden evening, and we sit sipping wine in the lush tropical garden filled with frangipanis, mango trees, birds of paradise and bougainvillea. Rob and Lachie have spent hours mowing lawns, mulching, weeding and tidying, preparing the place for sale. All of us have scrubbed and cleaned. Emily and I cook a simple Italian meal with antipasto, chicken-basil-tomato-and-chorizo pasta, green salad and a dessert of blueberries, strawberries and coffee ice-cream. There are tears, but lots of laughs and funny stories. It is a gorgeous celebration of friendship and family. The next day we load the car, lock the door and drive back to Sydney.

As a family, we pull together to manage the many medical appointments, practicalities and legalities, juggling everything in between our hectic full-time work schedules over the next six weeks. Dad's follow-up scan shows the aorta is worse, and the vascular surgeon tells us that high-risk surgery is the only way to save his life.

Dad ends up back in hospital with pneumonia while I'm in Melbourne visiting schools.

Rob and my three children are amazing in their support, helping to share the load. My children make Dad endless cups of tea and snacks, entertaining him with stories from their day. My friends shower me with love, hugs, meals and the odd glass of chardonnay.

It reminds me that, in tough times, it is those people who really love us who help us get through.

🌿

I wonder who helped Charlotte in those dark, dark days of grief. Did John and Jane Atkinson help and support her? Or were they too caught up in their own financial problems and their busy life with a large, young family? When James died, there was a legal dispute over which land belonged to him and which to John, which was not resolved for two years. Did the neighbours, like Charles and Betsey Throsby, do what they could? Or was it restricted to a few sympathetic smiles after church on Sunday? In those days, death was far more commonplace, and people were supposed to toughen up and get on with life, even if you had lost a beloved child or the love of your life.

Charlotte was in a tough position, running multiple vast estates in remote and wild country. Oldbury in those days was isolated. Most of the workers were male convicts who took little notice of the directions of a woman, and her own knowledge of farming was limited. Without James' experience and firm hand, the convicts became difficult.

In managing the estates, Charlotte turned for help to a friend of her husband—George Bruce Barton, a miller and farmer at Belanglo, who had arrived from Kent in 1832. James had appointed him as superintendent helping to run the various estates, and he was in charge of the Oldbury mill.

James Atkinson had left a will, written two-and-a-half years before his death. In it he left all his personal property and real estate to his *dearly beloved wife*, to be held by her during her life, or while she remained a widow. After her death, the Oldbury estate was to be inherited by their son James, with the remainder of the property to be divided equally among the children as soon as they all turned 21. He had made an allowance that if Charlotte married again she was entitled to £1,000 for her sole use, with the remainder to be held in trust by the executors until the children all reached 21. It was a relatively simple will.

An inventory was done, which was signed by Charlotte Atkinson and George Barton on 5 July 1834. The total property, comprising financial investments, land, livestock, the house and all its goods and furnishings, was worth more than £3,500. The livestock included about 3,000 sheep, among which were 49 merino ewes, and 200 cattle. James and Charlotte had done very well—a tribute to their hard work and innovative farming practices.

The executors of this will were Charlotte herself, as well as James' friends Alexander Berry, Edward Wollstonecraft and John Coghill. John Coghill had been master of the convict ship *Mangles* (on which James had taken passage to England in 1824) and was now a landholder and magistrate at Braidwood. Edward Wollstonecraft had died in 1832, after a long illness. Alexander Berry was a conservative and brusque man, who had not liked Charlotte when he first met her—he had a reputation for being easily stressed and irresolute, particularly after his business partner Wollstonecraft died.

Charlotte was an independent woman, accustomed to making decisions about her finances, her children and her life. She was used to managing a large household with many servants and being involved in running the family estates with James. Inevitably, Charlotte and Berry clashed. As well as the difficulties of dealing with the executors and running the estates, Charlotte had to contend with prolonged drought, and an economic depression.

According to notes made by Charlotte's daughter Louisa for her unborn child:

Charlotte ... professed throughout her life brilliant talent & great clearness of mind. No words could too highly paint her excellence & worth. Warm in disposition & affectionate, she was too marked a character not to meet with persons to whom her uprightness & courage made her obnoxious and after your grandfather's death ... [she suffered] ... great trial.

A few months after his death, James' friends John Godden Colyer and William Bowman raised over £100 to commission a memorial statue to Charlotte's husband that would stand outside the Mitchell Library in Macquarie Street. William Bowman was a local pastoralist, who established the Argyle Inn at Bong Bong. While Charlotte initially gave her permission, she later withdrew her support for the project.

In 1857, Louisa Atkinson would write a novel called *Gertrude the Emigrant*, which was set during the late 1830s at an estate called Murrumbowrie, inspired by Oldbury. One of the characters, the widow Mrs Doherty, is believed to have been based on Charlotte Atkinson.

In a plain dress and sun bonnet, marching round her fields, or counting in a flock of sheep, she was at home. She might have changed places with half the hardier sex, and filled their station in a thoroughly manly spirited manner.

In one conversation, the heroine, Gertrude, comments that they rarely receive visitors.

Mrs. Doherty was seated at the window with a lot of cheese cloth in her lap, which she had been cutting up for the dairyman ... 'No child,' she said ... very sadly, 'we have no visitors.' ...

'in Dr. Doherty's time we had many ... travellers, and persons bringing out introductions from home ... sometimes for months—waiting till something offered suitable for them, or gaining experience, if they were going to settle ... now many of these are influential men, and occasionally in Sydney we meet, and pass without recognizing; these sort of obligations are soon forgotten ... and they don't like to remember that there was a time when they were glad to eat at our table; and perhaps to borrow money of my husband, to start them in life—but' she added fiercely 'I want no patronage from any one.'

Mrs Doherty later discussed dealing with another character, which probably reflected something of Charlotte's relationship with Alexander Berry: *'You could not reason with [him]; he never admitted an error in his own judgment, I used often to argue with him to no purpose.'*

Someone who did visit Mrs Doherty was the estate superintendent, who lived in the old homestead cottage but would come down in the evenings to talk about the day's work.

Louisa described their working relationship:

Several times during the morning, when she passed a small office at the back of the house she had seen Mrs. Doherty and Tudor, apparently busied over accounts and letters, both wore grave and businesslike countenances; and when the former came in rather late to dinner, it was with a weary air.

This friendship may have been the relationship that Charlotte Atkinson developed with her own superintendent, George Barton. Charlotte took an active role in running the Oldbury estate—checking stock, bookkeeping and supervising workers.

Charlotte was an excellent horsewoman and rode out with George Barton to visit the various outstations at Belanglo and Wollondilly, to provision the workers and check on the sheep and cattle. This was most unconventional for a woman of the times.

These horseback expeditions were dangerous, riding through rough and lonely countryside, down steep gorges, across rivers and through dense bushland. Bushrangers continued to terrorise the neighbourhood, raiding the station huts, holding up travellers, stealing stock and robbing drays.

On the morning of 30 January 1836, Charlotte rode out with George Barton to visit her sheep stations near Belanglo. After riding about ten miles, they dismounted to descend a steep mountain track, Barton leading the horses. Two masked bushrangers sprang from behind a rock, brandishing pistols and in the *most diabolical language* ordered them to stop and hand over their valuables.

George Barton was tied to a tree and then viciously flogged with an *uncommonly thick [and] exceedingly heavy* stockman's whip made of green hide. The bushranger lashed Barton's back *with all his strength, in the most deliberate manner,* giving him 30 stripes. They planned to give him 30 more lashes, but Charlotte stood up to the bushrangers and intervened on George Barton's behalf, although she was also threatened with the stockwhip and pistol.

Charlotte and Barton were eventually released but forbidden from continuing their journey.

This brutal attack by bushrangers must have been terrifying. From George Barton's description, this flogging would have flayed his skin, causing deep and painful lacerations that would take weeks to heal. Barton was never the same again. The flogging left both physical and emotional scars that would last for many years. Afterwards he absolutely refused to ride out to the stations, and he appears to have suffered a nervous breakdown or post-traumatic stress disorder. He began drinking heavily, perhaps to reduce the pain or to cope with the fear and anxiety.

Barton provided a sworn statement to local magistrate Charles Throsby five days after the attack—perhaps he waited until he was sufficiently recovered to speak about it. Barton's statement was reported in *The Sydney Herald* one week later and was undoubtedly widely discussed in colonial society, provoking scandal. The report highlighted that Charlotte had been riding out alone with Barton, far from home without a female chaperone. There may also have been whispers about what else might have happened during the attack. An attack involving two violent bushrangers and a defenceless and attractive woman.

The Sydney Herald Thursday 11 February, 1836
FLOGGING OF AN EMIGRANT SETTLER BY
RUNAWAY CONVICTS.

THE following statement was sworn before me at Oldbury, on the 4th February, 1836:—

George Bruce Barting states that he left Oldbury on the morning of the 30th ult., to visit his farm at Belangola and some of Mrs. Atkinson's sheep stations in that neighbourhood; he had proceeded about ten (10) miles, when, in going down a steep mountain, at the time leading two horses, he was suddenly stopped by two bushrangers who sprung from behind a rock close to him, presenting, the one a double-barreled percussion gun, and the other a pistol, close to his head, and in the most diabolical language ordered him to stop. This order he complied with; they then told him to turn the horses loose, this he refused to do; then to take his jacket off, this was done, deponent think[s] they intended to take it. The deponent's money was next demanded; this he gave them to the amount of 21s. The man who acted as leader, told the man with the gun to keep it levelled at the deponent, and to fire directly he gave the order. He then took deponent's handkerchief from his neck, and proceeded to tie him to a tree; this he would not submit to till persuaded by Mrs. Atkinson, who was with deponent at the time, deponent still thinking the bushrangers only meant to detain him. The leader then tore out the back of deponent's waistcoat and shirt, and told the other bushranger, who still kept his gun presented at deponent, to give him the cat. He immediately gave the leader an uncommonly thick stockman's whip, very short in the thong, made of green hide, and exceedingly heavy. The bushranger, a very strong man, then began to lash deponent's back with all his strength, in the most deliberate manner; and in answer to deponent, who asked how many stripes he was to expect? replied thirty, about which number were inflicted. The rascal then said he would give deponent ten minutes' rest, and then ten minutes' more punishment; this through the intercession of Mrs. Atkinson, was not inflicted; but he directed Mrs. Atkinson to untie deponent, which she did. The bushranger then brandished his whip over Mrs. Atkinson's head with one hand, and holding a large pistol close to her face with the other, declared, although he never had struck a woman, he had a good mind to serve her as deponent had been served, as she allowed her men to

be treated so very bad in her establishment; *this she denied, and defied him to name any man that could complain; he said he did not have his information from her servants, but from a Gentleman, a Mr. Munn (who is the son of the professor of that name in Edinburgh); the leader then told deponent that he was not the only one that was to be served in that manner, as he considered it his duty to go round and flog all the Gentlemen so that they might know what punishment was, this he repeated twice; deponent was then ordered to return: the bushranger declaring deponent should be shot if he attempted to proceed on his journey; deponent further states, that within these* last twelve months, *his own and Mrs. Atkinson's stations have been robbed at least ten times, and he believes by* the same party; *that the bushrangers are constantly shooting a bullock when they want meat, taking of the same as much as they require, leaving the remainder to spoil; that the shepherds are continually loosing their shoes and clothes, and that, although some of the stations are twenty-five miles distant, they are obliged to be rationed weekly as the huts are constantly being ransacked by bushrangers; deponent feels satisfied there was one, if not more of the party that stopped him that did show themselves; one of whom was called Simmons.*
GEORGE BRUCE BARTING.
Sworn before me at Oldbury,
this 4th February, 1836.
CHARLES THROSBY.

I hereby certify, that I have sheep stations within a few miles of Mrs. Atkinson, and that they have been frequently robbed during the last twelve months, and was reported to have been so by two armed bushrangers about a fortnight ago.

I further certify, that no complaints (of any description) have ever been made to the Bench in this District by the Assigned Servants from Oldbury.
(Signed) CHARLES THROSBY.
Oldbury, 4th February, 1836.

One of the bushrangers was John Lynch, *usually regarded as the most callous and brutal of the bushrangers in New South Wales.* Lynch was a convict assigned to Oldbury, but later became Australia's most notorious serial killer, brutally murdering at least ten people with a tomahawk. He also raped one of his victims, 14-year-old Mary Mulligan, before killing her, along with her whole family.

While there is no evidence, many members of our extended family fear that Charlotte may have been raped during the attack. Kate and I chat to several relatives at a reunion lunch. All the attendees are descended from Charlotte and James Atkinson, mostly through our own great-great-great-grandmother Charlotte Elizabeth, and her daughter Flora.

'It was a brutal attack and I think Charlotte was probably raped,' says Robin Corban, our mother's second cousin. 'Those bushrangers were particularly vicious.'

Elaine Holdom agrees that Charlotte was raped. 'It was the brutality of those times. I think the attack brought Charlotte and George Barton closer together. They had both experienced and witnessed something shocking.'

Whether it was to silence the gossips, or to provide protection for herself and her children, Charlotte took a momentous step that was to change everything.

The Sydney Herald reported the attack on 11 February 1836. Two days later marked Charlotte's fortieth birthday. On 3 March 1836, Charlotte married George Barton, by special licence, at All Saints Church at

Sutton Forest. Charlotte Elizabeth was eight, Emily was six, James was four and Louisa was two. This wedding must have been very different from Charlotte's joyous marriage to James, nine years before.

The next day, 4 March, an Oldbury convict, Thomas Smith, was bludgeoned to death by other Oldbury convicts including John Lynch and John Williamson. Smith had been locked up at Bong Bong for a few days on suspicion of stealing a saddle and bridle during a journey to Sydney, but was released without charge, as requested by George Barton. The Oldbury convicts believed that Tom Smith had been released in return for snitching—giving evidence to George Barton, naming John Lynch and John Watts as the bushrangers who had attacked Charlotte and Barton. John Watts was later captured and hanged for his crimes.

The Sydney Gazette 29 March 1836
CASE OF MURDER.—*We are given to understand that eleven or twelve assigned servants belonging to the estate of Mrs. Atkinson, of Sutton Forest, are lodged in the gaol at Bong Bong, charged with the murder of one of their fellow servants. The manner in which this horrible crime has been perpetrated is said to be wantonly cruel, the head of the deceased appearing to have been smashed to pieces with bludgeons or waddies. No particular cause has been assigned, except a little petty jealousy existing among the men themselves for the perpetration of the horrid deed.*

Lynch and Williamson were indicted for the murder of Tom Smith. However, the jury found them not guilty due to insufficient evidence. George Barton was summoned to Sydney as a key witness, having seen Lynch near the body on the day of the murder. Barton's evidence was rejected because he appeared in court *in such a state of intemperance that his testimony was valueless*, and he was fined £50 by the judge for contempt of court. *The Sydney Herald* later claimed that John Lynch's spree of brutal murders would never have happened if Barton had given evidence at the first trial.

The murder of Tom Smith was just one of many violent attacks near Oldbury during the 1830s. *The Sydney Monitor* claimed there were *more robberies committed in this district, than in any other in the Colony,* while James Atkinson's friend John Colyer wrote that his home had been plundered *three times within a few months … my family brutally driven out … myself shot at.* One thing in particular surprised me about the local bushrangers. I had always believed they were runaway convicts, fugitives hiding in the bush, preying on travellers and coaches. In fact, many were convict labourers assigned to various farms in the area, including Oldbury, Mereworth and Throsby Park. John Colyer believed the landowners were aware of the problem but didn't want to lose their free convict labour.

Just a few weeks before the wedding, the rectory of All Saints Church at Sutton Forest had been invaded by four masked bushrangers, armed with pistols and cutlasses, who imprisoned and robbed Reverend John Vincent, his wife Eliza and their nine children, along with their servants. John Vincent was threatened with death and was only saved by the courage of one of his servants, who escaped and fetched their neighbour with his muskets.

I believe that John Lynch planned the attack on Charlotte and her overseer, knowing that they were riding out to Belanglo that morning and which route they would take. He hated George Barton and took delight in exacting his revenge. I also have this creepy feeling that he had been watching Charlotte at Oldbury, and enjoyed humiliating her.

It must have been terrifying for Charlotte knowing that there were such dangerous and ruthless men living all around her home. Barton was certainly petrified, which may explain much of his irrational behaviour. What is interesting is the way that the two dealt with the trauma. While Barton holed himself away drinking, Charlotte continued to ride out to the stations, to run the many estates on her own and to manage the convict workers. Her courage and strength were formidable.

Louisa later wrote: *two years after the death of my father she married a Mr Barton his friend; a clever man but who shortly became a furious maniac & had to be kept under restraint.*

One thing that surprised me was that James' brother John wasn't more help to Charlotte in this time of trial. The brothers had been very close, working together in partnership at Oldbury, naming their sons after each other and living as neighbours. James did not name his brother as an executor of his will, nor did John seem to help Charlotte with the court battles to come. Around this time, John was experiencing stressful financial difficulties. When James died there was confusion over which property belonged to James and which to John. In 1836, John's ownership of Mereworth was confirmed by an inquiry and John converted his beautiful home into an inn called the Kentish Arms, to try to make ends meet. One of his regular customers was George Barton. I'm sure John didn't like Barton and didn't approve of Charlotte's marriage. The relationship probably wasn't helped when Barton later accused church warden John Atkinson of harbouring bushrangers and prisoners of the Crown!

Kate and I have been to the little sandstone church at Sutton Forest many times. Yet we've never been inside. It is always securely locked. Once more, fate or Charlotte is smiling down on us. On one of our visits, our plans for an early departure from Sydney are foiled by a punctured tyre, so we arrive at the church much later than we'd hoped. From inside, we hear stirring organ music and joyous hymns. We look at each other.

'Shall we?' I ask.

'Definitely,' Kate replies. We creep inside to join the service. Inside, the church is simple and beautiful, with its ancient pews, dark rafters, colourful crocheted knee rugs and the commandments painted on the wall. The sermon is personal and inspiring. Praying for rain to ease the drought. Praying for local parishioners who are sick. Praying for wisdom.

On the wall above our heads are three marble memorial tablets. One for Caroline Louisa Waring Calvert, daughter of James Atkinson. One for her daughter Louise Snowden Annie Cosh. One for Louise's daughter Janet Louise Cosh. This little church was the heart of the Sutton Forest community in Charlotte's day.

After the service, Reverend Jeremy Tonks welcomes us. I introduce myself and Kate and gesture towards the tablets above our heads. 'We're the great-great-great-great-granddaughters of James and Charlotte Atkinson of Oldbury.' A twitter of interest runs around the congregation as they file past.

'We're writing a book about Charlotte,' explains Kate.

Jeremy is welcoming, and invites us to afternoon tea in the church hall, but first he offers to show us the new memorial plaque in the churchyard, dedicated to the victims of John Lynch who are buried here. There is Thomas Smith of Oldbury, killed in 1836. The Mulligan family—John, Bridget, 18-year-old John junior and 14-year-old Mary, murdered in August 1841. Kerns Landregan, murdered on 20 February 1842. There were at least another four victims, who are buried elsewhere. John Lynch was captured and hanged at Berrima Gaol in 1842. The memorial plaque gives me chills.

Kate and I visit our family vault, where James and Charlotte are buried, and talk to Jeremy about how he would like to raise funds to renovate the vault and put up new plaques to share the stories of the Atkinson family. Of course, we would love that.

In the hall, we are offered cups of freshly brewed tea from a giant tea pot. The table is laden with home-baked biscuits, cakes and sandwiches. We nibble on slices of lemon-and-passionfruit sponge, as light as angel wings. It is delicious. People ask us questions about our project and inquire if we've been to Oldbury.

Two local women come over for a chat. They are warm and friendly and full of interesting stories.

One leans over to me and asks 'Why do you think Charlotte married Barton? What was she thinking?' The question makes me laugh. Here we are, in a tiny church hall, chatting with total strangers, who ask me questions about my ancestor as though it happened last week.

'I don't know,' I confess. 'Was it the scandal after the bushranger attack? Was she raped by John Lynch? Or was she just sick of trying to manage everything on her own?'

She nods her head. 'John Lynch was vicious. Charlotte and Barton were lucky to escape with their lives.'

I think back to the memorial plaque in the churchyard. All those people whom John Lynch cold-bloodedly bludgeoned to death with a tomahawk. Probably the worst serial killer in Australian history, he thought he had God's blessing to murder at will. Charlotte and George Barton *were* incredibly lucky to escape with their lives. I take a sip of my tea and am so very grateful that Charlotte wasn't one of his murder victims. Whatever happened there in the bush that day, Charlotte had the strength and courage to overcome it, and to stand up for George Barton.

Chapter 9

CHANGING THE WORLD

Written by Kate

to endeavour to discover
Charlotte Waring Atkinson

———⊰◈⊱———

In April 1834, as James Atkinson lay dying and his wife Charlotte faced a dark and uncertain future as a widow with four young children to support, a young man wrote from Argentina to his sister Catherine:

> *There is nothing like geology; the pleasure of ... hunting cannot be compared to finding a fine group of fossil bones, which tell their story of former times with almost a living tongue.*

That young man was Charles Darwin.

He had been born in Shrewsbury, in Shropshire, into a family of clever, creative thinkers. His father was Robert Waring Darwin, son of Erasmus Darwin, a naturalist, inventor and poet. His mother was Susannah Wedgwood, daughter of Josiah Wedgwood, the famous potter and designer. Charles counted many writers, artists and scientists among his cousins, including—distantly—our ancestor Charlotte Waring.

Charles Darwin's great-great-grandmother, Anne Waring, was the third cousin of Charlotte's great-grandfather, Richard Waring. This means Charles Darwin was Charlotte's fifth cousin, once removed. She was almost 13 years older than him to the day, since Charlotte was born on 13 February 1796 and Charles on 12 February 1809.

There are other eerie similarities. They both lost their mothers at a young age (Charlotte was two and Charles was eight). Both were sent away to boarding school as children (Charles at eight and Charlotte at ten). Both were interested in insects and botany.

In autumn 1826, when Charlotte was employed by Harriet King and first met her husband-to-be James Atkinson on board the *Cumberland*, Charles was at university studying medicine (which he loathed), and flirting with his cousin Emma Wedgwood.

In winter 1831, when Charlotte was building her life with James in Australia, the 22-year-old Charles sailed from Plymouth on board HMS *Beagle* on its famous journey around the world.

Three years later, Charles wrote to his sister Susan: *We all on board are looking forward to Sydney, as to a little England: it really will be interesting to see the colony which must be the Empress of the South.*

The *Beagle* dropped anchor in Sydney Cove on 12 January 1836. Darwin's diary says: *In the evening I walked through the town & returned full of admiration at the whole scene.—It is a most magnificent testimony to the power of the British nation … My first feeling was to congratulate myself that I was born an Englishman.*

Darwin was distressed to find no letters from home waiting for him. As he wrote to Susan: *probably, when we reach England, I shall not have received a letter dated within the last 18 months. And now that*

I have told my pitiable story, I feel much inclined to sit down and have a good cry.

Darwin wanted to see some of the interior landscape and so, on 16 January, he hired some horses and a guide and set off for Bathurst, writing:

> *the first stage took us through Paramatta, a small country town, but second to Sydney in importance ... In all ... respects there was a most close resemblance to England; perhaps the number of Ale-houses was here in excess ...*
>
> *At Sunset by good fortune a party of a score of the Aboriginal Blacks passed by, each carrying in their accustomed manner a bundle of spears & other weapons ... their countenances were good-humoured & pleasant & they appeared far from such utterly degraded beings as usually represented.*

The road through the Blue Mountains had only been open two years. Darwin stopped at Wentworth Falls and Govetts Leap, then stayed the night at Wallerawang, which means 'place near wood and water' in the language of the local Wiradjuri people. A man named James Walker had been given a land grant there, on the western rim of the Blue Mountains, in 1824, 11 years after the first European crossing of the Blue Mountains by Gregory Blaxland.

The next day, Darwin was taken out to hunt kangaroos. Although no kangaroos were seen, Darwin did spot a potoroo (a marsupial the size of a rabbit, often called a 'rat-kangaroo'). He was also, he wrote, impressed by the *most beautiful* parrots.

> *In the dusk of the evening I took a stroll along a chain of ponds, which in this dry country represents the course of a river, &*

had the good fortune to see several of the famous Platypus or Ornithorhynchus paradoxicus. They were diving & playing about the surface of the water; but showed very little of their bodies, so that they might easily have been mistaken for many water Rats. Mr. Browne shot one; certainly it is a most extraordinary animal.

It was during this journey through the Blue Mountains that Darwin reflected *on the strange character of the Animals of this country as compared to the rest of the World ... An unbeliever in everything beyond his own reason, might exclaim 'Surely two distinct Creators must have been [at] work' ... It cannot be thought so.—The one hand has surely worked throughout the universe.*

This revelation was to prove the beginning of a paradigm shift in Darwin's thinking that led, eventually, to his seminal work, *On the Origin of Species by Means of Natural Selection*, the book that—more than any other—helped change the world.

During his return journey to Sydney, Darwin had lunch at The Vineyard, the home of Hannibal Hawkins Macarthur in Rydalmere, where nine years previously Charlotte had worked as a governess. Darwin's diary entry reads:

The house would be considered a very superior one, even in England ... It sounded strange in my ears to hear very nice looking young ladies exclaim, 'Oh we are Australian, & know nothing about England'.—In the afternoon I left this most English-like house & rode by myself into Sydney.

On 30 January 1836, Charles Darwin sailed out of Sydney Harbour on the *Beagle*, heading south for Hobart.

On the same day, Charlotte was attacked by bushrangers in Belanglo.

According to our family's oral history, Charles Darwin met with his cousin Charlotte while he was in Sydney. My mother was told so when she was a child, and so were her second cousins Jan Gow and Neil McCormack—all by different relatives.

Yet there is no mention of Charlotte in Darwin's diary.

There are, however, quite a few days where he did not update his journal.

In January 1836, it was a day's journey from Sydney to Berrima in a gig. So it is possible that Darwin raced southwards on one of his missing days, stayed with Charlotte at Oldbury for a night, then raced back the next day.

If Darwin drove to Oldbury to see Charlotte, it would have been a long, hot, dusty, bone-jarring journey, with little opportunity to take out his notebook and write his impressions. Her four young children would have been pulling him by the hand to show him their toys and amusements, scarcely giving him a chance to catch his breath, let alone sit down and write in quiet contemplation for an hour or two.

Their mother Charlotte might have showed him her sketchbooks with their detailed drawings of Australian flora and fauna. They might even have gone beetle-hunting together. Darwin somehow managed to collect 97 different species of insects while he was in New South Wales, 42 of which were entirely unknown to science.

She would have cooked him the best meal she could manage, despite the heat and her primitive oven. Perhaps she told him something of her struggles, a widow alone with four children, so far from civilisation, and dependent on the goodwill of trustees who had spurned her.

Darwin's diary for 28 and 29 January—the days where he does not note his whereabouts—says, with a great many crossings-out and amendments:

On the whole, from what I heard more than from what I saw, I was disappointed in the state of Society. The whole community is rancorously divided into parties on almost every subject. Amongst those who from their station of life, ought to rank with the best, many live in such open profligacy, that respectable people cannot associate with them ... The whole population poor & rich are bent on acquiring wealth; the subject of wool & sheep grazing amongst the higher orders is of preponderant interest. The very low ebb of literature is strongly marked by the emptiness of the ~~Booksellers~~ booksellers shops; these are inferior to the shops of the smaller country towns of England.—~~To families~~ There are some very serious drawbacks to the comforts of families, the chief of ~~which~~ these is perhaps being surrounded by convict servants ~~must be dreadful~~. How disgusting to be waited on by a man, who the day before was ~~perhaps~~ by your representation flogged for some trifling misdemeanour? The female servants are of course much worse; hence children acquire the use of ~~such~~ the vilest expressions, & fortunately if not equally vile ideas. ~~I heard of one instance where the dear little innocent must have perfectly astounded its Mama.~~

I cannot help but wonder if that dear little innocent, swearing like a trooper, could have been my great-great-great-grandmother, Charlotte Elizabeth, running wild at Oldbury? Though Binny says our Charlotte would never have permitted her daughter to swear!

I can imagine Charlotte pouring out her heart to Darwin, expressing the difficulties of managing such a vast property with only convict labour to assist her, venting her frustrations at having no one to talk to about books and art and ideas, worrying about her impressionable children, left fatherless at such a young age.

Perhaps Darwin refrained from naming Charlotte out of a desire to keep her confidence, knowing his diaries would be published on his return to England?

Perhaps.

F.W. and J.M. Nicholas, authors of *Charles Darwin in Australia*, note his careful choice of words in his letters and diaries, as he knew they would be read by friends, family and the wider public and did not wish to offend anyone.

There are three more clues that seem to support the possibility that Darwin knew of Charlotte's life in Australia.

The first is that Darwin—when he was entertained by the Macarthurs at The Vineyard—was apparently called upon to recite some poetry. He is said to have chosen verses by one of his Waring kin, whom he named as his favourite poet. According to family lore, he chose a poem that would act as a kind of reproof to the Macarthurs, or as a sign of solidarity with his cousin Charlotte.

We do not know for certain what poem Darwin quoted. There are quite a few writers in the Waring family, including Robert Waring, a friend of Ben Jonson, who wrote 'Effigies Amoris, or the Picture of Love Unveil'd' in the mid-1600s; Anna Letitia Waring, poet and composer of hymns including 'Go Not Far from Me, O My Strength'; her father the Reverend Elijah Waring, a poet and biographer, who wrote *Edward Williams: The Bard of Glamorgan*; her uncle Samuel Waring, author of *The Minstrelsy of the Woods* and *The Traveller's Fire-side*; and their cousin Mary Waring, who published a diary of her ecstatic religious experiences in 1810.

I think—given the suggestion that the poem was chosen as a subtle reproof—that it was most likely to be 'The Poet's Apology', written by the Reverend Elijah Waring in 1809:

And blame not, ye worldlings, the choice he has made ...
He minds not whom honours or riches await;
But, grant him the smiles of the good—
he cares not a whit for the great.

That last line could clearly be interpreted as a rebuke to the worldly, ambitious Macarthur tribe.

Secondly, after his return to England, Darwin wrote to his sister Susan asking her for an explanation of their connection to the Waring family. His letter has been lost, but her reply, dated October 1839, has been preserved. Susan Darwin writes: *the Warings originally were a Staffordshire family—Nicholas, is written Esquire & styled of Wolverhampton in Henry the eights reign—Robert Waring was settled in Wilsford, in the Country of Nottingham & was Grandfather to Anne, wife of William Darwin of Cleatham—who was your great great Grandfather.*

Finally, he named his youngest son Charles Waring Darwin, acknowledging the importance of the kinship in the way families have for millennia (just as my middle name is Emma, a traditional family name, and Binny's daughter is named Emily Jane Charlotte).

On the Origin of Species was published on 24 November 1859, with a print run of 1,250 books. The entire first edition sold out that day.

The same year, an article on rare beetles appeared in the *Entomologist's Weekly Intelligencer*, by Darwin, Darwin and Darwin—the authors being Franky, Lenny and Horace, aged ten, eight and seven (written, one might suppose, with the help of their famous father).

The Darwin children were intimately involved in their father's experiments. They helped feed his pigeons, chased floating dandelion seeds in order to see how far they could travel, followed bumblebees through hedges and over meadows, collected frog's eggs from ponds in jars, and drew all over the draft pages of the handwritten *On the Origin of Species* manuscript.

It reminds me of my own childhood. My father was a scientist too, and my first journals were written in his old laboratory diaries.

One of my earliest memories is going to visit my father at Sydney University, where he was a Teaching Fellow at the Department of Veterinary Physiology.

I can remember Dad in a long white lab coat, giving us teacake with pink icing on top (something we'd never be allowed to have at home). I remember a long room, rows of fluorescent lights, shiny metal tables, and cages on top of cages, filled with mice running back and forth and squeaking in distress. Many of the mice were white, with demonic red eyes. Mostly I remember the smell. That distinctive ammoniac tang always triggers the memory for me, which is perhaps why I remember it so clearly even though I was so young.

'Your father was a genius,' I remember being told by a friend's father, who had gone to university with him. 'He would never study, spent all his time at the pub, and still got honours.'

His academic brilliance showed itself young. When he was just 14, he won a competition to be one of a contingent of schoolboys to travel to England to see the Queen's coronation. Boys aged 14 to 16 had to sit a written examination, and then undergo an interview in which judges considered *the boys' personality, appearance, alertness, deportment, speech and interests—and ... their ability to represent Australia creditably on the tour.*

The RMS *Oronsay* called at ports in Fremantle, Colombo, Aden, Naples, Marseille and Gibraltar, before docking at Tilbury.

Another 'Youth Travel' boy wrote of the coronation:

London, 3rd June, 1953

It was like a fairy tale come true, the Queen looked like a fairy Queen riding in her golden coach ... London on Coronation Eve was really a sight—all the decorations were lit up; everything was sparkling and the whole city shone ... I had a first-class view of all the events, 'smashing' view as they say over here. I saw the Queen on her way to the Abbey to be crowned. This wasn't till 11 o'clock. What a wait in one spot! She was preceeded by many colourful regiments and military bands. The actual crowning ceremony took place in the Abbey and was relayed to us listening outside by a system of loud speakers. When the Queen was crowned a Royal Salute was fired within 15 seconds of the crowning. We could hear the guns thundering in the distance. Then commenced another long wait until 2.45 p.m. when the whole procession passed once more ... the Queen and the Duke [came] riding in their golden coach. The Queen wore her crown and the Duke wore a cocked hat. They waved to us as they passed. You should have heard the crowd cheer—it was deafening ... I should imagine the eyes of the world were on London, and here was I right in the middle of the great event.

After witnessing the coronation procession, the boys toured England, Scotland and Wales, being away from home for more than 13 weeks.

I have a photo of my father in the regulation green blazer with the Australian coat of arms emblazoned upon the pocket.

By the early 1960s, my father was a scholarship student at Sydney University, studying a Bachelor of Science in Veterinary Physiology. His professor was Clifford Emmens, who had been brought out from London in 1948 to set up this new area of speciality. His particular research interest was reproductive biology. In 1952, Emmens set up a cooperative venture with what later became the CSIRO Division of Animal Husbandry.

The department's early interests were concerned with experiments in the freezing of bull and ram semen, which were crucial in the development of artificial insemination. Later, research focused on oestrogens and anti-oestrogens, in a bid to understand both fertility and anti-fertility. Their research was supported by the Ford and Rockefeller foundations, and was aimed at developing a form of safe contraception for women.

In 1957, the Federal Food and Drug Administration of America approved an oral anti-fertility pill for severe menstrual disorders. After a massive surge in women reporting intense period pain, the Pill was approved for contraceptive use in 1960.

In 1961, my father graduated from his first degree. He was 22 years old. To celebrate, he and his friends took part in a sculling contest to see who could drink the fastest. To his chagrin, he was beaten by a New Zealand footballer. In the after-party shenanigans, Dad tripped and fell on a barbed-wire fence, cutting his chin open. He was taken to the Accident and Emergency Department at the Royal Prince Alfred Hospital in Camperdown, bleeding heavily. The doctor sewed my dad up, and Mum—who was then studying nursing at the RPA—gave him a tetanus shot.

'I love you!' he declared. 'I'm going to marry you.'

Mum thought nothing of it, drunken patients being a hazard of the job. But then Dad tracked her down.

'I was living at St John's College,' he tells me, 'and the nursing college was just across the road. We were strictly segregated in those days. I needed permission if I planned to stay out past 10 pm, but your mother needed permission if she was allowed out at all.'

They used to meet when they could, at parties and university balls and at a café in Newtown that had a television set. After graduating, Dad did his service with the State Department of Agriculture, but then he was offered the chance for postgraduate study and so returned to Sydney. It did not take long for the romance to rekindle. 'Neither of us had any money, of course, but we decided to take the plunge anyway,' he tells me.

He bought her a golden Labrador pup called Sammy and they were married on 1 December 1962, at the age of 24.

'We were so poor!' my mother says. 'If I bought half-a-dozen eggs, I had to choose whether to make an omelette that month, or a cake.'

While Dad was studying his PhD, he worked as a Teaching Fellow at the university. He hated it. 'It interfered with the real work,' he told me, 'which was, of course, the research.'

By all accounts, he did not shine as a lecturer. Both Binny and I and our cousin Pete (who is a vet himself) have heard from numerous sources that he could be brusque and impatient. 'He was so brilliant, he just could not comprehend that his students could not understand things as quickly and easily as he did,' one of his students told Binny.

I have read some of my father's published academic works. They have titles like 'The Development of Viable Embryos after Ovum Transfers to Long-Term Ovariectomised Mice' (*Steroids*, 1967); and 'Mechanisms Concerned in Ovum Transport' (*Advances in the Biosciences*, 1970).

In mid-1968—when I was two years old—my father removed 45 fertilised eggs from pregnant merino ewes in Sydney, transplanted them into the wombs of three rabbits, and then carried the rabbits across the Tasman Sea to the Ruakura Agricultural Research Centre in New Zealand. Another 14 fertilised eggs were transported 'in vitro' (which means 'in glass'), in thermoses containing sheep serum.

In New Zealand, my father and a Kiwi scientist named Dr Robert Welch then transplanted the fertilised merino eggs into the wombs of ten Romney ewes. None of the eggs carried in the thermos flasks survived. However, two months later, two of the Romney ewes were pregnant.

The idea of using live rabbits as egg incubators was not new. However, the successful implantation of these surrogate lambs was a breakthrough. My father was one of a number of scientists around the world working on theories that would lead to the first IVF ('in vitro fertilisation') embryo transplant, in 1975, and to the first IVF baby, in 1978.

My father was still a PhD student when he undertook his ground-breaking experiments. He was also working as a vet a few days a week at a Sydney racecourse, trying to earn enough money to support us.

My mum—looking ahead to the future—bought a house on the Pacific Highway with some money they had inherited, and they set it up as the Artarmon Vet Hospital. 'Your father loved animals,' she tells me, 'but disliked people. And he was still teaching at the university so could only take clients in the evenings. I was trying to manage the vet hospital and take care of you two little girls. It was hard.'

On 1 October 1968, I was attacked by a dog in the backyard of the vet hospital. It was a Doberman brought in to be put down for savagery. Rushed to Royal North Shore Hospital, I had more than 200 stitches on my face and scalp, including sewing back my left ear, which had almost been severed. Afterwards, I lay in a coma for six weeks.

After that, my father gave up his work as a research scientist. He finished his PhD at the age of 29, and then was offered work in a research lab in Boston. My mother did not want to go and live in the USA. Her friends and family were here in Australia, and she wanted a more stable home environment for their two little girls than could be offered by the precarious world of science.

Research that my father had spent many months on—inducing artificial pregnancies in rats—had been published by a rival scientist in the UK. The development of the Pill meant that the university had lost its funding for fertility research. In addition, the brave new world of IVF and surrogate pregnancies aroused ethical considerations in a government already rattled by the thalidomide scandal. It was not a good time to seek employment as a scientist in this country, with newspapers of the time reporting a 'brain drain' as many of my father's colleagues sought employment overseas.

Our mum always used to say: 'your father was so brilliant! He was in his element as a scientist, but there was just no money to be made in research and so he went into private practice to support his family and children.'

I have often wondered what incredible discoveries my father might have made if he—like Charles Darwin—had come from a wealthy and well-connected family. Darwin did not need to make his living from his research. He was a man of means who could afford to spend decades reading, thinking, observing, measuring, experimenting and writing.

Unlike our dad.

In the distant future I see open fields for far more important researches, Darwin once wrote. *Light will be thrown on the origin of man and his history.*

I like to think that my father was part of science's bright illumination of our world. He taught us to be endlessly curious, adventurous and resilient, and to interrogate everything. He believed every child should witness both birth and death, and so we helped rub life into newborn puppies and held our beloved cats in our arms as they died.

I am proud to be his daughter.

I finished writing this chapter at 4.30 am on Wednesday 13 March, after rising early to work in the dark and the silence of the night.

A few hours later I discover I have a sister I have never known.

Her name is Emma Jane, which is my middle name and Binny's middle name.

I write in my diary that night: *the thing is I'd spent the morning working on the Darwin chapter ... and thinking about blood & family & inheritance & people's desire to know where they come from ... it was eerie & unsettling.*

A few pages later, I write: *it's very strange but also rather wonderful to know I have another sister—a half-sister. Family has always been so important to us—it's weird to think that she's been there all these years, not knowing us, not knowing her father.*

For the next few weeks, I struggle to sleep. I cry at books and movies. I write poetry.

One poem is inspired by the hurt and grief I felt when our father left us.

It reads:

the centrifugal void
black hole spinning at my core

Binny and Nick and I arrange to meet our new sister at the end of the month. *I'm a little nervous, I admit,* I write in my diary. *The real reason has got to do with Dad, not with her. It's stirred up some old bad feelings.*

After our meeting, I write: *yesterday was wonderful and emotionally tumultuous and exhausting—strangely so, because all we really did was sit and talk.*

Slowly we build a bridge between us.

On my flight to England, two months later, I think about how our family—mine and Binny's and Nick's—is so uncannily similar to that of the Atkinsons.

Our family was broken slowly, over many years, as my parents fought and parted, and then reconciled and repaired, only to break apart once again.

Charlotte's family was broken swiftly and irrevocably.

Our father left us. Their father died.

We both ended up with stepfathers. Ours was a godsend. Theirs was a nightmare.

And most strangely, most startlingly ...

Theirs was a family of four. Two girls, then a boy, and then another little girl.

We always thought we were a family of three: two girls and a boy. Yet all the time—unknown to us—we had a little sister. We were a family of four too.

Chapter 10

TRAPPED

Written by Kate

Oh! dear! poor things. How melancholy to be left
[without] any thing to aid their escape

Charlotte Waring Atkinson

———◆———

If Charlotte entertained her distant cousin Charles Darwin for dinner in the sultry-hot summer of 1836, it would have been her last happy day in a very long time.

For the day he sailed away from Sydney, towards a brilliant future, was the day that Charlotte was attacked by Australia's worst serial murderer.

Whatever happened that day in Belanglo—and we fear the worst—Charlotte was consequently trapped in a marriage with a man who was increasingly unpredictable and dangerous.

The bare facts of the next few years of Charlotte's life show that the violence escalated. There was another murder, on 19 February 1837, at John Atkinson's pub, the Kentish Arms. Three Oldbury servants were indicted.

The following year a bullet was fired through the parlour window at Oldbury. It whistled past George Barton's ear, knocked him to the ground, and then ricocheted off the wall to land at Charlotte's feet. Our grandfather, Papa, told us the bullet hole could still be seen in the glass when he visited Oldbury in the 1930s.

George Barton wrote a letter to the editor of *The Sydney Herald*, claiming it was John Lynch who had shot the gun, having sworn to kill Barton.

In May 1839, a man named Andrew Shandy was attacked and seriously injured when his dray was held up at Sutton Forest by seven Oldbury convicts. He died after nine days.

A few weeks later, the trustees of the farm informed Charlotte that due to George Barton's fecklessness they had decided to turn him out of Oldbury and sell the stock. On 1 June 1839, Alexander Berry wrote to Charlotte:

> *it is entirely on account of Mr Barton that I fear for the children's property. He is your Husband—his intemperance is known to the whole world—and I know from yourself and others that he is a useless idler who neglects his concerns ... some time ago he told me that having been flagellated he was afraid [to ride out to check the stock] ... under these circumstances there is reason to fear that everything will be squandered. Therefore ... I intend ... to put the remainder of the property beyond his control.*

Of course, finding a new tenant for Oldbury meant that Charlotte and her children would have to leave too. Despite her protests, Oldbury's prized flock of merino sheep were put up to auction on 1 October 1839.

Nobody made a bid. It was a time of drought and depression, and many thought the value of the flock had been too greatly diminished by Barton's mismanagement. Berry threatened legal action against Barton, writing: *I consider him ready to deprive your children of their last morsel.*

This was a dark and terrible time in Charlotte's life: the death of her darling husband, the long hard struggle as a widow with four young children, the bushranger attack, and then her marriage to a drunkard and a wastrel.

By now, our great-great-great-great-grandmother is a living woman to us. She has inhabited our minds and our hearts for many months. It is awful to see her suffering. And we are haunted by questions. What happened that day in Belanglo? Why did she marry George Barton? How could our clever, strong, determined Charlotte make such a hideous mistake?

☙

In London, the rain pelts down upon us. We are cold and exhausted. Jet lag is an iron ball on a chain that we drag every step. We have so much to do and so little time; urgency beats in our blood.

We are meeting with Emma Darwin, the great-great-granddaughter of Charles Darwin and our ninth cousin, twice removed. She has written a book entitled *This Is Not a Book about Charles Darwin*, which is a fascinating blend of memoir, family history and fiction. Emma is known for her intelligent, subtle historical novels, and this hybrid memoir is a departure for her, an attempt to grapple with her family heritage, which almost kills her after she suffers a coronary artery dissection following months of intense creative labour. Her book, she writes, is *strung painfully on the tension-line between the responsibilities of the storyteller and the responsibilities of the historian.*

Binny and I feel that painful tension too.

We plan to meet on the roof garden of the Queen Elizabeth Hall in Southbank. The idea is to enjoy a gin and tonic among wildflowers, herbs and fruit trees, gazing out over the River Thames and London's iconic skyline. It is midsummer. It should be warm and sunny. I'd imagined us in floral dresses, the light lingering long into the evening.

Instead we huddle inside, damp and shivering, broken umbrellas dripping. My hand is so cold I find it hard to write. My feet pulse with pain. It has been a very long day.

We talk about the difference between fiction and non-fiction, and the difficulty of writing about our own families. We are so afraid of getting it wrong. Emma wrote in her book: *On every shelf of the library, in every Darwin expert, enthusiast or nut, and above all in my own mind, there waited a judge whose hand was poised to clap over the mouth of my imagination, and silence me.*

This strikes home. We too have felt the weight of that condemning hand.

'How do you overcome that fear?' I ask. 'We want to get it right, but it's so hard to know what right is … and we don't want to be held back, limited, by worry of what people will think.'

'In fiction, I am empress of all I survey,' Emma says. 'I can make up my own rules. I only need to make my story *seem* authentic. The problem with non-fiction is that a well-documented archive can be a potential censor.' She advises us to draw up a rule book for ourselves, and to flip the censor off. I write these words in capital letters, and draw a box around them in my notebook.

FLIP THE CENSOR OFF.

Emma tells us how Toni Morrison was inspired to write her Pulitzer Prize-winning book *Beloved* by the true story of Margaret Garner, a slave in pre-Civil War America, who had escaped but was then recaptured. Margaret Garner killed her young daughter to save her from being returned to slavery. Toni Morrison chose to reimagine these events in a novel, rather than as non-fiction reportage, for the imaginative freedom that fiction brings.

This chimes with us strongly. Some years earlier, the Children's Book Council of Australia had named a literary prize for aspiring children's authors after our ancestor—the Charlotte Waring Barton Award. We begged them not to use the name of THAT man, but they pointed out it is the name by which she is known to posterity. It was wonderful to have Charlotte honoured in that way and we did not wish to seem ungrateful, so we did not argue the point too vehemently. We were asked to speak at the presentation of the award at the Lady Cutler Dinner that year, and so Binny and I chose to tell Charlotte's story together. We were overwhelmed with the response. So many people came up to us afterwards, saying 'what an extraordinary story ... why is it not better known ... this is a story you must write!'

Binny and I shared a cab home after the presentation. We were exhausted, but exhilarated.

'I think I need to tell her story,' Binny said to me. 'Do you mind?'

'Not at all,' I said. 'You'd tell it so well.'

So Binny wrote a historical novel for young adults, called *The River Charm*. The title was inspired by an old family story that Charlotte had picked up a pebble from the bank of the River Darent in Kent before she left English shores forever. The stone from the river of her homeland became a talisman for her, reminding Charlotte why she had left. Charlotte wanted to forge a new life for herself, and the pebble gave her courage and hope for the future. Whenever life grew too hard, she drew the pebble out of her pocket and rubbed it. The pebble reminded her where she had come from and where she hoped to go.

After her death, her daughter Charlotte Elizabeth found the pebble in her mother's jewellery box. She had it polished and encased in gold, and hung it from a bracelet that she wore about her wrist. She added other charms—a cameo of a gumnut carved by her sister Louisa, an old gold locket. In time, the bracelet was inherited by her daughter Flora. She too added her own charms, and so did her daughter Sarah Mabel.

The charm bracelet was eventually inherited by my great-aunt Bobby (christened Elvira but called Baby all her life, till she rebelled and declared a new name for herself). When I was a little girl, we used to visit Aunty Bobby. She would sit me on her lap and show me the charm bracelet, and tell me the stories behind every charm. My Aunty Bobby had added many herself, as she travelled the world and had many adventures—a golden Eiffel Tower, a prayer scroll from Jerusalem. But my favourite tale was always the story of the small brown pebble, picked up on the banks of the River Darent by my great-great-great-great-grandmother so long ago.

When my great-aunt died, the charm bracelet was inherited by my mother, and she often wears it. It is very old, very beautiful and utterly priceless.

The River Charm is my favourite book by my sister (and I love them all!) It is told from the point of view of Charlotte Elizabeth, the oldest of the four Atkinson children, and it illuminates how awful it must have been for them all, living at Oldbury with a violent drunkard of a stepfather and an unhappy mother. When Binny wrote *The River Charm*, she had to walk that tightrope between the known historical facts and the need to spin a compelling yarn.

All this is going through my mind as Emma Darwin talks. She is telling us about what kind of rules we should make for ourselves—don't be overwhelmed by the research (too late for that, I think!), don't give ownership of our story to others but claim the right to tell our own understanding of the facts, don't judge people of the past by the attitudes of today ...

'Remember the context,' Emma says. 'Your ancestors were shaped by their times, but you need to find a parallel that speaks to now.'

'We don't want our book to be just a dry biography,' I said.

'No,' Emma said. 'The kind of book you are writing is akin to fiction in many ways, and that means the inner life can be explored as well as the outer. The interior life is the novelist's true work.'

At that point, Binny reaches across and writes in my notebook: *Charlotte's inner life.*

This is a moment of epiphany for us.

What was Charlotte thinking, feeling, suffering, during those years as Mrs Barton? We had to try and understand, if we were to make sense of the decisions she made.

Whenever I need to understand something, I turn to books.

So I read *Trauma and Recovery: The Aftermath of Violence—From Domestic Abuse to Political Terror* by Judith Lewis Herman, an American psychiatrist who has focused on the study of post-traumatic stress disorders in women. She begins by saying:

> *The ordinary response to atrocities is to banish them from consciousness. Certain violations of the social compact are too terrible to utter aloud ...*
>
> *The essential element of rape is the physical, psychological, and moral violation of the person. Violation is, in fact, a synonym for rape. The purpose of the rapist is to terrorize, dominate, and humiliate his victim, to render her utterly helpless. Thus rape, by its nature, is intentionally designed to produce psychological trauma.*

The only defence against the distress of sexual or domestic violence, she says, is denial, repression and dissociation, a state that Freud called *double consciousness*. It's a kind of psychic numbing, which can lead to a paralysis of the body and the mind, both during the traumatic event itself and in the months afterwards.

This altered state of consciousness might be regarded as one of nature's small mercies, Herman writes, *a protection against unbearable pain.*

As the #MeToo movement has shown, sexual assault is all too common in our society. According to the Australian Institute of Health and Welfare, one in five women in our country has been sexually assaulted or threatened since the age of 15. To speak about such experiences is extremely difficult, even today when we have a much greater understanding of its prevalence and traumatic impact.

How much harder must it have been for Charlotte?

Whatever happened that day in Belanglo, it would have taken her a long time to recover. Science shows us that, long after the danger has passed, traumatised people relive the incident as though it were happening again. The traumatic moment becomes encoded in a fixed and involuntary memory-image, which manifests itself as flashbacks during waking states and as nightmares during sleep. Small things, like leaves rustling or the stench of sweat, trigger memories that return with all the immediacy and emotional intensity of the violation itself.

Everything feels dangerous.

Some retreat into themselves, like a wounded creature seeking refuge. Others are compelled to re-create the moment of terror, either literally or in disguised form. Freud named this *the repetition compulsion*.

It is believed this compulsion may be an attempt to master the overwhelming feelings of the traumatic moment, as if by facing their fears the victim can overcome them. However, in their attempts to undo the traumatic moment, survivors put themselves at risk of further harm. The psychological impact of violence can also lead, Herman believes, to later involvement in high-risk relationships.

Like Charlotte's marriage to George Barton.

The early spring months in the Southern Hemisphere are marked by the rising of a constellation of misty blue stars known as the Seven Sisters.

The ancient songlines of the Seven Sisters stretch across Australia, passing through a multitude of different language groups and geographies. Their rising heralds the coming of fair weather and flowers, and the season of birth and regeneration. Baby magpies shriek for food, and their protective parents dive-bomb anything seen as a threat. Dingo pups tumble and play, and snakes wriggle out from their long hibernation.

The core motif of the Seven Sisters story is the relentless pursuit of a group of unwilling young women by a man. The women finally escape into the sky, and are transformed into the star cluster known to astronomers as the Pleiades, from the Greek myth that, fascinatingly, follows a similar pattern of action.

In October 1839, when the Seven Sisters rose over Mount Gingenbullen and the land quickened with spring, Charlotte quietly sent some of her furniture to Sydney. She packed as many of her possessions as she could fit onto the back of three bullocks, including her little writing desk and the family's pet koala. Then she and her four children rode away from Oldbury. Charlotte Elizabeth, the eldest, was eleven. Louisa, the youngest, was five.

Oldbury and everything they knew was left in the possession of a man Charlotte called *a raving lunatic.* Ahead was only uncertainty.

ᕱ

In order to gain their freedom, survivors may have to give up almost everything else, Herman writes. *Battered women may lose their homes, their friends, and their livelihood. Survivors of childhood abuse may lose their families. Political refugees may lose their homes and their homeland. Rarely are the dimensions of this sacrifice fully recognized.*

The story of how Charlotte so bravely set off into the unknown has always reminded me of *The Tenant of Wildfell Hall,* Anne Brontë's second novel, which was published in 1848 under the pseudonym of Acton Bell. It tells the story of a young woman named Helen, who flees her drunken, violent husband and takes refuge in a tumbledown country house with her young son. There she supports herself with her painting. Apparently, the novel was inspired when a young woman came to Anne's father Patrick, who was the vicar at Haworth parsonage, seeking advice on how to deal with her situation of domestic violence. She took his advice and escaped, and was able to build a new life for herself.

Our Charlotte could not have been inspired by *The Tenant of Wildfell Hall,* since it was published nine years after her own flight. But whenever I read it, I think of my brave ancestor and wonder if she too felt the pain and anguish expressed by the novel's protagonist, Helen:

Oh! when I think … how cruelly he has trampled on my love, betrayed my trust, scorned my prayers and tears … crushed my hopes, destroyed my youth's best feelings, and doomed me

to a life of hopeless misery, as far as man can do it, it is not
enough to say that I no longer love my husband—I HATE him!
The word stares me in the face like a guilty confession, but it is
true: I hate him—I hate him!

Binny and I set off to retrace Charlotte's extraordinary journey in the
thin, bright sunshine of early spring.

As the road leads us out of Sydney and south towards the Southern
Highlands, I feel the familiar quickening of excitement in my blood.
Ever since I was a little girl, this journey has been one of anticipation
and adventure.

We went often as little girls, as our grandparents told us the sad and
romantic stories of our ancestors' past. Then, when I was a young woman,
I brought the man I had fallen in love with, and we peered through the
tangled hedgerows while I shared the story with him. Greg asked me to
marry him, a few years later, at beautiful Milton Park in Bowral, only
a hop, a skip and a jump away. His parents then moved down to the
Southern Highlands, living in Burradoo. We have had many a happy
weekend down there with our three children, foraging in bookshops
and antique stores, lunching at the atmospheric old pubs, exploring the
countryside. One of my favourite things to do was to peruse the real
estate advertisements, looking at country houses for sale. If I could not
buy back Oldbury, as I had determined to do as a kiddie, then I wanted a
house just like it, somewhere equally beautiful. My mother-in-law Elaine
always said to me, 'I'm sure you'll end up living down here one day, Kate!'

I have been thinking a lot about landscape and memory this past
year. What I have realised is that story acts as a magnifying lens upon

the landscape. Whenever we visit a place that we are deeply connected to—by blood, ancestral memory, or knowledge of its story—we feel an intense hyperfocus. Everything is charged with meaning.

I have always felt that deep affinity in the Southern Highlands. Perhaps the powerful connection I felt when I first travelled to Kent was simply a shock of recognition: it looks like the countryside around Sutton Forest. Perhaps I was feeling a reversal of the recognition James and Charlotte felt when they first came to this beautiful part of the world.

The Grounds adjoining Mr Throsby's Hut are extremely pretty— gentle Hills and Dales—with an extensive rich Valley in his Front—; the whole Surrounding Grounds having a very Park-like appearance—being very thinly wooded ... The Situation of the New Settlers 4 miles South West of Throsby-Park, is particularly beautiful and rich—resembling a fine extensive Pleasure Grounds in England, Lachlan Macquarie wrote in 1820.

Charles Throsby was, of course, the Atkinsons' neighbour. When Oldbury was dissolved by the trustees, he bought the steam flour mill.

A cathedral of eucalypts arches over our head as we drive down towards the Meryla Pass where Charlotte and her small family rode almost 180 years earlier. The road is rough and rutted. Civilisation seems a million miles away.

All around, light glances through shifting grey leaves and delicate silver trunks. The red slash of mud is the only colour.

The road follows an ancient Aboriginal track. In 1818, Throsby was commissioned by Macquarie to find a route from the Southern Highlands down into Kangaroo Valley. He was guided by an Aboriginal man called Timelong (which is such a beautiful, evocative name). They made their way down through impenetrable bush, following landmarks only Timelong could see.

Following in his tracks, in my brother-in-law Rob's Land Cruiser, it is hard not to be a little nervous. The bush stretches as far as the eye can see, seemingly unchanging, strangely claustrophobic. We have no signal. Our phones are useless. We see black cockatoos, as lofty and inscrutable as eagles, their tail feathers flashing primrose-yellow. A burnt-out car, abandoned miles from anywhere.

How brave she was! I write in my diary.

The road winds its way to the edge of a sandstone escarpment, then plunges hundreds of feet in a series of narrow hairpin turns. Far, far below, a valley is filled with the blue shimmer of trees like an ocean. Far, far away, magnificent red cliffs glow in the sunset light like headlands. We stop the car and walk down the steep track. All I can hear is the susurration of wind in the leaves, and the faint, clear ting of a bellbird. The air is crisp, oxygenated. The silence is a breathing presence.

Twilight under the trees, shadows gathering close around.

I imagine Charlotte, white and tired, her hands bruised by the reins, and night closing in. I imagine the four drooping children, trying so hard to be brave. I imagine the horses' hooves slipping in the mud, and that great fall of distance reeling away.

Many years later, Louisa Atkinson wrote about the dangerous descent:

The pass had been improved by cutting steps down the face of the rocks, and the oxen ... stumbled down as best they could, while the horses groaned audibly, trembled, and even in some instances sunk powerless on the dangerous declivity, not encouraged by the sight of the gully yawning at the side of the narrow road ... Onward trudged the travellers ... Darkness gathered round early in that deep narrow vale, where mountains rose abruptly on either side.

Charlotte and the children made camp at the creek that flowed through the deep valley, and waited there with their young servant, Charley, for the bullocks that carried their tents and provisions.

Louisa writes:

But total darkness closed above them, and the absentees came not; all ears were strained to catch the first sound of them; conversation had flagged, then ceased ... the fire had died down—it was a darkness which could be felt ... suddenly appeared a small light, scarcely larger than a spark. 'Charley, what is that?' inquired several tremulous voices. 'Debel, debel, I believe,' returned the lad in a tone as if his teeth were chattering. On came the light, about two feet from the ground. 'Nonsense, Charley; what can it be?' Charley again hinted the possibility of the presence of his Satanic Majesty—while the little luminous speck crept cautiously onwards towards the horrorstruck group. 'Can it be a bushranger?' whispered the lady. 'I believe so, missus,' returned the aboriginal.

In Louisa's account of this nerve-racking encounter with a firefly, 'the lady fainted' at the thought of bushrangers. It is hard to know if Louisa is exaggerating for dramatic or comic effect, or if her mother Charlotte—overwhelmed with terror—truly swooned. Binny is sure it's not true: 'Charlotte was far too brave to faint helplessly and leave her children in danger!' she says.

The alarms of the night were not over. In Louisa's words:

Still the men and the pack bullocks did not arrive; the chill dews of evening were falling, and no tents erected, no supper to refresh and invigorate the weary travellers. Fear held possession of all hearts ... presently was heard the tramping of heavy feet; one of the pack bullocks was running wildly down the mountain, dragging behind him a heavy body.

Everyone feared the ox had knocked down its handler and killed him, and was now dragging the man's lifeless body behind it.

Once again, the truth proved to be an anti-climax. The children's pet koala—described by Louisa as a *rather portly gentleman*—had been secured in a pannier tied to the bullock's back, balancing the hamper of china and Charlotte's writing desk. He had unsurprisingly disliked the steep jolting descent. *This was too much for any choleric gentleman, who had nerves,* Louisa wrote in her usual ironic manner. *Maugie waxed wrath, and stuck his long claws through the wicker-work into the bullock's back,* with predictable results.

The next morning, the small party of intrepid explorers continued down the gully towards the Kangaroo River, which winds its way through thick rainforest in a series of cascades and waterfalls until it converges with the Shoalhaven River.

Later, Charlotte wrote of her son James: *I remember a little Gentleman ... who bravely rode his horse through a deep Salt Water River, while his Mamma was afraid to venture, till this little Gentleman had returned more than once, to re-assure her.*

Beyond lay Kangaroo Valley, the traditional lands of the Wodi Wodi people. The rainforest was so thick with vines, fig trees and cabbage tree palms that a horseman was unable to ride through unless a track was first cleared. Charlotte and her children probably rode along the Wodi Wodi's traditional trackways, shown to James Atkinson by Errombee, the Aboriginal Elder who had saved his life there some years earlier.

Charlotte and her children lived at Budgong for seven months. At the time, it was a place set in deep wilderness. The men who came into the forest to cut the cedar trees had to do so by hand, and then somehow get them down to the river for transportation from Shellharbour and Kiama. A few dairy farmers settled in the cleared pastures; they could only sell butter and cheese, since it took days to carry their produce out of the valley.

Food would have been simple and scarce, and all water drawn by hand from the stream. The children would have had to gather firewood, and help wash and mend the clothes and cook the meals. Yet there would have been time for play and laughter as well, and Charlotte made sure she took the time to teach them their lessons.

It must have been lonely and difficult for Charlotte, so far away from any kind of support network. It is known that at least one of the children fell ill, for Charlotte had to call a doctor and the bill for his services went unpaid for several years.

✹

Recovery unfolds in three stages, Herman writes. *The central task of the first stage is the establishment of safety. The central task of the second stage is remembrance and mourning. The central focus of the third stage is reconnection with ordinary life.*

In 1840, George Barton—described by Alexander Berry as 'half-insane'—was finally forced from Oldbury. Charlotte and her children returned there briefly, knowing they were not permitted to stay. It must have been a bittersweet return to the home where she had been so very happy with her first husband and so very unhappy with her second.

In Charlotte's *A Mother's Offering to Her Children*, the mother, Mrs Saville, says:

The [local] tribe ... were very much attached to your dear lamented father. You know they never mention the name of a deceased person; but they were giving me to understand, the regret and sympathy they felt at his loss. I had the locket with me at the time, which has a lock of all our hair in it. I showed this to them, pointing out his (to us) much valued brown curl; when they uttered a piercing cry; and all turned away; holding down their heads a short time: when they looked up I saw they were in tears. One of the women stepped aside; and whispered to me 'Bail you show that to blacks ebber any more missus.' This of course I promised to refrain from. I was much surprised and effected at their manner; having wished to give them pleasure. It was six years after our bereavement.

It is clear Charlotte still grieved very much for James, even so long after his death. But it was time for her to make a new life for herself. This time she and her children rode for Rose Bay, a small harbourside village near Sydney Town.

Like Anne Brontë's heroine, she was *free and safe at last!*

Chapter 11

A NOTABLE SHE-DRAGON

Written by Kate

Our future destiny is so veiled in obscurity, that it is quite impossible
to say, with truth, what any of us will do at a distant day

Charlotte Waring Atkinson

———⊰◆⊱———

At the age of 45, Charlotte had lost everything. The love of her life, her home, her financial security, her sense of who she was in the world.

She was a now single mother with four children under the age of 13, living in the small fishing village of Rose Bay, struggling to find some way to support her family.

One of the first things Charlotte did was apply to the Sydney police for protection against George Barton, chilling proof that he had been physically violent towards her during their marriage.

Charlotte had no income at all from Oldbury, supporting her family by the sale of her clothes and jewellery, and by borrowing money and running up debts. So she applied to the courts for the proceeds from the estate to which she was entitled under James' will.

She began with a petition to the Chief Justice, Sir James Dowling, on 1 September 1840, in which she listed her complaints about the executors' administration of James Atkinson's estate. Under their mismanagement, the petition said, the value of Oldbury had diminished from £6,000 to only £500. She and her children were in a state of destitution as a consequence. *Her situation is extremely distressing,* her solicitor wrote. *She assures me she and the Children are literally starving.*

And Charlotte was someone who valued the true meaning of words. When she said 'literally', she meant 'actually and exactly'.

Charlotte wished to be appointed guardian of her children, and to be given an adequate income from the estate to feed, support and educate them.

In retaliation, Alexander Berry and the other trustees declared that she was *incapable and unfit to be guardian of her own children,* and applied to the courts to have Charlotte Elizabeth, Jane Emily, James John and little Louisa given into the guardianship of a stranger. It did not matter who, as long as it was a man.

As a woman in the 1840s, Charlotte did not have any of the basic legal rights that we take for granted. She did not have the right to manage the estate as she saw fit, nor even the right to decide how her children should be educated. These decisions belonged by law to her new husband, George Barton, and to the executors of her dead husband's estate.

Mary Wollstonecraft once famously described marriage as *legal prostitution,* since a woman lost any power over her own body and actions once she was married.

In December 1837—not quite three years before Charlotte was accused of being *incapable and unfit*—an English politician, MP John Temple Leader, addressed the British House of Commons:

As it stands at present, the law is entirely in favour of the husband, and oppressive to the wife. A man ... may be drunken, immoral, vicious, and utterly brutalised … the wife, in such a case, has no redress … there are hundreds of women now suffering in silence, pining for the children whom a stern law has torn from them … eagerly hoping that the representatives of the people will save them from the terrible alternative which forces them to choose between being the abject slaves of a brutal husband, or of being deprived of the very sight of their own children.

It did not matter that Charlotte had fled her violent and abusive husband. She was still his chattel.

I do not mean that metaphorically.

According to nineteenth-century English common law, a married woman had no legal rights of her own. She and her husband were seen as a single legal entity. An unmarried woman was named, in law, *feme sole*, or 'single woman'. A married woman had the legal status of *feme covert*, or 'covered woman'. This principle of coverture was described in William Blackstone's *Commentaries on the Laws of England* in the late eighteenth century:

By marriage, the husband and wife are one person in law: … that is, the very being or legal existence of the woman is suspended during the marriage, or at least is incorporated and consolidated into that of the husband: under whose wing, protection, and cover, *she performs every thing.*

This meant a married woman was not permitted to own property, or indeed, anything of her own. Anything that belonged to her before the wedding automatically became the property of her husband as soon as the marriage certificate was signed and witnessed. She could not sign a contract, execute a deed of gift, or write a will without her husband's consent. She could not seek education without permission, nor keep any money she earned for herself.

A few years before Charlotte was forced to fight for the right to custody of her own children, another young woman writer faced a similar battle in the UK. Caroline Norton had made a convenient marriage urged upon her by her penniless mother. Her husband, George Norton, the younger brother of Lord Grantley, was a vicious spendthrift who probably caused the miscarriage of her fourth child. Caroline Norton wrote poetry and plays to support her family. According to the law, all of her earnings went straight to her husband.

Caroline left her husband in 1836. He then sued her close friend Lord Melbourne, the Prime Minister, for 'criminal conversation', then the legal term for adultery. In *March, Women, March*, Lucinda Hawksley writes: *It was not Caroline who was being sued: Norton was suing Lord Melbourne for sullying his 'property'—a wife being merely a possession of her husband's.*

The jury cleared Lord Melbourne, but the damage to Caroline was incalculable. At that time, a divorce could only be obtained by a Private Act of Parliament. Men could ask for a divorce on the grounds of adultery, but women could only initiate a divorce if their husband's adultery was accompanied by life-threatening cruelty. It cost a fortune, and so only the very wealthy could afford it. Despite all the evidence of her husband's violence, Caroline was unable to obtain a divorce. Norton not only continued to live at her expense, but he kept her three sons hidden from her. One died soon after she left her husband, and she was not permitted to see him on his deathbed.

In her grief and anger, Caroline undertook a period of intense campaigning to change the law. She wrote numerous pamphlets arguing for the natural right of mothers to have custody of their children. This led to the passing of the Custody of Infants Act in Great Britain in 1839, which allowed judges some discretion in deciding who should have custody of children after a divorce. Although fathers were still automatically given guardianship, a mother was now allowed to petition the courts for custody of children up to the age of seven and for access to older children.

As Australia was a colony of Great Britain, Charlotte was subject to the same unjust laws that ruined Caroline Norton's life. In fact, Australian courts were not fully freed from British supervision until 1986.

Because of these gender injustices encoded in the law, Berry and the other executors—men who were not related to the Atkinson children in any way—were able to decide that they should be taken away from their mother Charlotte and raised by strangers.

Charlotte was not a *fit and proper person to be the Guardian of the Infants ... in consequence of [her] imprudent conduct ... since her intermarriage with George Bruce Barton*, the executors declared. A formal school would educate the Atkinson children better than *Charlotte Barton could possibly educate them*. She was, they said, as much to blame for the marriage breakdown as Barton. She *had thrown many obstacles in the way of the Executors in settling matters for the benefit and advantage* of the children, they asserted, and suggested that the two children over ten, Charlotte Elizabeth and Jane Emily, be sent away to school, with James John to follow as soon as he was old enough.

The legal system is designed to protect men from the superior power of the state but not to protect women or children from the superior power of men, Judith Lewis Herman wrote in 1992. *If one set out by design to devise a system for provoking intrusive post-traumatic symptoms, one could not do better than a court of law.*

It must have been so hard for Charlotte, a woman alone, penniless and powerless, struggling to keep her children at a time when the world thought women were as stupid as dolls.

The courts made many suggestions for possible guardians for the Atkinson children. Their uncle John Atkinson refused the role, either because he did not want to betray Charlotte or because her re-marriage had opened a rift between them. It is impossible to know which is the truth. John Atkinson had been dealing with his own financial troubles, and had consequently mortgaged Mereworth and leased out the Kentish Arms inn.

Charlotte fought for her children like a tigress.

She asked the courts for permission to rent Oldbury, offering to pay £550 in the first year and £600 thereafter, which would allow her to access the income from the estate and accumulate some capital for her children. Her petition was refused.

This may be because George Barton—who was a defendant in the case, as he was still lawfully her husband—made a series of shocking allegations against her. His deposition reads: *[he] had every reason to believe the said Charlotte Barton has had improper and criminal intercourse with convict men and various other persons.*

He accused her of riding out into the forest with convicts (which is more than likely, since someone had to take care of the sheep runs).

Charlotte Barton ... was away with said Convict for a week or ten days ... and did on several other occasions commit the same offence with another convict man during these years and the following year and on the said Charlotte Barton's return to Deponent's house after [he] had gone to rest [he] refused to admit her to his bed and remarked ... [he] was not going to keep illegitimate children of Jews and convicts.

Herman writes that *in order to escape accountability for his crimes, the perpetrator does everything in his power to promote forgetting ... If secrecy fails, the perpetrator attacks the credibility of his victim. If he cannot silence her absolutely, he tries to make sure that no one listens.*

Barton's lawyer later offered to withdraw these accusations, but the damage had been done. In the small, insular world of colonial Sydney, such accusations must have caused much scandal and shame for Charlotte. She defended herself with what Patricia Clarke calls *a blistering petition.* She denied all the allegations, declared that she had not been guilty of improper conduct and that she lived apart from Barton because *his habits of constant intoxication render him unfit to live with and comparatively if not altogether insane.* He was, she avowed, *violent and dangerous.*

Charlotte also denied the executors' allegation that the breakup of the marriage had been as much her fault as Barton's. She had left because of *his intemperate habits and bad treatment,* she wrote, and because of her *anxious desire to remove her children from his control and example and to devote herself to their moral and intellectual improvement.*

She set out to prove her own ability to raise and teach her children, giving evidence of her unusually thorough education and long experience as a governess. She also begged that her daughters not be sent away to boarding school, saying she did *not consider that Ladies can be educated properly at a school even in England and that consequently it would be less possible to educate them properly at a school in this Colony.* If they were placed under her charge, she promised they would be brought up with *stricter attention to their morals* than any school could provide. This plea seems to come from the heart, and probably arises from her own misery at being sent away to school when she was so young.

Nonetheless, the Master in Equity found that—because of Charlotte's *peculiar circumstances* (being a woman who had fled her violent drunkard of a husband)—she was not fit to be guardian of her own children. He appointed a 28-year-old solicitor named Edward James Cory as their temporary guardian.

Charlotte refused to submit. *His youth … his local inexperience and his position in society render him an unfit person to be guardian of the said infants*, she declared.

She also denied that the *children … were often left alone in their residence without any person to be in charge of them in consequence of Mrs Barton's frequent visits to town on business.* Charlotte replied angrily that she had always left them in the care of a responsible person whenever she needed to leave her home *as she has been frequently obliged to do to consult legal advisers upon the subject of this suit.*

Rumours that George Barton had been married before, and was therefore a bigamist, could not be proved, and her pleas to delay the inquiry were ignored.

The Master in Equity demanded the children be brought to his office, where he examined them individually on their skills and knowledge.

After each of the four children had sat their exams, the Master found they had all been instructed with care and attention, and in some branches of education not generally taught at public schools. It was a resounding vindication for Charlotte.

Nonetheless, the court case had now dragged on for many months and the cost was a sucking drain on the estate left by James Atkinson, with legal costs already escalating to the enormous sum of £1,475.

In July 1841, Charlotte gained the right to proceed separately from George Barton. She then begged the court not to confirm the interim report of the Master in Equity, which would have removed her children from her, asking that it be referred to the Chief Justice, Sir James Dowling, instead.

The case was summarised as follows:

> *a bill had been filed by the children of James Atkinson, deceased ... against the executors and trustees of their father's will, praying an account and maintenance ... It had been referred to the master to appoint a guardian ... and a maintenance for the minors: the master made his report, recommending the appointment of a guardian ...*

> *Mr. BROADHURST, for the defendant, Charlotte Barton, submitted that the plaintiffs' proceeding was irregular: that he should have proceeded by petition instead of motion ... [this being] so much cheaper and shorter ... the better to save the estate from expense, and the sooner to supply the wants of the minors, who were now in a state of complete destitution.*

On 9 July 1841, the Chief Justice heard Charlotte's case. The Equity Court had described her petition as *impertinent and scandalous*. Charlotte was ordered to pay the costs of referral because of this supposed impertinence.

I love this. I imagine her, only a little over five feet tall, wearing a rather shabby dress, for she had no money to buy a new one, a shawl wrapped around her shoulders against the chill of the courtroom in winter, her back straight, her chin high, gazing up at Sir James Dowling at his judge's bench, his white wig and black robe giving him a dour air as he reprimands her for her impudence.

I imagine, though, a twinkle in his eye and a smile suppressed at the corners of his mouth, for Sir James Dowling found emphatically in

Charlotte's favour. He declared that her separation from George Barton was *irrespective ... of any personal demerit on her part*, and that the suggestion that she was unfit to care for and educate her children *was without foundation.*

He ruled that *it would require a state of urgent circumstances to induce the Court to deprive them (all of whom are under thirteen years of age) of that maternal care and tenderness, which none but a mother can bestow.*

He refused to deprive *the infants of that most essential part of education the cultivation of filial piety, of the affections of the heart—and of those social duties of domestic life which constitute the most sacred bond between parent and child ... I see no reason why she should not still have the guardianship of them ... The comfort, the happiness, and the advantage of the children, indicate this determination.*

It was a resounding victory, both for Charlotte and for the rights of Australian women.

'It's not only the first time that a woman was given custody of her own children in this country, but also one of the first cases of maternal custody in the world,' my brother Nick says. He is a top corporate lawyer and managing partner of the law firm Hamilton Locke, as well as a bestselling author.

In England, the only time a mother had been granted custody of her child—a six-year-old—was in the Blisset Case of 1774, when it was proven that the father had mistreated them both. This was not at all the norm. In 1804, for example, a newborn daughter was forcibly returned to her father, even though she was an infant *then at the breast* of the mother.

In the USA, the first decision to defy the unassailable rights of fathers was awarded in the Prather v. Prather case of 1809. The court ruled that the youngest child, a five-year-old girl, was to be returned to her mother's care after her husband had turned her out of the house and installed another woman in an act of open adultery. However, the South Carolina court noted: *The Court is apprised that it is treading on new and dangerous grounds, but feels a consolation in the reflection that if it errs, there is a [higher] tribunal wherein the error can be redressed.*

I can only imagine the giddy relief and joy that Charlotte felt that chilly winter's day in 1841, knowing her beloved children would not be removed from her and given into a stranger's care.

The battle was not over yet, however. The trustees still refused to pay Charlotte the money owed to her. In April 1842, the Chief Justice declared the will of James Atkinson proven and ordered that his debts, funeral expenses and legacies be paid. Patricia Clarke, usually so impartial and objective, writes: *eight years after his death!*

That exclamation mark from her is like a string of furious emojis from anyone else.

The Chief Justice also found against the executors in some matters. Alexander Berry was required to pay back £95 to the Oldbury estate. *The whole is a fine specimen of legality,* Berry wrote to Coghill, *and of course I must submit to repay the money out of my own pocket—as it is now impossible to alter the accounts ... All the lawyers say that you acted quite wrong ... you will most likely be made liable to the children to the amount of £600 ... This no doubt must be very annoying to you but is far more annoying to me because being originally totally averse to having any connection with such a notable she-dragon I was only prevailed upon to act at the earnest remonstrance of Mr Norton & yourself.*

His malicious description of Charlotte as *a notable she-dragon* is to me the finest praise anyone could bestow. Charlotte had no weapons but her intelligence, her facility with words, and her indomitable spirit. She fought the world to save her children, and she won.

It was during this harrowing time that Charlotte somehow found the time to write.

Every evening—after a long and exhausting day spent in court—Charlotte gathered her four children about her and told them stories, creating an enchanted circle for them where they could feel safe and loved. When they were asleep, she took up her pen and she wrote the stories down.

We should never, my dear children, say we cannot bear this, or that, she wrote one night. *It is impossible to set bounds to human endurance. Who can tell how much misery may be borne, and yet the sufferer live to tell it!*

On 18 December 1841—five months after she had won her court case—*A Mother's Offering to Her Children* was published, in time for Christmas. Charlotte had struggled through almost impossible obstacles to become Australia's first children's author.

Chapter 12

RETURN TO OLDBURY

Written by Belinda

it would afford us much delight ... We should find
abundance of subjects for our pencils

Charlotte Waring Atkinson

———❖———

In the 1840s, fewer than half the children in the colony received any form of schooling. Most girls received little or no education, except for domestic skills. It was extremely rare for girls to learn such a broad-ranging syllabus as Charlotte taught her children—covering art, music, science, languages, literature, geography, zoology, conchology, geology and botany.

Charlotte's passion for education and determination to educate her own children was unusual for the time and is one of the characteristics that I most admire about her.

In February 1842, Charlotte moved her family from Rose Bay to a cottage in Woolloomooloo, which was then a pretty bayside suburb of fashionable villas and gardens, closer to Sydney. The move was so her children could attend school for the first time. Of course Charlotte chose an outstanding school, one with progressive educational principles, focusing on academic subjects as well as 'ornamental' accomplishments, which aimed *to substitute the discipline of kindness … for the usual harsh system of flogging and beating.*

She chose College High School near the corner of Elizabeth and Market streets, opposite Hyde Park, run by James Rennie, who had been Professor of Natural History at London University. The Young Ladies department was run by Professor Rennie's daughter Christina, and cost two guineas per quarter for juniors and three guineas for seniors.

The 1842 academic results for College High School were published in *The Sydney Morning Herald*, and Charlotte and James Atkinson did brilliantly, a shining testament to the education they had received from their mother. In the first half of the year, Charlotte Elizabeth, nearly 14, came first in drawing and geography, second in Italian and ornamental needlework, and third in history and 'Letter Writing and Keeping a Daily Journal'. Her brother James, aged ten, came first in geography and second in drawing. At the prize-giving ceremony at the end of that year, Charlotte was dux of the girls' section, receiving the medal for general superiority in all classes. Her brother James came first in drawing for both junior and senior boys, as well as being among the top three students for most of his subjects. Results for later years were not published, but Charlotte Elizabeth received several medals for academic excellence, which she treasured all her life.

When my own children were six, eight and ten, I decided to take on the daunting challenge of home schooling them for two years, while we travelled. Our family spent six months gallivanting around Europe, and 18 months exploring the remote outback of Australia in a four-wheel drive caravan, having the most amazing adventure, filled with incredible experiences and so much special family time. While we travelled, I taught Nick, Emily and Lachie myself, preferring not to enrol them in distance education.

Over the two years, we used our travels as the basis for the children's education, studying art, music, French and German language, cooking, history, geography, geology, science, English, Aboriginal culture and maths. The hardest for me was maths, so Rob helped with this, and with science experiments, as well as teaching the kids life skills such as fishing, building campfires, map reading, playing guitar and carpentry.

Their learning experiences ranged from studying French and art in Paris, to exploring ancient archaeological ruins in Greece and Italy, searching for 20-million-year-old fossils in the desert and snorkelling over the Great Barrier Reef. There were always piles of books to read, and writing every day. It was the most wonderful experience for us all. I particularly loved the chance to be so involved in my children's education for an extended period. The two years of home schooling stood them in good stead right through high school and university.

A highlight and enormous privilege was living for three weeks with a Bardi family, near Ardyaloon, on Western Australia's Dampier Peninsula. We absorbed Bardi cultural and spiritual traditions, learned from male and female Elders, and witnessed their ancient connection to country. It was a life-changing experience—gathering bush tucker and medicine, making spears, hunting turtle and stingray, swimming with sharks, creating art, listening to Dreaming stories, learning some of the Bardi language, hearing first-hand about the Stolen Generation and discussing the many complex challenges facing Indigenous Australians. Bardi Elders Frank and Maureen Davey believe it is vital to teach young Australians, like my kids, to understand and respect Aboriginal culture, history and empowerment. This intense immersion, with the Elders' blessing, inspired characters and stories in several of my books, and motivated me to become involved in literacy programs supporting Indigenous students in remote areas. Much later, my son Lachie worked as a volunteer in the Buru homeland of Far North Queensland, was initiated into their mob and wrote his own story exploring the consequences of Aboriginal dispossession.

Like me, Charlotte must have been enormously proud as she saw her children grow up to be so clever and accomplished. Like me, she also taught her children to be strong, adventurous, inquisitive and independent.

My great-great-great-grandmother Charlotte Elizabeth Atkinson was very like her mother. She was clever, artistic, opinionated and strong-willed, with curly black hair and dark eyes. Sometimes mother and daughter clashed, as Charlotte Elizabeth sought to forge her own independent path.

On 5 March 1844, aged only 15, Charlotte Elizabeth sought permission from the Court of Equity to marry 18-year-old William Cummings of Liverpool. Her mother had already consented to the marriage. It seems unbelievable that Charlotte had given her permission for her daughter to marry at such a young age, but perhaps she was swayed by the fact that she herself had left home and was living independently at 15.

The court granted the request for an inquiry, wishing to ensure Cummings was a man of substance, as Charlotte Elizabeth was so young.

William was a wine and spirit merchant, the son of Mary and William Cummings senior. The Cummings family had owned several respectable hotels for many years, including the Sydney Arms, a coffee house and tavern, which was a favoured venue of the colonial gentry. The family later moved to Liverpool—after William's father became ill—where William junior helped his father run the Ship Inn. The family were wealthy, but a combination of the economic depression in the 1840s and William senior's poor health meant their fortunes waned.

Shortly after his proposal, William Cummings junior was granted a licence to operate the Liverpool Arms. But, by the end of the year, William Cummings senior was declared insolvent and the younger William was in financial difficulties. Whether the Court of Equity refused permission or Charlotte Elizabeth changed her mind, the marriage did not go ahead.

On 7 April 1846, James John Oldbury Atkinson turned 14, and Charlotte brought her family home to Oldbury so he could learn to run the property. Charlotte Elizabeth was 17, Emily was nearly 16 and Louisa was 12. Charlotte was 50.

Oldbury had been rented out to multiple tenants since the family had left it six years before and was in a poor state of repair. In her novel, *Cowanda*, Louisa later described the family home as *it was then empty, and so gone to decay … the glass was broken in many places, and the walls cracked and damp-stained.*

With the economic depression, the estate was not producing enough income, and Charlotte's allowance had therefore been reduced to £200 per year. Her letters to the court show that she was struggling to make ends meet, particularly with so many repairs to undertake at Oldbury.

The family lived quietly and happily—drawing, sketching, walking, observing nature, discussing botany, playing music, reading, cooking, gardening and raising wildlife. Louisa later wrote about rearing pet koalas, possums, lizards, echidnas and birds, including a pair of curlews called Petrea and Peter. She wrote about a pet kangaroo: *So strong is this power of attachment … that I have known a hand-reared and partly grown one fret to death during the temporary absence of the person who reared it, even though surrounded by other kind friends.* Of course, this reminds me of the orphaned possums and baby wallaby that we raised as children in our back garden at Gordon.

Charlotte seemed to enjoy this time with the children—now they were older and less reliant on her for their education, she was able to spend more time drawing and painting, as evidenced by her surviving sketchbooks. Her drawings reveal her ongoing fascination with travel, faraway lands, exotic people and strange animals. She drew everything from 'esquimaux' and Aboriginal people to picturesque scenes copied from books, and plants and insects drawn from life. Her 1848 sketchbook includes portraits of the famous adventurer Lady Hester Stanhope, who grew up at Chevening, near Shoreham, and Stanhope's physician, Dr Madden, dressed in Turkish garb. Some paintings and sketches attributed to Charlotte Elizabeth, Emily and Louisa also survive from this period.

Charlotte and her family continued their friendship with the local Aboriginal community, especially Errombee.

Jem Vaugh [Errombee] and his tribe were encamped on Oldbury, in the neighbourhood of Berrima, and the old chief came to visit the friends he had known on the Shoalhaven; he found some of the family engaged in making pastry in the kitchen, and while he stood talking, a Bathurst black who was visiting the tribe entered and asked for flour, then for an order on a miller on the estate, and finally for sixpence; all these requests being denied he retired, and it was presently discovered had stolen a sixpenny coin which lay on the table. Jem was made acquainted with the loss; he stepped into the verandah and uttered a rapid 'hi, hi, hi'. The culprit, who was at some distance, immediately returned, put down the money in silence, and withdrew, evidently bowing to the rule of the chief whose subject for the time being he was. This was the only act of dishonesty I ever knew any of them guilty of, and their honesty arose not from want of opportunity, as the reverse has frequently been the case.

Oldbury was no longer the centre of the district's social and political life. Charlotte was judged harshly by conservative colonial society as a woman who had left her husband, even though he was a violent alcoholic. Her reputation was scarred by the scandal of the bushranger attack, her very public humiliation through the court cases, George Barton's history and her own outspoken and forceful personality as *a notable she-dragon.*

The neighbourhood had also changed. John and Jane Atkinson had suffered ongoing financial difficulties due to drought and the economic depression. Mereworth was mortgaged and had to be sold, as did their land in Berrima. In 1843, while Charlotte was living in Sydney, John and Jane Atkinson moved to Tumut with their family, horses and cattle, to become some of the first farmers in the district.

With their financial and social circumstances reduced, young Charlotte Elizabeth may have had difficulty meeting men of her own background. At the age of 18 she fell in love with a handsome and charming scallywag called Thomas McNeilly, who was employed at Oldbury as a coachman. He was a dark-haired Irishman, about 30 years old, with *winning ways,* who had been born in Connaught.

According to family lore, Charlotte Elizabeth ran away with Thomas McNeilly, as her mother would never have approved of the match. Not only was he a servant, he was illiterate, an Irish Catholic and probably a former convict. He must have been sexy!

Charlotte was devastated. It was hardly the match she would have wished for her beloved daughter. However, Charlotte found the runaways, brought them back to Oldbury and arranged for them to be married by Catholic priest Father McGinty. They were married at Oldbury on Charlotte Elizabeth's nineteenth birthday, 22 July 1847. Thomas couldn't write his name, so marked the register with an X.

In Charlotte's 1848 sketchbook there is an exquisite wedding sketch of a beautiful bride in her delicate wedding dress and veil, with curly black hair and dark eyes just like her mother's. Finding this sketch of my great-great-great-grandmother Charlotte Elizabeth was such a joy. One of the absolute highlights of our research.

Very little is known about Thomas, although it is believed that he was probably a farm labourer, born Thomas McNally, who at the age of 17 was sentenced in Mayo to seven years transportation for firearm offences. Thomas McNally arrived in the colony in 1834 on the *Parmelia* with his brother Edward. According to family lore, Charlotte Elizabeth encouraged him to change his name to the more respectable McNeilly.

Charlotte and Thomas McNeilly lived for some time at Oldbury in one of the farm cottages, perhaps Swanton, a four-room sandstone house about two miles from the main homestead, on the other side of Mount Gingenbullen.

Ten months later, on 1 May 1848, Charlotte McNeilly had a daughter called Florence Charlotte, known as Flora—my great-great-grandmother. Flora was born at Oldbury and baptised by Father McGinty in Berrima on 11 August. Flora was the only child of the McNeilly family to be christened as a Catholic. The remaining children were all brought up as staunch Anglicans.

Four years later, Charlotte Elizabeth and Thomas had a *beloved and only* son, Thomas James Louis McNeilly, but he died on 1 February 1853 *aged nearly thirteen months after a few days' severe illness* and was buried at All Saints Anglican Church at Sutton Forest. I can only imagine how devastated the whole family must have been at the death of a much-loved child. Charlotte McNeilly gave birth to another son, Charles James Edward, several months later.

In April 1853, James John Oldbury Atkinson turned 21 and the family once more applied to the courts, this time to give James permission to take over possession of Oldbury.

Encouraged by Charlotte and keen to earn money, Louisa pursued an ambitious literary career. At the age of 19, Louisa's articles and drawings were published in *The Illustrated Sydney News*. The series was called 'Notes of the Month', with the first published on 15 October 1853, along with two articles on Aboriginal culture and artefacts, called 'The Native Arts'. The first of these was accompanied by Louisa's sketch of the traditional burial mound with carved funeral trees on Mount Gingenbullen. This was the beginning of Louisa's writing career, as the first Australian-born woman to write a long-running series of newspaper articles.

A joyous occasion occurred in 1853, when 23-year-old Emily was married to a local grazier, James Johnson Warren, at All Saints Church on 12 October. James Warren had taken over the farm at Mereworth (but not the inn) after John Atkinson's family had moved away. Charlotte would have been much happier about this marriage. The joy was not to last. Ten months later, on 24 August 1854 *at Oldbury, the residence of her mother, Jane Emily, the much beloved daughter of Mrs C. Barton, and wife of Mr. J.J. Warren died aged 24 years, of puerperal fever, after three weeks of intense suffering, leaving an infant son.* She was buried in the family vault with her father James.

The whole family was heartbroken. Gentle and kind, Emily was adored by everyone. Her baby son, Henry Warren, was cared for at his father's farm at Mereworth, but died eight months later and was buried with his mother in the family vault at All Saints.

The loss of beloved Emily and two infant grandsons in such a short time must have been devastating. In early nineteenth-century Australia, nearly 40 per cent of children died before their fifth birthday. They fell victim to accidents, diarrhoea or dysentery caused by poor sanitation, and infectious childhood diseases such as whooping cough, measles and diphtheria.

Another event had occurred earlier in 1854 that must have revived many distressing memories for Charlotte and her family. George Barton was charged with the wilful murder of one of his employees, William Rogers, at his farm at Bathurst. The case was widely reported in the newspapers, including the salacious details that Barton and his employees were all drunk and as usual had been drinking rum all day. Barton had been in bed with *the mistress,* a woman called Catherine Byrnes, when Rogers burst into the bedroom wielding an axe, saying, *now I have got the axe I'll knock the old beggar's head off.*

Barton grabbed his shotgun and shot Rogers in the lower stomach, in what he claimed was self-defence. The man took eight days to die, in excruciating agony, and at the trial the judge observed that Barton was not overly concerned about his victim's fate. The jury returned a verdict of manslaughter and Barton was sentenced to two years hard labour. This was the violent drunkard from whom Charlotte had fled. George Barton survived his sentence and went on to outlive most of the Atkinson family, dying at Barraba, New South Wales, on 2 January 1880, aged 81.

The grief of Emily and Henry's tragic deaths triggered a period of ill health for Louisa, who had been delicate since birth. While she had many periods of remission, when she was healthy and active, she suffered periodically from issues caused by pulmonary tuberculosis and a weak heart. The only treatment was rest, eating well, fresh air and exercise outdoors. It was about this time that Charlotte and Louisa decided to move from Oldbury, leaving James junior to run the estate.

Charlotte and Louisa moved to the quiet village of Burwood, surrounded by bushland, on the railway line to Sydney, perhaps to be closer to Louisa's publishers.

Here Louisa began writing her first novel, *Gertrude the Emigrant*, under the pseudonym of An Australian Lady. The book was published in 1857, with her own illustrations, when Louisa was 23 years old—the first novel written by an Australian-born woman. Charlotte actively encouraged her daughter's literary career, and Louisa's writing reflects many of Charlotte's own beliefs, interests and family stories.

Gertrude the Emigrant follows the adventures of its orphan heroine, making her own way alone in the world by working hard, before she marries the man she loves, just like Charlotte did when she left England in 1826. The story is set in the 1830s, on a station inspired by Oldbury, much as it was when Louisa was a child. It is filled with authentic and lively scenes of Australian colonial domestic and farming life—cooking, harvesting, sheep washing and shearing, cattle duffing, bushfires and mustering. These everyday scenes made Louisa's writing very popular with Australian readers.

What is most notable about *Gertrude the Emigrant* is the novel's strong, capable and independent female characters, running businesses and overcoming difficulties with courage and resourcefulness. Louisa's heroines have an outstanding work ethic. She rejects typical nineteenth-century English notions of idle ladies, and promotes an ideal of hard-working, industrious and competent women. This theme runs through all of Louisa's novels and reflects the feminist philosophy she learned from her mother. Louisa's writing also echoed her mother's beliefs about the inadequacy of education available to girls of the time. Louisa prefers girls who can ride horses and bake and manage a dairy to girls who embroider and simper in the drawing room.

I love reading Louisa's books. Her descriptions are detailed and engaging, providing a tantalising glimpse into mid-nineteenth-century Australian life. The only aspect I struggle with is her intrusive religious themes. Louisa, like her mother Charlotte and her sisters, was deeply religious. Yet their religious beliefs were not dogmatic but based on helping the poor and sick, educating local children, being involved in the local community and spreading an understanding of Christian moral values.

Like Charlotte, Louisa's writing showed a deep fascination with and affection for the Aboriginal people and their culture, describing corroborees, artefacts and customs. Scenes of Aboriginal life were to appear in much of Louisa's work. From our perspective her attitudes to Indigenous people seem condescending, but for the mid-nineteenth century her attitudes are remarkably sympathetic.

In 1859, when she was 63, Charlotte decided to move to the Blue Mountains for Louisa's health. Charlotte had a house built on about five acres at Kurrajong, north of the Bells Line of Road, which she called Fernhurst. The *delightful, romantically situated cottage residence* had eight rooms, two servant rooms, a cellar and storerooms, with outbuildings including a detached kitchen, stables, gig house, pigsties and poultry house. There were three acres of vegetable and flower gardens with a large orange and apple orchard.

Mother and daughter lived at Fernhurst for about six years— sketching, painting, gardening, raising poultry, writing, birdwatching and 'botanising'.

Charlotte began a small boarding school, taking four resident pupils and teaching them *a sound English education, to ground them thoroughly in spelling, grammar, geography, writing, arithmetic, French, drawing and sketching from nature. Terms, £50 per annum.*

For an additional fee, students could also learn *piano, with composition* or harmonium.

Charlotte was adamant that she did not want 25-year-old Louisa to marry, because of her frail health and the deadly risk of childbirth.

Louisa's second novel, *Cowanda*, was set in her new home of Kurrajong, where she also wrote two popular ballads, *Cooee!* and *The Light from the Mountain*, which were performed by well-known opera singers.

Louisa was known for her cheerful, kind and gentle personality. She was active in the local community, wrote letters for the illiterate, taught local children, began a Sunday school at Fernhurst and visited the sick and poor. She also learned dissection and taxidermy, preserving many birds and animals as stuffed specimens.

Her health improved enormously in the clear mountain air. Here she delighted in exploring the gullies and steep mountain slopes on horseback, accompanied by friends and her dog Aime. One of her frequent companions was her dear friend Emma Selkirk, from Richmond, who was also a keen plant collector. The pair caused snide gossip in the neighbourhood by choosing to wear practical trousers on their jaunts.

Louisa loved travelling and made many horseback journeys, as she had done as a child with her mother and siblings, as far afield as Springwood, Mount Tomah, Colo, Richmond and Wisemans Ferry. On these arduous journeys she would spend many hours in the saddle, riding up to 45 miles per day, sometimes camping out overnight. She wrote about the joys of camping in the bush, with *a saddle [for] a down pillow* and the stars overhead. The travellers enjoyed drinking billy tea from the *tin quart* and eating salt beef with damper cakes cooked over the coals.

On these expeditions Louisa would collect many plant specimens, some of which had never been identified before, storing them in a homemade leather plant wallet. These would be pressed, or planted in the garden at Fernhurst.

In 1859, Louisa began writing a series of articles called 'A Voice from the Country', which appeared monthly in *The Sydney Morning Herald* and *The Sydney Mail*, and ran for several years. Her natural history series was popular, covering topics as diverse as flora, fauna, conservation, changing seasons, explorers, geology, bushfires, Aboriginal people and her intrepid excursions. Louisa also wrote articles for the *Horticultural Magazine*.

Her third novel, *Debatable Ground*, was published in 1861 as a long-running weekly serial in *The Sydney Mail*. The story is complicated, but again explores several of Louisa's recurring themes, including strong, independent heroines, one of whom is a young governess: *To earn an independent and respectable livelihood, and to be useful, was the sum of her ambition.* She also pokes fun at the false gentility of the upwardly mobile classes and the generally poor education available to children.

While Louisa's writing and artistic career was remarkable, her greatest talent was as a practical field botanist, at a time when few women did original scientific research—a tribute to the outstanding scientific education she received from Charlotte. Many people have commented on the fact that Louisa received no formal education, totally ignoring the fact that Charlotte taught her most of what she knew, through daily discussions, practical demonstrations and a lifetime of excursions into the bush.

Louisa worked closely with William Woolls and Baron Ferdinand von Mueller, as well as other eminent botanists. Von Mueller named several of Louisa's plant discoveries in her honour. Louisa Atkinson was an extraordinarily talented Australian woman, whose story, like her mother's, has been forgotten in the mists of time.

Chapter 13

CHARLOTTE'S LEGACY

Written by Belinda

the cheering hope of a happy hereafter!
Charlotte Waring Atkinson

———◆———

In 1863, Charlotte and Louisa returned to Oldbury to stay with James for a few months.

Louisa wrote several newspaper articles inspired by her trip home, including three about Aboriginal culture and spirituality. She wrote about the charm stones that the local Aboriginal women always carried: *the smooth white stone she carries in her wallet … a reference to spirits … which shall be carefully kept a mystery from the curious white invader.* I loved Louisa's description of the European invaders, which displayed an unusual sensitivity for the time.

Louisa wrote about a visit to the Fitzroy Ironworks at Mittagong. James Atkinson was an investor in the company, which had high hopes of mining and smelting iron ore for railway contracts. Charlotte and Louisa must have taken the opportunity to visit Charlotte Elizabeth McNeilly, who lived nearby.

By this time, at the age of 35, our great-great-great-grandmother was doing it tough. On 5 October 1863, she gave birth to her tenth child, Edwin Thomas McNeilly, at Berrima. The birth certificate recorded that Charlotte Elizabeth had four older children living, but that five babies (three boys and two girls) had died. I cannot begin to imagine how heartbreaking this must have been. Flora Charlotte, the eldest, was now fifteen. Charles was ten, Ernest was four and Louisa Emily was two. Flora and her mother were very close.

Three months before her sister Emily's death in 1854, Charlotte Elizabeth and her husband Thomas bought 40 acres of land at Cuttaway Hill, about three miles north-east of Berrima, using money from her inheritance. Three years later they bought another 38 acres next door. The McNeillys farmed there successfully for several years, and Thomas opened a stall close to the Fitzroy Ironworks to sell their produce.

The business was thriving, until Thomas had a horse-riding accident while delivering produce. He was severely injured. Unable to work, he was declared insolvent and they lost the farm. In 1861, the family moved to Goulburn, where Thomas worked as a labourer, trying to feed his large family. Louisa Emily, named for Charlotte Elizabeth's beloved sisters, was born there.

In 1863, *full of hope*, the McNeillys returned to Berrima, where Thomas was employed as a carrier and construction labourer at the ironworks. Unfortunately, like many other workers, he was not paid regularly, and the family lived on credit.

Around this time, they were living in a bark-and-wood hut that Thomas had built on someone else's land, a far cry from the grandeur of Oldbury. I am sure that Charlotte Elizabeth, as her mother had at Budgong, made a welcoming although simple home—her *rough slab hut rendered quite an object of beauty, by having the common scarlet geranium trained against its walls; while a few saplings made into a rustic porch … clustered over with roses.*

Charlotte Elizabeth, like her mother before her, delighted in telling her children enthralling and romantic stories about her childhood at Oldbury and her family background in England. Perhaps in their time of desperate poverty, after a long day of relentless labour, she found comfort in telling her children about her aristocratic ancestors and the splendour of their former homes. These stories were lovingly told to her children and later grandchildren and great-grandchildren, just as we were told them by our mother and grandparents. These stories were later written down and shared.

Kate and I drive to Canberra to trawl the archives of the National Library of Australia. We are particularly keen to see the papers of Janet Cosh, Patricia Clarke and Marcie Muir. When we arrive, we discover a treasure trove of letters, newspaper articles, interview transcripts, depositions and photographs in dozens of boxes, neatly labelled and numbered. Most exciting for us is the chance to see Charlotte's original shipboard journal from 1826. It is so fragile and precious. Kate and I are in tears.

One of the highlights of our trip was an invitation to lunch with writer, journalist and historian Dr Patricia Clarke. Patricia is a true inspiration, still writing fascinating and meticulously researched books in her nineties. Patricia wrote *Pioneer Writer*, her biography of Louisa Atkinson, 30 years ago, yet recalls tiny details as though it were yesterday. She talks about Louisa with empathy.

'Pat, your memory is extraordinary,' I say.

Patricia smiles. 'When you spend years researching someone's life and writing their biography, you get to know them intimately.' Kate and I nod vehemently. We know exactly what she means.

We sit in Patricia's dining room, surrounded by books, artworks and antiques, chatting about Charlotte's life. The table is set with crystal, silver, fine bone china and platters of cold meat, salad and cheese.

Patricia is keen to know what we have discovered about Charlotte's early life in England—especially her training under John Glover and her career as a governess.

'I think Charlotte was a very independent woman, a fighter, and very brave in tackling the legal establishment,' says Patricia. 'She was highly ambitious for Louisa, particularly after Charlotte Elizabeth eloped and Emily died. But I do think she could be abrasive. People didn't always like her.'

Kate and I agree that Charlotte could be opinionated.

'I think the difficulties she faced after James' death would make anyone abrasive and difficult,' I say. 'You can see how frustrated and angry and *determined* she was in her court depositions trying to justify why she should be able to keep her children. I think a gentler woman would have lost them.'

'Isn't it funny how men who stand up for themselves are leaders, but women who stand up for themselves are abrasive?' observes Kate.

'Things haven't changed that much, have they?' I reply.

There are many interesting facts that we discover trawling through the National Library of Australia archives. Some of it confirms information we already knew. Other information sheds a new light on our understanding.

Both Charlotte Elizabeth and Louisa wrote accounts of their family history. Charlotte McNeilly's was written when she was 77 years old and was published in both the *Evening News* and the *Town and Country Journal* in August 1905, and *The Molong Argus* in January 1906, and later was included in a book, *History of the Founding of the Wool Industry of Australia*. Louisa's unfinished notes are held in the Mitchell Library. Both accounts are fascinating and have slight inaccuracies.

Louisa's granddaughter Janet Cosh wrote a detailed family history, based on her mother's stories as well as her own extensive historical research. Janet Cosh's observations helped inform the research of Patricia Clarke and Marcie Muir for their books.

Among my favourite discoveries were accounts written by Charlotte Elizabeth's descendants, which offer a view very different from the account written by Louisa's descendant, showing the challenges of family oral history.

Flora McNeilly, who clearly adored her grandmother, wrote a newspaper article about the Atkinson family. It claimed aristocratic Charlotte de Waring was the daughter of the Honourable Albert de Waring, younger son of the Earl of Somerset, Lord Saye and Sele of Broughton Castle. This romantic and wildly exaggerated version was told to my grandfather Beric as a boy. While I haven't found Flora's published article, there is a handwritten copy by her daughter Bertha Bruck in the National Library archives.

Of course, there are snippets of truth in the story. The Warings were once a wealthy family, and many centuries ago were known as de Waring. Charlotte did have an ancestor with a relationship to Lord Saye and Sele of Broughton Castle in Oxfordshire, but it was her great-great-great-grandmother Ann Mayern Waring, who had previously been married to John Twisleton, a baronet and heir of Baron Saye and Sele. The story is a perfect example of family oral history exaggerating and embellishing the facts. In April 1909, when Flora's youngest daughter,

Bertha Adelia, married William Bruck, *The Molong Argus* stated: *The bride is a niece of E.T. McNeilly, Esq., J.P. of Orange, and great niece of the late Earl of Somerset (the Hon. Albert de Waring), Belvidere Castle.*

In the National Library archives was a letter from Bertha to Janet Cosh, recording a visit to Oldbury and the Atkinson vault with her niece Dorothy (genealogist Jan Gow's mother) and her nephew, my grandfather Beric. My mother Gilly was thrilled when we discovered this mention of Papa. Bertha couldn't read the faint wording on the grave, but Papa could. This reminded me of our adventures in England, visiting Mereworth with Jan Gow, searching for the grave of James Atkinson's parents and our excitement when we found it, with Emily and Ella on their knees deciphering the ancient inscription.

❧

Charlotte and Louisa returned to Fernhurst at Kurrajong. In 1865, at the age of 69, Charlotte suffered a severe fall, breaking her arm in several places, dislocating her elbow and injuring her spine. Shortly afterwards, Louisa's tuberculosis returned, making it impossible for her to continue her active lifestyle.

Charlotte decided to sell Fernhurst and move back to Oldbury, to live with James. The return home was poignant, reviving both happy memories and recollections of stressful incidents during their life there. Charlotte remained a *confirmed invalid*, suffering from her injuries for the next two years. She was extremely deaf, and Louisa found her difficult in her old age. Caring for her mother, Louisa had little time for creative endeavours.

I imagine that in the many hours that they spent together, Charlotte told and retold stories about the old days. Tales about her childhood growing up in London and Kent, romantic memories of the Warings' aristocratic Norman forebears, reminiscences of England and stories about Oldbury in its heyday, when James was alive and the house rang with joyful laughter. I am sure she shared these tales with her granddaughter Flora, and the younger grandchildren Charlie, Ernest, Emily and baby Ted. I love to think of Charlotte, in her old age, surrounded by the adoration of her family.

On 24 April 1866, Charlotte's first-born grandchild, Flora (our great-great-grandmother), who was 17, married George Garlick, a teamster from Nattai, near the Fitzroy Mines. At the time, Flora was living with her parents in a timber hut close by. According to her daughter, Flora met George when she was staying at Oldbury and he was working on a nearby farm.

Charlotte Elizabeth and Thomas McNeilly were still struggling, as a result of the financial troubles of the Fitzroy Ironworks. Many of the workers and investors, including her brother James, lost money. Thomas was declared insolvent for the second time in 1866. He stated that his only asset was the bark hut he'd built on a friend's property. Thomas said: *I have a helpless family and nothing before me for the future but to support them by a day's labour.* You can feel the heartbreak in his words.

At the age of 38, Charlotte McNeilly gave birth to her eleventh and last child, Eva Henrietta, on 20 April 1867, at Nattai.

Six months later, on 10 October, Charlotte Waring Atkinson Barton died. She was 71 years old. The notice in *The Sydney Morning Herald* said: *at Oldbury, after a long and painful illness, Mrs. C. Barton, the dear and excellent mother of J.J.O. and Louisa Atkinson, in perfect peace, trusting in her Redeemer.*

Her children were distraught.

Charlotte was interred in the family vault at Sutton Forest churchyard with her first husband James, beloved Emily and baby Henry Warren.

I am so sad, writing about Charlotte's death, as though I am grieving the death of my own grandmother, rather than someone I have never met. I was in tears reading the death notices of Emily and babies Thomas and Henry, as though I'd lost my own sister or child. Over a family dinner, Kate and I discuss it.

'I know exactly what you mean,' says Kate. 'I get so sad too.'

Kate's husband Greg is surprised. 'How can you feel upset about someone who died so long ago?'

'I guess that is the power of stories,' I say. 'I feel like I know them all. And I feel so much empathy for them. Mothers losing children. Daughters losing mothers.'

Their difficulties help me put my own smaller problems into perspective. This year has made us face the mortality of our beloved parents. Both Mum and Dad have recovered from their near-death experiences six months ago. But they are frailer. Their lives have become an endless round of medical appointments, tests and treatments, which is frustrating for them and for us. Mum tells me that inside she still feels like she's 30 and she hates her body letting her down.

Dad and his rambunctious dog Toby are still living with us as he recovers after his operations, which has been a huge adjustment for us all, but we love having Dad around and the chance for him to spend time with his grandchildren.

Another joy has been getting to know our half-sister Emma and her mother Annie. We've had many gatherings of the extended clan, including a cattle mustering weekend at my brother's farm. Emma and Annie have been a wonderful help, entertaining Dad and checking on him when I've been away. Emma's daughters adore their new cousins, and my children have fun playing with her girls, digging out old toys. Emma tells me she's loved the chance to get to know her dad. So, our family is more complex than it was a year ago, but richer.

What made me particularly sad about Charlotte's death notice was that Charlotte Elizabeth was not mentioned. Janet Cosh, Louisa's granddaughter, believed that there was a rift within the family. Louisa may have been angry that she carried the burden of their mother's illness and crotchetiness. Charlotte Elizabeth may have felt envious that Louisa had the time to develop her creative talents in a way that she couldn't with six young children. Or perhaps the sisters had simply grown apart during the decade that Charlotte and Louisa had lived away in Burwood and Kurrajong.

I can't imagine sisters not being close. While I can disagree with my sister Kate from time to time, we adore each other. We live five minutes apart. Our children are similar ages and are great friends. We walk our dogs together as often as we can, share family dinners and beach holidays. We lecture each other on doing too much or getting exhausted. Best of all we support each other's writing, commiserate with disappointments and celebrate each other's successes. No one else truly understands the difficulties and highlights.

Louisa lived with her brother James at Oldbury for more than a year. On 11 March 1869, at the age of 35, she married 44-year-old James Snowden Calvert. He was a keen botanist who, as a 19-year-old, had been an explorer with Ludwig Leichhardt's expedition across the Top End of Australia, during which he had been severely injured in an Aboriginal attack.

They lived for 15 months at Cavan, James Calvert's sheep station, near Yass. The couple were blissfully happy. Louisa continued writing novels and articles, drawing and painting, dissecting birds, collecting plants and working on an illustrated book of Australian plants and animals, which was to have been published by the University of Strasbourg in Germany.

Two months after their marriage, they returned to Oldbury for a week, to help celebrate the marriage of Louisa's brother, 37-year-old James John Oldbury Atkinson, to Sarah Annie Horton, the 28-year-old daughter of the local minister at All Saints.

In 1870, Louisa and James Calvert moved back to Oldbury, and lived at Swanton, one of the stone farm cottages on the estate, while they looked for their own property to buy.

Here, Louisa gave birth to a daughter, Louise Snowden Annie Calvert, on 10 April 1872. While Louisa was pregnant she wrote some family notes for her unborn child, based on the many stories her mother had told her. She began with the de Warennes of Normandy and Charlotte Waring's family. These notes, kept in the Mitchell Library, are a priceless source of information.

Kate and I are devastated when her reminiscences finish halfway through a sentence. Are the other pages lost? Or did Louisa stop writing mid-sentence?

Two weeks after Louise's birth, on 24 April 1872, Louisa looked out of Swanton's window and saw her husband's horse gallop into the yard without a rider. Louisa, imagining the worst, had a heart attack and dropped dead. When James Calvert limped home a short while later, he found his wife's lifeless body beside her baby's cradle. James was distraught, and never recovered from his loss.

Louisa was buried with her parents and sister in the Atkinson family vault at All Saints Anglican Church in Sutton Forest. Her last novel, *Tressa's Resolve*, was published as a serial in *The Sydney Mail* after her death. Baby Louise was looked after at Oldbury by her uncle James and aunt Sarah, who already had two infant sons, Horton William and Austin Waring Atkinson, with another son, Tertius Trafford, born soon after.

James Calvert lived for a time at Winstead at Nattai, which was the property he and Louisa were building when she died. Calvert became deeply depressed after Louisa's death. Two years later, he fought with the Atkinsons and took his daughter to Botany, a suburb of Sydney, where she had a lonely childhood, brought up by housekeepers. When Louise Calvert was 12, her father died, and she returned to Oldbury for a few months to live with James and Sarah Atkinson.

James had established the Berrima Coal Mining and Railway Company, with a coal mine on the Medway Rivulet and a private railway to Moss Vale. He was running Oldbury as a dairy with his four young sons. Louise said her uncle was kind, but quiet and melancholy. He was not a good businessman like his father and had lost much of his inheritance through disastrous investments. Sarah Atkinson was an invalid, having suffered a stroke, and was unkind to Louise.

Eight months later, on 13 March 1885, James John Oldbury Atkinson died when he fell from his horse on Golden Vale Road, riding back from Sutton Forest. He was 52. Poor orphan Louise was sent to live at the rectory at Sutton Forest. She later said this was the happiest home she'd known.

Two years later the coal mining company had gone into liquidation, and Sarah Atkinson decided to sell Oldbury. She summoned 15-year-old Louise Calvert to collect some of her mother's drawings. Louise had to walk three miles each way and could only take what she could carry. She picked at random in a hurried visit, gathering sketchbooks, drawings and paintings by various members of the Atkinson family.

Everything else, including mountains of drawings, paintings, letters and papers, was burned in a massive bonfire. My heart aches for all those precious records destroyed. Illogically, I am so furious with Sarah for selling Oldbury and burning everything! Yet, I am so grateful that young Louise managed to carry away as much as she did. It is these salvaged artworks that make up the bulk of the Atkinson family collections in the Mitchell and National libraries.

These invaluable collections were donated by Janet Cosh, Louise Calvert's only child. Janet was also a talented artist, botanist, teacher and historian, and spent many years researching the Atkinson family, collecting letters, birth and death certificates, interviews, photographs and newspaper articles. She was of course particularly interested in the life and career of her grandmother, Louisa.

In contrast, Kate and I are particularly interested in the life and career of Louisa's eldest sister, Charlotte Elizabeth McNeilly, our great-great-great-grandmother. We know she was exceptionally clever, being dux of her school and winning several gold medals for academic and artistic excellence. We know she was strong-minded and had a tough life, marrying Thomas McNeilly against her mother's wishes, having 11 children and losing her inheritance through bad luck. Yet, despite all the difficulties, she fought for her children and the chance for a creative career.

After her mother died, Charlotte Elizabeth and her husband decided to pack up their tribe and move to Orange. Flora and George Garlick went too, with George working as a carrier between Orange and Sydney.

Here the McNeillys worked hard to build a new life. Charlotte Elizabeth began a private school for girls, which she ran for many years, on the corner of Byng and Sale streets. The Orange *Leader* newspaper later wrote: *many will have reason to remember with gratitude the good*

... *lady who taught them so thoroughly.* She continued her passion for music and art, which she'd learned from her mother.

Soon after Charlotte Elizabeth moved to Orange, she painted a beautiful landscape featuring the Anglican church and parsonage, which still hangs in Holy Trinity Church. Her painting of Cockatoo Island is in the Mitchell Library and a pastoral painting of the 'Canobolas Mountains' is privately owned. She was also commissioned to create paintings of the Lucknow Gold Mine near Orange, to encourage investment in the mine. One was sent to London and the other to Paris. Two of her paintings, one of Penrith Bridge and one of Oldbury House, were submitted for the art exhibition that was held in 1938 to mark 150 years since the landing of the First Fleet, but were lost.

She took after her mother in having a fiery temper. In one family story, Charlotte Elizabeth and Thomas McNeilly disagreed about religion. Charlotte Elizabeth was an involved member of Holy Trinity Church and had brought up her children as Anglicans. Like her mother and sisters, she was deeply religious: *a real solicitor for the poor people in Orange, helping them in every way ... She was a wonderful woman.*

Thomas McNeilly remained a staunch Catholic, however. Charlotte Elizabeth discovered that the local priest from St Joseph's had taken to visiting Thomas when she was out, to convert the children to Catholicism. She was furious. So, she pretended to leave the house, hid around the corner, and then, when the priest arrived, confronted him, whacking him with her umbrella! The McNeilly children remained firmly Church of England.

Thomas worked as a farmer and carrier, droving stock and carting timber. For a while, the McNeillys seemed to be doing well for themselves, buying property and becoming respected members of the local community.

Then tragedy struck again. In 1873, their eldest son, Charles, died at the age of 19. He was the same age as my beautiful Lachie, and Kate's son Tim. A year later, Thomas McNeilly left his family.

Charlotte Elizabeth claimed that Thomas was drinking heavily, *idling about and doing hardly any work*, taking all her income from the school, insulting the parents and students, and *commenced to treat her with great cruelty and severity*, threatening her life. He kicked her *so violently that her body was black and bruised … and [she] was ill for several days*. She wrote that she was terrified for her life, and recounted several instances of being choked, and of being beaten senseless and left covered in blood. Thomas also injured one of his sons in a rage, when he tried to protect his mother.

When Thomas absconded in April 1874, Charlotte Elizabeth *was left with her children in a most cruel and destitute state—no wood, no food, no clothes, no money and the poor children almost naked, creeping around the fences in the wet and cold to get some chips of wood to light a fire*. On one occasion she went for three days without food.

The four children at home were Ernest, aged 15, Emily, 13, Edwin (Ted), 11 and Henrietta, 7. Flora, at 25, was married and living in Orange with three young children, and pregnant with her fourth child, Sarah Mabel, who would be my great-grandmother.

Charlotte McNeilly, like her mother, was a fighter. She took in needlework and went to work as a nurse for two local doctors and *managed to keep her children alive*. Later she took in boarders.

I find Charlotte Elizabeth's detailed descriptions of Thomas McNeilly's violence and threats *to murder her* deeply distressing. The domestic violence is reminiscent of George Barton's heavy drinking and vicious fury. She claimed that Thomas had squandered her inheritance and taken all the money she earned to spend on his drinking. Married women still had no legal right to own property or manage their own money. Everything legally belonged to her husband, to use as he wished. Like her mother, Charlotte McNeilly took on the law to protect her interests.

Three years later, when Charlotte Elizabeth was 48, she tried to divorce Thomas McNeilly for desertion, adultery and cruelty. This was one of the earliest suits for divorce in New South Wales. In her deposition in 1876, she wrote that *from that time they never lived on happy terms together*, and she produced a witness, a boarder in Thomas' house, to support her claim of his adultery. Thomas represented himself and simply denied all charges. He still couldn't write, signing his deposition with an X.

Incredibly, the judge, Justice Hargrave, dismissed Charlotte Elizabeth's petition because it was her word against that of Thomas. Judge Hargrave had a reputation for being a misogynist and regularly decided against women.

After the failure of the divorce case, Charlotte Elizabeth and Thomas McNeilly were eventually reconciled and lived together. Not surprisingly, Charlotte Elizabeth became a strong advocate for sobriety, establishing a Temperance Lodge in Orange.

She wrote many letters to newspapers and journals about issues of the day and corresponded with Sir Henry Parkes about universal education. According to the Orange *Leader* newspaper, Charlotte McNeilly *wielded a facile, graceful pen and was a frequent contributor to the polemics of the time … She was remarkably well-informed on a variety of subjects … [with] many controversial combats with the late Mr. N [Nicholas] Head, when that gentleman was editor of 'The Liberal'.*

Tragically, in 1885 Charlotte Elizabeth's second daughter, Emily, who *was very beautiful, went on a picnic, … sat on the wet grass, became sick and died.* She was not yet 24. I'm beginning to think that I gave my daughter a cursed family name—they all died so young!

Thomas died shortly afterwards, aged 68 years, of stomach cancer, after two years of intense pain. He was buried in the Catholic cemetery. There was something very strange about Thomas McNeilly's death certificate. Firstly, there were discrepancies with dates such as his age at marriage and length of residency in Australia. Secondly, the death certificate listed Thomas as having another family with seven unnamed children—four sons and three daughters!

I'd heard rumours from distant cousins about Thomas having a second family. One family tree shows Thomas McNeilly married to Margaret Purvis in Belfast in 1826, but a quick fact-check shows our Thomas would have only been nine years old, which clearly is impossible. His death certificate in the National Library archives has a handwritten note from Janet Cosh saying a second family was *highly unlikely.* I did hours of research but could find no records.

I write to Jan Gow, our family genealogist, to ask if she can shed any light. Jan had heard that Charlotte Elizabeth added the information after her son Ted had registered Thomas' death, to keep it secret from her children. I wonder if Thomas had a de facto relationship with another convict before his marriage to Charlotte Elizabeth? Did he abandon the poor woman and all those children to elope with a young heiress?

These revelations do not shed a positive light on our great-great-great-grandfather. Yet Flora and other descendants remembered him fondly, describing his charm, goodness and generosity. When Thomas died, Charlotte Elizabeth moved in with her son Ted's family, where she lived for another 26 years.

All her life, Charlotte Elizabeth was very close to her children and grandchildren—teaching them, telling them stories and encouraging them to be the best they could be. The family stories were celebrated in the names that were passed on. Charlotte Elizabeth had one grandson called James Atkinson McNeilly and two granddaughters called Emily. Ted called his house Oldbury.

The McNeillys were remembered as a leading family of Orange. Charlotte Elizabeth and Thomas' son Ted became Mayor of Orange, serving for eight years (including a term during the First World War), and was an alderman for 32 years. Ted McNeilly spent his career improving the lot of the poor, especially women and children.

Nineteenth-century women didn't leave much of a trace behind them. It was unusual that when Charlotte Elizabeth McNeilly died on 17 March 1911, aged 82, after a fall on the verandah, the Orange *Leader* ran a long and glowing obituary, listing her many achievements and qualities. *Mrs. McNeilly was that type of woman, whose removal hence represents a distinct and great loss.*

Only three of Charlotte Elizabeth's children survived her, but she left 19 grandchildren, 14 great-grandchildren and 4 great-great-grandchildren.

When Ted died in June 1929, his obituary was detailed and emotional, but I particularly loved this tribute to his mother:

The roots of his spiritual life were watered by the loving teaching and devotion of a good mother, who watched her son's progress in the service of the people with delight. He used to say that he wanted to leave this world a little better than he found it, and she gave him unmeasured help and inspiration as he energetically sought to realise his ideal.

I loved the family value of striving to leave the world a better place. It is an ideal that we have tried to follow in our own lives and encourage in our children's lives, through helping friends in tough times, supporting charities, being actively involved in our community, teaching and working hard in meaningful careers.

Our great-great-grandmother Flora Charlotte McNeilly was also strong, clever, creative and a golden storyteller like her mother and grandmother before her. Flora had 11 children, although most of hers survived to reach adulthood. She and her husband George Garlick ran a successful blacksmith business in Molong for 40 years. Flora died aged 92, in 1940, at Bondi, where she was living with her daughter Gertie, whom my grandfather knew as 'the Mater'.

I don't know much about my great-grandmother Sarah Mabel, known as May, although she had a *bright, sweet and loveable disposition, the sunshine of her parents' home.* She was born in Orange on 16 October 1874, and trained as a nurse in Sydney before marrying an Englishman, Herbert Charles Wood. May died of pneumonia in 1915, leaving behind four young children. My grandfather Beric was only two years old.

Just as they had when Charlotte Waring's mother died, the family called on an aunt to raise the children. May's younger sister Gertie moved in, later marrying her sister's widower. Papa's father died when he was just 13, leaving him an orphan to be raised by his aunts and grandmother Flora.

My grandfather was a young, poor engineer when he met my grandmother Joy on a yacht with friends. She was an elegant and clever teacher from a wealthy Newcastle family, and was with her fiancé. Nonnie said she took one look at Papa, who was handsome, charming, dapper and a true gentleman, and realised she could never marry her fiancé. It was love at first sight. When she married Papa, Nonnie kept it a secret so she could continue to teach, a profession that she loved. Incredible to believe that in the 1930s she was not allowed to work as a married woman.

Like her forebears, my mother, Gillian Mackenzie-Wood, is a marvellous storyteller and exceptionally clever, having been dux of her school as well as head girl. Her dream was always to study medicine. Unfortunately, in those post-war years there was not enough money to pay the large university and college fees, and the money was put aside to educate her younger brother. Instead, Mum studied nursing at Royal Prince Alfred Hospital, and eventually became matron of Gordon Nursing Home. Her medical knowledge is phenomenal and better than most specialists'. She would have been an incredible doctor. Mum has always been strong, opinionated, caring, interested in people and a staunch feminist.

Later, Mum ran her own businesses, everything from our family vet hospital, a private nursing home, renovating derelict Balmain terraces and interior decorating, to breeding Rhodesian ridgeback dogs and Himalayan cats. As a single mother she worked incredibly hard so that we could have the best possible education. She always believed that it was even more important for girls to have a brilliant education, to help them overcome the intrinsic biases of a patriarchal world.

When I was a teenager, Mum enrolled at Macquarie University. She began studying Law, but became fascinated with psychology, behavioural science and medical anthropology, gaining straights As. She wrote articles for journals and magazines and charmed all her lecturers with her dedication.

Mum has always been a huge supporter of our careers, and has attended dozens of book launches, library events and festivals over many years to cheer for us. She's always keen to chat with us about our inspiration, progress and plot problems.

Of course, she adores her grandchildren and is actively involved in their lives and academic studies—encouraging them all to be the best they can be. She tells them to 'Aim for the moon, and if you fail, you'll fall among stars'. She tells us that writing is in our blood and I think she might be right.

We are all so proud that my daughter Emily is embarking upon her own writing career. Like Kate and me, she studied Media, together with Literature and Creative Writing, at Macquarie University. Soon after we returned from England, one of her folktales was published in *The Quarry*. She has edited a children's novel for a friend and written travel articles about our trip.

There have been many writers and storytellers in our family, going back hundreds of years. Telling stories helps us make sense of our world, our lives and our experiences. The stories that we choose to share, reflect who we are and shape who we become.

I know I come from a long line of strong, empowered, clever women who fight for what they believe in. My forebears had fascinating, busy and creative lives. Like Charlotte Waring Atkinson, they faced tough times with dignity and strength, overcoming almost impossible odds. They fought to give their children the best education they could and taught them to try to make the world a better place. They celebrated family with boundless love.

It reminds me that life is a rollercoaster of ups and downs, and not always easy. However, while there will be difficulties and disappointments along the way, there is always hope and joy and family.

Chapter 14

ANON.

Written by Kate

Tell us some little story then, if you please Mamma?
Charlotte Waring Atkinson

———⟫◆⟪———

When I was 12 years old, I won a writing competition at my school.

My prize was to attend the official opening of Children's Book Week, which was being held in The Rocks at the Argyle Tavern, one of Sydney's oldest buildings. Sir Roden Cutler, who was then Governor of New South Wales, was opening the event, and the awards were being presented by his wife, Lady Cutler.

It was 10 July 1978, and one of those bright glittering days you can get in Sydney during the winter. I was shivering with both cold and excitement. I desperately wanted to be a writer, but I had never met one. It seemed as if the books I most loved were written by people who lived far, far away and long, long ago.

There was one shining exception. That year I had read a novel by an Australian author which had utterly enraptured me. It was called *The Nargun and the Stars* and it was written by Patricia Wrightson.

Her books had that sense of magic and mystery and wonderment for which I longed. I was thrilled to the marrow of my bones because I would be meeting her that day. Patrica Wrightson's newest book, *The Ice is Coming*, had been shortlisted for the Children's Book Council of Australia Book of the Year, and I had the honour of sitting at her table. No wonder I was trembling!

My aunt had given me her new book for my twelfth birthday, a little over a month earlier. It began: *The old south land lies across the world like an open hand, hollowed a little at the palm.* I loved the poetry of these words. On the next page, it read: *the oldest race of all lives among them and is hidden. This is a race of creatures born of the land itself: of red rocks and secret waters, dust-devils and far places.*

This idea of Australia as a place of ancient hidden power fascinated me. *The Ice Is Coming* reminded me of Lloyd Alexander and Ursula Le Guin and Susan Cooper, those masters of high fantasy I revered. Yet it was set in Australia, my homeland. I had never thought of Australia as a place of myth and magic.

The event was held in a long room with walls of convict-hewn sandstone, the ceiling held up by battered wooden pillars. It had big glass windows that looked out towards the harbour. I was at Table 20, sitting next to Patricia Wrightson herself. I remember her as an elderly woman with short grey hair and a kind face. She greeted me warmly, but I was so shy and tongue-tied I could only stammer a few words in response to her remarks.

Our meals were brought. I stared down at my plate in dismay. It held a hunk of desiccated chicken schnitzel with flaccid chips and nuclear-red ketchup.

The waiter put down Patricia's plate. She had a plump chargrilled steak with creamy mushroom sauce, fresh green vegetables and tiny roast potatoes. She must have seen the look on my face for she said, 'My goodness, what a big meal they've brought me. I couldn't possibly eat all this. Would you mind helping me?'

I nodded my head shyly, and she divided her meal in half and shared it with me. As I tucked into my half with gusto, she asked me how I came to be at the lunch. Timidly I told her about the prize I had won, and how much I wanted to be a writer when I grew up, and she was so encouraging that my bashfulness fell away.

'I've already written three books,' I told her, and she was most interested.

'That's wonderful, when you are still so young,' she said. 'What are they called?'

Just then, our conversation was interrupted as Sir Roden Cutler got up to make his speech. So I wrote my name and the titles of the three books I had written on the back of my official yellow invitation. She read my scribbled words, and smiled, and whispered, 'Well done, you must keep on writing. Don't give up, if that's what you want to do.'

Then it was announced that Patricia Wrightson was the winner of the Book of the Year award, and she had to get up and go and receive her prize from Lady Cutler. As I watched her turn her smiling face towards the cameras to be photographed, I knew that I too wanted to be a published prize-winning author one day, holding up a beautiful book with my name on it.

After that everyone wanted to speak to her, and she was kept busy chatting and signing books. I ate my vanilla ice-cream, served in a paper cup with a tiny wooden spoon, then practised signing my name on the back of the invitation, in preparation for the day when I was famous.

Then it was time to go.

'Hunting the Giraffe', from Charlotte's 1848 sketchbook, is one of several illustrations of African animals and scenes that she painted, inspired by her visit to the Cape of Good Hope.

A hungry blackbird and a frightened frog, from Charlotte's 1848 sketchbook.

From top to bottom: Portraits of Emily, James John and Louisa Atkinson circa 1845, attributed to Charlotte Elizabeth Atkinson, held in the State Library of New South Wales.

Watercolour views of Oldbury, painted by Charlotte Waring Atkinson (top) and Louisa Atkinson (above).

Oldbury House, built in 1828 as a wedding present for Charlotte.

Oldbury House in Kent, where James Atkinson was born in 1794

Kate, aged six, and Belinda, aged eight, as bridesmaids at our beloved
Auntie Rozzie's wedding.

It was such a thrill to read Charlotte Waring's 1826 shipboard journal at the
National Library of Australia.

Emily, Ella, Kate and Belinda enjoying the summer sunshine on our research trip to England.

Our mother's heirloom bracelet, with its river pebble charm. According to family stories, before Charlotte left England she picked up this pebble from the riverbank to remind her of home and where she came from.

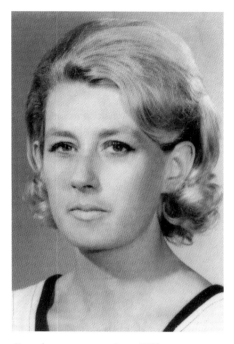

Our glamorous mother, Gillian Mackenzie-Wood.

Our father, Gerry Humphrey, aged 14, ready for his UK tour.

Our grandparents, Nonnie and Papa (Joy and Beric Mackenzie-Wood), told us so many wonderful stories about the Atkinson family. Papa was Charlotte's great-great grandson.

'Would you like me to sign your book for you?' Patricia Wrightson asked, seeing me getting up.

I did not know that you could ask authors to sign their books, and so I had not brought my copy. My eyes stung with tears of disappointment. She found a scrap of paper, and signed her name on it for me.

When I got home, I sticky-taped it inside my copy of her book. It is still one of my greatest treasures.

❦

I had indeed written three novels already.

The first was called 'Runaway'. I wrote it longhand in a school exercise book, and gave it a title page and a publication page and dedicated it: *To my family, for all the kindness they have ever given me.* Inscribed on the title page were the words *London. New York. Sydney.* So even as a little kiddie, I knew I wanted to be an internationally published author.

I wrote it in the summer holidays when I was only seven-and-a-half years old. It was 29 pages long.

My next novel was called 'Far, Far Away', and was written the following summer. By then my illustrations were a little better. The title page declares it was published by *Belinda Humphrey & Co*, and Binny drew the cover for me. Many of the pages are also copied out in her handwriting, as it was much neater than mine.

The title of my third novel was 'Daughters of the Mountain'. I wrote it the summer between Years 5 and 6, when I was ten. The first chapter is about a kitten who is abandoned on the side of the road. The story, however, soon changes into an adventure tale, with smugglers and a mysterious missing uncle. I can remember that my original plan had been to write about the lost kitten, but Binny had thought that was boring, and began to rewrite it. I ran, crying, to my grandmother Nonnie. She put me on her knee and cuddled me, saying that it was only because Binny loved me so much that she wanted to help me. I was comforted, and went back to where Binny was carefully drawing the two girls whose adventures she'd been writing into my book.

They were named Emily and Ellen. One was blonde like Binny, and one was brown-haired like me.

Isn't it strange and wonderful that we now have daughters named Emily and Ella? One of us—I can't remember who—even described Emily as being 'tall and slender with hazel eyes and naturally curling hair'.

I wrote the book as a Year 6 project, and my teacher wrote her comments at the end: *Excellent work—you write particularly well for your age. Keep writing & maybe I'll be buying your books one day. I hope so.*

I did keep on writing. Daniela, my best friend at school, and I worked on a fantasy trilogy together all through our first years at high school. We'd write chapters in turn, passing them to each other in class and reading under our desks. On the weekend, we'd dress up and act out our favourite scenes.

When I was 16, I wrote a novel called 'Harp Moon Rising', which I sent to the publishers Angus & Robertson. Although they did not accept it for publication (unsurprisingly), they did write me a very gentle and encouraging rejection letter. I was, nonetheless, heartbroken.

I began another novel soon after, called 'Towradgi', a word apparently derived from the Dharawal word Kow-radgi, meaning 'guardian of the sacred stones'. It was a novel set on the south coast of New South Wales, drawing upon Aboriginal myths but focusing on a girl whose father was dying, possibly as a result of foul play. It was rewritten again and again during my last two years of school. I was utterly determined that I was going to be a writer. In my final year at Abbotsleigh I won the school's Elizabeth Robbins Prize for Creative Writing, and was given a beautiful red-leather bound copy of Dylan Thomas' poetry as a prize. It too is one of my greatest treasures.

Binny and I are often asked if we became writers because we were inspired by Charlotte's example. After all, it is incredibly special to be descended from Australia's first children's writer.

Charlotte's story was just one of many wonderful family stories, however. Our Scottish great-great-grandmother, for example, was sent to Australia to make a new life for herself when she was only a girl. Or there is the romantic tale about how an ancestor of ours was washed up on the shore of Ireland after the Spanish Armada was blown off course by a storm in the sixteenth century, which is why we have so many brown-eyed, olive-skinned babies in our family. One of our great-uncles was a Rat of Tobruk. His brother, who was also a veteran of the Second World War, went out one day for a pint of milk and never came home.

We come from a family of marvellous storytellers, particularly on my mother's side of the family. Our lives were enriched by their stories, many of which had been handed down through the generations. My mother Gilly bought us books, and encouraged us to write and draw and act out our plays, always applauding us warmly. Every night—after what must have been a very long and tiring day as a working single mother—she listened as I stumbled and stammered my way through a passage of Shakespeare as she sought to help me overcome my stutter. Her encouragement and emboldening was, I think, the primary reason we all ended up so creative.

Binny and I were also very lucky in our teachers, like my lovely Year 6 teacher who wrote such a beautiful comment about my writing. Binny had always dreamed of being a vet like our dad, because she loved animals so much and wanted to help and heal those who had been hurt. When she was in her final years of school, our headmistress said to her, very gently, that her real talent was her extraordinary ability to write. 'It would be such a shame not to use your God-given gift,' she said. So Belinda stopped struggling with science, and went on to study literature and communications, building a very successful career as a public relations consultant, freelance journalist and travel writer. She was actually the first one of us to have a book published, when she was 22, a professional publication for the Department of Water Resources, entitled *Water and the Natural Resources of New South Wales*.

When we were children, no one else in the world knew about Charlotte Waring. Few people had heard of *A Mother's Offering to Her Children by a Lady Long Resident in New South Wales*. Those who had, thought it had been written by someone else. In 1978, when I was shyly confessing the secret ambitions of my heart to Patricia Wrightson, there were only a few battered copies of the book left in the world.

In 1979, when I was 13, Jacaranda Press published a tiny hardback edition of the book. Its introduction, written by Rosemary Wighton, begins: *Nearly a century and a half has gone by since the publication in Sydney in 1841 of* A Mother's Offering to Her Children, *the first Australian children's book.*

Rosemary Wighton—who was a lecturer and reviewer of Australian children's literature—went on to say: *For many years it was believed, because of a hand-written note in one of the surviving copies, that the author was Lady Gordon Bremer ... this attribution now seems increasingly dubious ... [for] she never visited Australia at all.*

At the moment, she wrote, *it is only possible to suggest that the compiler was someone with a closer knowledge of Australia than a visitor would be likely to have … both the identity of the author and the sources of all the material remain unclear.*

Charlotte had published her book anonymously, and that veil of secrecy had not been pierced.

It was usual for women of the time to publish anonymously or under a male pseudonym. Examples are Jane Austen, whose books (published between 1811 and 1816) were attributed simply to 'A Lady'; Mary Shelley, who published *Frankenstein* without any author attribution in 1818; Amantine Lucile Aurore Dupin, better known for her *nom de plume*, George Sand; the Brontë sisters, who wrote under the pseudonyms Currer, Ellis and Acton Bell; and Mary Ann Evans, who published novels such as *The Mill on the Floss* (1860) and *Middlemarch* (1871) under the name George Eliot.

Interestingly, *Frankenstein* is written as a series of letters to Mrs Saville by her brother, the explorer Robert Walton, who rescues a frozen and emaciated man named Dr Frankenstein on his way to the North Pole. Mrs Saville does not reply to the letters, or take part in the exciting events of the story. She is both absent and silent. The initials of her name 'Margaret Walton Saville'—M.W.S.—are the same as those of Mary Wollstonecraft Shelley. Many feminist critics believe this is a subtle comment by the author on the silencing of the female voice in her book, and in literature in general.

When disguising her children under false names in *A Mother's Offering*, Charlotte gave them appellations that began with the same initial as their own name. Her eldest daughter Charlotte Elizabeth is called Clara, Emily is Emma, James is Julius and Louisa is Lucy. Charlotte did not use the same alphabet code when disguising her own identity by giving herself a surname beginning with A. She takes Mary Shelley's alias Mrs Saville as her own.

In *A Room of One's Own*, Virginia Woolf writes:

Genius of a sort must have existed among women ... Now and again an Emily Brontë ... blazes out and proves its presence. But certainly it never got itself on to paper. When, however, one reads of a witch being ducked, of a woman possessed by devils, of a wise woman selling herbs ... then I think we are on the track of a lost novelist, a suppressed poet ... some mute and inglorious Jane Austen, some Emily Brontë who dashed her brains out on the moor ... crazed with the torture that her gift had put her to. Indeed, I would venture to guess that Anon, who wrote so many poems without signing them, was often a woman.

Why did Charlotte publish her book as 'a Lady Long Resident in New South Wales'? It was clearly not to conceal her gender, like the Brontë sisters who *did not like to declare ourselves women because ... we had a vague impression that authoresses are liable to be looked on with prejudice.*

The historian Amanda Foreman writes that Jane Austen may have chosen anonymity because:

Writing for money was akin to taking on paid work—something that few gentlemen, much less gentle ladies, would ever consider ... for a woman, there was the added burden of societal expectations regarding 'female respectability,' which characterized any sort of publishing or public display of talent as not just vulgar but unchaste behavior.

Charlotte needed to find some way to support her family until her son James could inherit Oldbury, and so making money from her writing was a necessity. She had also just spent months fighting a scandalous court case, which had threatened the loss of her children. Her second husband's depositions had been scurrilous. Charlotte could not risk losing sales because of any tarnish attached to her name, nor risk attracting any more scandal. She had to protect her identity.

As Rosemary Wighton writes in her introduction:

I have already mentioned the author's insistence on total truth in her work. 'I am not at liberty to invent,' says Mrs Saville on page 124 ... it does seem unlikely that the author of a work of this kind would practise such a deliberate deception as to describe herself as 'a lady long resident in New South Wales' if she were not ... Until research at present under way is completed, both the identity of the author and the sources of all the material is unclear.

Rosemary Wighton goes on to compare *A Mother's Offering* unfavourably with Charles Dickens' *A Christmas Carol* (published in 1843) and Frederick Marryat's *Children of the New Forest* (1847), but then says:

children living in Australia who read this book in the 1840s must have had some pleasant surprises. For example, the author describes in detail the beauties of Australian scenery, flora and fauna ... all must have seemed extraordinary references to children in the colony whose other books referred entirely to British natural history.

Just as I was astonished by Patricia Wrightson, the first author I had ever encountered to celebrate the Australian landscape and the extraordinarily rich myth and history of its Indigenous people.

As a 12-year-old, I had no idea that Charlotte Waring's book had been re-published, nor did anyone in my family. It was not the kind of book that appeared on the shelves of Shearer's Bookshop in Gordon, where we were allowed to choose books for our birthdays and Christmas.

We also did not know that a book lover named Marcie Muir was doggedly working to discover the identity of Australia's first published children's writer. She had, in the 1950s, begun compiling a list of all published books produced for children in this country, not knowing what a herculean task it was. Most people knew of such famous Australian children's books as *Seven Little Australians*, published in 1894 when the author Ethel Turner was only in her early twenties; *A Little Bush Maid*, the first of Mary Grant Bruce's famous 'Billabong' books, which was released in 1910; *Tales of Snugglepot and Cuddlepie* by May Gibbs, and Norman Lindsay's *The Magic Pudding*, both published in 1918; and *The Complete Adventures of Blinky Bill*, written by Dorothy Wall in 1939. Marcie Muir, however, was determined to find every single Australian children's book, no matter how obscure.

She spent many thousands of hours poring over old diaries and letters, rummaging through libraries and second-hand bookstores, and slowly scrolling through microfiche screens looking at ancient yellowing newspapers, for these were the days before the digitisation of information. Marcie Muir was not being paid for all her hard work. She simply believed that our literary heritage should not be forgotten.

A Bibliography of Australian Children's Books was published in 1970, 15 years after she began. Beautifully illustrated and more than a thousand pages in length, it gave detailed descriptions of more than 5,000 books published before 1967.

A second volume followed in 1976, bringing the bibliography up to the end of 1976, and including such wonderful Australian authors as Colin Thiele, Patricia Wrightson, Nan Chauncy and Ivan Southall. In her many years of investigation, Marcie Muir built up a library of over 7,600 rare and precious books, manuscripts and other ephemera, which was bought by the National Library of Australia in 2010.

During her long years of research and study, Marcie Muir wondered many times who had written *A Mother's Offering to Her Children*. She had ascertained that the author was not Lady Gordon Bremer, but had not been able to find any clues as to the identity of the mysterious 'Lady'.

In December 1978, Marcie Muir flew to Sydney to look through the newspaper collections at the Mitchell Library. She knew *A Mother's Offering* had been published in 1841, and so she doggedly read through the entirety of each newspaper of the year, hoping against all odds for a clue, a lead she could follow.

She found a small review of the book tucked away at the back of the very last edition of *The Sydney Gazette* for the year, published on 23 December 1841. It read:

[A Mother's Offering to Her Children] which embraces a variety of useful and entertaining matter, is got up under the form of dialogues, between a mother and her children. It is to be hoped that others will follow the noble example set by Mrs. Barton ... nothing sooner gives young persons a taste for refined literature than books ... which while ... interesting, are also instructive.

She had at last found a name—Mrs Barton—but there the trail of gingerbread crumbs ran out. Though she searched tirelessly, Marcie Muir could not discover who Mrs Barton was. *It seemed hopeless,* she wrote, *nothing could be proved—nothing was known. I went on with other work.*

So Marcie Muir turned to solving another mystery. She had for many years been trying to identify the author and illustrator of *The Australian Alphabet of Natural History* (1859), the earliest children's book produced in Australia with coloured illustrations.

She had found an advertisement for it in the back of Louisa Atkinson's novel, *Cowanda, the Veteran's Grant*, published the same year, and began to wonder if Louisa could have been its author. Researching her life and work, she discovered to her astonishment and delight that Louisa Atkinson's mother—Charlotte Waring—had remarried when Louisa was only two, to a man named George Barton.

Could the mother of the first Australia-born female novelist also be the author of Australia's first published children's book?

Marcie Muir at once noticed that the names of the four children in *A Mother's Offering* began with the same letter of the alphabet as the four Atkinson siblings. It seemed a compelling clue.

Then she discovered the paper written in 1929 by Margaret Swann in the *Journal of the Royal Australian Historical Society*, which said: *[Louisa Atkinson's] mother appears to have been a remarkable woman. Some of her writings had been published, she was clever at drawing and painting, and was also a keen observer of nature.*

Another persuasive piece of evidence.

Marcie Muir began to read all she could find on the Atkinson family. There was frustratingly little. Then, in 1979, the Kurrajong Heights Garden Club published a pamphlet entitled *Louisa Atkinson of the*

Kurrajong, the first attempt at a biography of Louisa. Marcie Muir wrote to the garden club, and her letter was passed to Janet Cosh, Louisa Atkinson's granddaughter and only living relative, who had helped the author with his research.

Janet Cosh was then 78 years old, and a keen amateur botanist herself. She had inherited some drawings and papers from her mother Louise Snowden Calvert, which she showed to Marcie Muir, proving conclusively the identity of the anonymous 'Lady'.

Marcie Muir subsequently wrote a slim, limited-edition book about her findings (which was published in October 1980), called *Charlotte Barton: Australia's First Children's Author.*

The Age reported:

> *One of Australia's deepest literary mysteries seems to have been solved. The author of … the first Australian children's book has been identified, almost 140 years after [its] publication in Sydney … She is Charlotte Barton, who sailed for Sydney in 1826 expecting to become the governess in Hannibal Macarthur's household but found a husband on shipboard instead.*

Nonetheless, Marcie Muir's *brilliant feat of literary detection* was generally so unnoticed that even *The Oxford Companion to Children's Literature*, released in 1984, still stated that Lady Gordon Bremer was the most likely author.

It was not until the historian Patricia Clarke was introduced to members of our extended family in October 1988, during the research for her biography of Louisa Atkinson, that any of us became aware of any mystery attached to the authorship of *A Mother's Offering*.

I can remember my grandfather saying, 'if only they'd asked us!'

I was then in my final year of university, eagerly studying a Bachelor of Arts in Literature. It was a time of political and creative awakenings. Only a couple of decades earlier, Indigenous Australians had finally been granted the right to vote, startling those among us naïve enough to have believed they had always had it. In my study of Australian Literature, taught by the academic Mark Macleod, we had hotly discussed whether or not a non-Indigenous writer like Patricia Wrightson had the right to draw upon Aboriginal stories in her work. Was such cultural appropriation another form of white imperialist exploitation?

My class read her speech 'When Cultures Meet', given at a children's literature conference at Sydney University in 1978, where she explained that *it wasn't easy to swap Puck for pot-koruck; it was only, I felt, essential.* She went on to say that she had not wanted to work with imported European folklore and legends; she had wanted to bring Australian landscapes and mythology *as a vitalising force* into Australian literature. She had done her best to do so respectfully. *There has been enough violation of secret and sacred beliefs. Any more of it by writers of fiction would be unpardonable.*

In what has been called *an electrifying moment,* the Indigenous poet Jack Davis then stood up and, *in ringing tones bade the author 'Be brave, Mrs Wrightson, be brave'.* She must go on, he said, making sure that Australians of European descent knew the stories of the land in which they lived.

I was glad Jack Davis had defended her, even as I was troubled by the implication that she had trespassed on sacred ground. Shyly I admitted my love for her work, and how it had opened my eyes to the beauty and vibrancy of the Dreaming.

'I'm sure she had the very best of intentions,' I said.

'It doesn't matter,' someone else argued. 'They were not her stories to tell.'

I went home and cut out every single reference to Aboriginal mythology in 'Towradgi', the novel on which I was then working. It hurt a lot. I renamed it 'Monk's Gate'. Feeling that my book had been drained of mythic power, I tried to find other stories to draw upon, stories that I felt held no risk of cultural exploitation. Shakespeare's *The Tempest*. Hans Christian Andersen's 'The Little Mermaid'. Pablo Picasso's painting 'Guernica'. I was unsure what I could use, what was allowed to me. I struggled to find my own voice.

Nineteen eighty-eight—the year my family learned of Marcie Muir's revelation—was the year that 40,000 people marched through the streets on the bicentennial of British colonisation to celebrate the survival of Australia's Indigenous people. Nineteen eighty-eight was also the year I was accepted into the selective creative writing course at Macquarie University, and had my first poem published. The following year I graduated, and began work as a journalist.

Patricia Clarke's biography, *Pioneer Writer: The Life of Louisa Atkinson, Novelist, Journalist, Naturalist*, came out in 1990, when I was 24. My grandfather bought copies for us all, and we read it with enormous interest. I remember feeling so proud that I was descended from such strong, resilient and talented women and wondering if my lifelong determination to be a writer was born in me.

A few months later, I was rummaging around in Gould's Book Arcade, a rambling second-hand bookstore on King Street in Newtown, and stumbled upon a box of remaindered copies of the second edition of *A Mother's Offering*. I was utterly thrilled. I bought the whole box, and then I went home and read my great-great-great-great-grandmother's book for the very first time.

Chapter 15

FIRE DANCE

Written by Kate

This little work

Charlotte Waring Atkinson

—⫸⬧⫷—

The book was small—the same length as my palm—with a sentimental sepia image of a girl reading on the cover. Its pages were age-spotted like an old woman's skin. Inside the opening pages was Rosemary Wighton's introduction and its speculation as to the identity of the author. I skipped this, wanting to get to the story.

Then a dedication—dated 29 October 1841—to:

Master Reginald Gipps, son of His Excellency Sir George Gipps, Governor of New South Wales and its Dependencies, and of Lady Gipps ... the author hopes the incidents it contains may afford him some little entertainment in the perusal: its principal merit is the truth of the subjects narrated ... and perhaps it may claim some trifling merit also from being the first work written in the Colony expressly for Children.

So Charlotte knew she was writing Australia's first children's book, and she was savvy enough to dedicate it to the son of the Governor.

The opening chapter is entitled 'Extraordinary Sounds'. A mother, named Mrs Saville, is *engaged at her needle*. Her children are *Amusing themselves by Drawing*.

Emma asks her mother a question about some *tremendous noises* which had been heard at a place named Coolondal Mountain, most probably a pseudonym for Mount Gingenbullen behind Oldbury. This inspires her mother to tell her how changes in temperature cause rock to expand and contract, with references to shells embedded in stone and other geological oddities. The loving warmth between the mother and her children, and their affectionate interplay, breaks up the factual information.

Framing lessons within a conversational question-and-answer format was then a pioneering method of teaching the young, replacing long lists of facts and dates that had to be memorised by rote. It was inspired by *Emile, or On Education* by Jean-Jacques Rousseau, an influential writer of the Enlightenment who sought to revolutionise the way children were taught. Rousseau believed that small children must be breastfed by their mothers and allowed to play outside. Older children should have their curiosity about the world stimulated, so that they learned to love learning.

You are afraid to see him spending his early years doing nothing, Rousseau wrote.

What! is it nothing to be happy, nothing to run and jump all day? He will never be so busy again all his life long. Plato, in his Republic ... teaches the children only through festivals, games, songs, and amusements. It seems as if he had accomplished his purpose when he had taught them to be happy.

Today we see the value of engaging children's interest and firing their imaginations, but this was rare at the time. For example, in Charlotte Brontë's novel *Jane Eyre*—published six years after *A Mother's Offering*—school was described as *a place where young ladies sat in the stocks, wore backboards, and were expected to be exceedingly genteel and precise.*

Maurice Saxby, the first National President of the Children's Book Council of Australia, and Superintendent of Aboriginal Affairs from 1953 to 1958, wrote in *Offered to Children: A History of Children's Literature 1841–1941* that Charlotte's book *was published for a reading elite: the sons and daughters of officers, government officials and the more affluent free settlers ... and this is reflected in the linguistic demands ... made on the reader ... the authorial voice is that of a governess or instructing adult ... much of the book is didactic ... a thinly disguised and not very interesting lesson in natural science, geology and anthropology.*

Rosemary Wighton says *it was a conservative book even then,* and compares it unfavourably with books by Charles Dickens and Frederick Marryat.

I feel both are being unfair. *A Christmas Carol* and *The Children of the New Forest* were written primarily to amuse and divert. Charlotte Waring was a teacher. Her book had a pedagogical purpose; its aim was to educate as well as to entertain. *A Mother's Offering* should rightly be compared to such nineteenth-century textbooks as *An Abridgment of Lectures on Rhetoric* (1802) or *Dr. Scudder's Tales for Little Readers, about the Heathen* (1849).

Trust me when I say that *A Mother's Offering* is infinitely more appealing.

It occurs to me one night—as I lie sleepless, my brain on fire with thoughts and feelings about this book I am writing with my sister—that we are actually creating exactly the same kind of book as our ancestor.

We are taking historical fact and framing it within our own personal lives, creating what might be called a hybrid memoir. *A Mother's Offering* is really a cultural history of colonial times filtered through the everyday conversations of a mother with her young children.

I am not the only one to realise that Charlotte's book was not a novel. Dinny Culican-Ward, a lecturer and collector of children's literature, described it as a mix of *didacticism and delight,* while the literary critics Brenda Niall and Frances O'Neill defended it, saying that *A Mother's Offering* is *not a failed novel but a collection of facts and anecdotes within a fictional framework.*

I think it is necessary to understand exactly what Charlotte's motivations were in writing *A Mother's Offering*. She was a single mother, struggling to support and educate her children by herself. She needed her book to be a financial success so she could afford to pay the bills. Even today, earning an income from your writing is seen as 'selling out', as if creative artists are ethereal beings of spirit who do not need to eat or drink or pay for new shoes when the old ones fall apart. We are meant to starve in a garret and die drunk and delirious in a gutter.

Charlotte did not have the luxury of such a lifestyle choice. She needed to earn a living, a difficult task for a lady of genteel birth in the mid-nineteenth century. The Brontë sisters and Jane Austen struggled with the same problem—the latter was to write in 1814: *But tho' I like praise as well as anybody, I like what Edward calls 'Pewter,' too.*

Nowadays, women can be authors or astronauts or archaeologists if they wish. This was not the case in Charlotte's time. Women were not permitted to go to university, or vote—or to reject their husband's sexual advances, no matter how weary they were. It was considered shameful for a so-called 'gently born' woman to work. So Charlotte had to think very carefully about what she could do to bring in some income. She decided to write the kind of book that would most appeal to the wealthy settlers and administrators of this fledgling colony of the British Empire: one that explained its flora, fauna, geology and geography while highlighting the courage and determination of its pioneers and explorers.

In order not to offend the Governor and his ilk, Charlotte needed to be sure that her tone was appropriately meek and pious 'for a lady', even while teaching subjects that would normally have been considered unfit for a woman to discuss, such as natural science. So the framing device of a demure little mother sewing while she instructs the children sitting at her knee has a twofold purpose: as well as breaking up the lessons, Charlotte makes sure she positions Mrs Saville well within the usual expectations of a woman's role—she does not 'unsex' herself, to reference Lady Macbeth's famous shriek to be freed from feminine restraints.

Feminist scholars have used the term *double-voiced* to show how Jane Austen wrote conventional tales about courtship romances that nonetheless contrived to be, as historian Lucy Worsley has written, *secretly, subtly, subversive about rank and society and gender.* Charlotte Waring is also double-voiced. When asked by her son Julius to explain more about geology, Mrs Saville replies: *What little I know about the matter I shall be happy to relate to you, my love. A Gentleman was telling me [about it] sometime ago ... I will endeavour to repeat it, in his own words.*

She then goes on to teach her children, simply and clearly, about such truly fascinating objects as fossils, petrified wood, and gigantic bones that *had belonged to Animals much larger than any ever seen in this Country. Possibly they were Antideluvian Remains. That is, existed before the Deluge.* (She was, of course, talking about dinosaurs, which were not named or studied until 1842, after her book was published.)

Statements like the above have led critics such as Maurice Saxby to call her prose *sedate [and] genteel*. Although it is indeed polite, *A Mother's Offering* is not at all genteel. After all, it has a woman teaching her three daughters about palaeontology and mineralogy and, later in the book, conchology and cetology:

> *This is a trochus: the fish which inhabits this shell, is said to be most voracious ... The enormous though peaceful whale, remains not unmolested by this scourge of the ocean: which fastens firmly to its huge sides; and sucks its flesh, until it is satiated. All the efforts of the defenceless whale, to rid itself of its tormentor, prove unavailing. In vain does it lash the waves; and dive about in agony; spouting rivers of water from its nostrils.*

It had been 50 years since Mary Wollstonecraft called for women to be given the same educational opportunities as men, but the idea of instructing girls in such subjects was still considered radical. Queen's College in London—the first to offer academic qualifications for women in Britain—opened in 1848, seven years after *A Mother's Offering* was published. So Charlotte spoke the language of patriarchy—the only language she knew—but she practised the philosophy of feminism, a term that did not come into use for another 50 years.

The following chapters focus on storms at sea and shipwrecks and cannibals—cunningly designed to excite the interest and imagination of children of the time—then give charming accounts of swallows and beetles that show us a loving, lighthearted side of Mrs Saville. For example, she describes rescuing a *poor little white slug* from a beetle: *I snatched it away from the beetle and ran far away with it; laughing, and saying, now you will not be able to find it, you cruel ungrateful creature ... you know my dear children I am unwilling to destroy life.*

Lucy replies by reciting a verse her mother has taught her:

Take not the life you cannot give,
For all things have a right to live.

Saxby writes: *while* A Mother's Offering *stops short of preaching conservation it does, through the course of Mrs Saville's conversations with the children, seek to inculcate a knowledge and respect of the environment.*

Some of the writing is beautiful: *Swan Lake appears to me to have been the Crater of a volcano many years age. Its agitated appearance, the desolation and barrenness that reigns around, fills the mind with an indescribable sensation of awe.*

Elsewhere, Mrs Saville says: *Nothing can be more ingenious than the nest of a bird: so carefully and beautifully woven.*

In these passages Charlotte's own voice shines through, full of warmth and charm and lyricism.

She declares, in her preface, that some accounts were *drawn from printed sources*; it is these sections that are dry and didactic and, it must be said, imbued with all the imperialistic bigotry of the time: *[John] Ireland told the Captain that the treachery and cruelty of the natives was not confined to white people, for they used each other no better when offended.*

As I read my great-great-great-great-grandmother's book for the first time, I was taken aback and distressed by the many references to *dreadful savages* and *wretched blacks*, terms that have rightly been banished from our vocabulary. I have to remind myself that she was the product of a deeply racialised society, writing more than 100 years before the civil rights movement began in Australia.

In the second chapter, called 'Wreck of the Charles Eaton', Mrs Saville tells the infamous story of a British merchant ship that was wrecked on the Barrier Reef in August 1834. It is one of Australia's most shocking maritime disasters. Five crew members escaped with the lifeboat, and eventually reached Timor. The rest of the crew and passengers built rafts from the wreckage. They tried to row for shore but were murdered by Torres Strait Islander people. Only two survived, with the cabin boy John Ireland later writing an account of his adventures:

About as near as I can guess, an hour after I had been asleep, I was awoke by a terrible shouting and noise. I instantly arose, and on looking round, I saw the natives killing my companions by dashing out their brains with clubs ...

Not very far off, the other savages were dancing around a large fire, before which they had placed in a row, the heads of our unfortunate companions, whose bodies, after being stripped of their clothes, were left on the beach ... From these heads, I saw the savages, every now and then, cut the pieces of flesh from the cheeks, and pluck out the eyes, and eat them, shouting most hideously. This, I afterwards learned, it was the custom of these islanders to do with their prisoners; they think that it will give them courage, and excite them to revenge themselves upon their enemies.

Ritual anthropophagy, in other words.

John Ireland was eventually rescued, along with the skulls of those who died, and he wrote a book entitled *The Shipwrecked Orphans: A True Narrative of the Shipwreck and Sufferings of John Ireland and William Doyley, Who Were Wrecked in the Ship Charles Eaton, on an Island in the South Seas* (1838).

This grisly encounter is reported in *A Mother's Offering*:

Mrs. S.—They remained ... with the cruel natives about three months, when these bad people added to their crimes by murdering the defenceless boys. Master D'Oyley was a very handsome child, and they cut off his head to adorn the front of a canoe.

Emma.—This is monstrous! How could such thoughts enter their heads?

Clara.—Were they cannibals, Mamma?

Mrs. S.—Yes, my dear. They ate the eyes and cheeks of the shipwrecked people; this they do with the idea that it increases their desire for the blood of white people.

Clara.—What dreadful sanguinary creatures. It makes one shudder even to hear of it.

Maurice Saxby writes of this passage: *One of the most bloodthirsty scenes ... is a description of a massacre that causes Clara Saville to utter her insensitive and infamous epithet: 'What dreadful sanguinary creatures!'*

Much as I love Maurice Saxby, who has been affectionately called the Godfather of Australian Children's Literature, I have to take issue with this. Calling someone *a creature* was common in nineteenth-century literature. Elizabeth Bennet calls herself a *rational creature*; Catherine Earnshaw is described as *a haughty, headstrong creature* by Emily Brontë; and George Eliot calls her heroine of *The Mill on the Floss*, Maggie Tulliver, *a creature full of eager, passionate longings for all that was beautiful and glad.*

Whether or not John Ireland's account of what happened to the castaways is true, it was universally believed at the time, ritual sacrifice and anthropophagy being a much-repeated trope of colonial contact and conflict. Clara Saville was only 11 years old. I think it most likely she would exclaim in horror at the idea of people being murdered and eaten, though I imagine nowadays she would use different words. Admittedly I am biased, Clara Saville being the avatar of my great-great-great-grandmother Charlotte Elizabeth (who I really hope never used such derogatory terms in real life!)

Chapter 9 of *A Mother's Offering* details the famous case of Eliza Fraser, who was shipwrecked along with ten other survivors off the coast of Queensland in 1836. Mrs Fraser later claimed that she had been captured by the Badtjala people, who killed her husband and abused her cruelly. Sensationalist reports of her ordeal were reported in the London papers, and later led to the dispossession and massacre of the Badtjala.

The event has haunted the Australian imagination, famously inspiring a series of paintings by Sidney Nolan, Patrick White's novel *A Fringe of Leaves*, and screenplays by David Williamson and Tim Burstall. This chapter in *A Mother's Offering* was the first creative attempt to engage with the story. Mrs Saville says: *Mrs. Fraser was very ill; exhausted by sorrow, fatigue and famine … She passed that dreadful night in the utmost alarm, trembling at every sound … An awful solitude reigned around; and her state of anxious suspense was dreadful.*

Larissa Behrendt, an Indigenous lawyer, writer and filmmaker, has examined the incident in her book *Finding Eliza: Power and Colonial Storytelling*. She concludes the story was exaggerated and sensationalised for international audiences, both to shock and titillate, and also to justify the government's dispossession of traditional land owners.

Charlotte draws upon these sensationalised reports in her account. The Badtjala people are described as *inhuman savages*, who allowed the white captives *no other food, than the entrails of snakes, fish bones, and such like disgusting things … treating them with great barbarity.*

She also adds, with a certain irony, that one should not call Eliza Fraser 'poor': *as soon as she arrived in England ... the English people, who are very charitable, immediately subscribed one thousand pounds; so I do not think she would be poor.*

The final chapter is entitled 'Anecdotes of the Aborigines of New South Wales', and it is the most horrifying of all.

Telling her children about the death of 'Little Sally the black child', Mrs Saville says: *These poor uncivilized people, most frequently meet with some deplorable end through giving way to unrestrained passions.*

Little Sally is adopted by *Jane ... a young married woman, who had lost her own child sometime before [and] took a fancy to little Sally ... her mother agreed to leave the child; as soon as it was weaned.* Taken from her mother at the age of two, Sally was *naturally much distressed, when she found herself deserted by her mother.* She was alarmed at being put into a bed, and at last Jane put a blanket on the floor for her *and poor little sorrowing Sally covered it about her.*

Several times during the night, Jane and her husband heard the poor little girl moaning; as if she were lying lamenting her deserted state.

In the morning, *little Sally went and stood outside; looking in all directions; and uttering the most piercing coo-ee-es imaginable ... The forest echoed and rang with them; and Jane who is a kind-hearted young woman, felt her heart thrill with pity and fear.*

Lucy is distressed. *Oh! Mamma that is just what I should do, if I lost you: cry as loud as ever I could; and be so very, very sorry! What did they do for the poor little girl?*

Mrs Saville recounts how the white husband and wife tried to console her, and how gradually Sally became used to her new home. Then *the tribe came again; and with them her mother.* Sally was overjoyed and rushed into her mother's arms, but her mother *sent her child from her. Poor little Sally screamed and was refractory; when her mother whipt her severely, and left her.*

Emma cries: *Ah! Mamma, I am very sorry for the poor little thing. I wish you had taken it from such a bad mother; and then we would have done all we could to have made it forget, it ever had such a naughty, cruel mother. Why did she go near, to teaze her poor little girl?*

Mrs Saville agrees that Sally's mother Nanny *was very blamable to go near the place; to unsettle her child; but she was not in many respects a bad mother ... perhaps [she] considered that [Sally] was better situated with Jane, than she would be wandering about the forests, in search of precarious foods.*

However, Nanny is then murdered by *a black man named Woombi ... The blacks dug a cave near the spot; and buried her in a sitting posture: putting her tomahawk, pannikin, net, bangalee, and indeed, all her little possessions, with her in the grave.*

When asked why she was murdered, Mrs Saville explains: *The Blacks have a great objection to their women living among white people. Nanny was particularly fond of this; and it made the blacks angry.*

It is such a heartbreakingly sad story. The poor little girl given up by her mother, most probably under strong coercion, and weeping alone all night and cooeeing for her all day; and then the poor mother, trying to make her daughter understand that she must stay. It is the Stolen Generation in action.

It is clear that Mrs Saville and the other adults believe that taking little Sally from her mother is in the best interests of the child. Clara is not so sure: *Mamma, it seems unnatural for a mother to part with her child ... I think if I were ever so poor, I would not part with my children.*

Mrs Saville and her children also discuss the following supposed customs: *In a savage state they bury the living infant with its deceased mother: sometimes when several months old ... You know Jenny has left three infants to perish in the bush; because, she said, it was too much trouble to rear them ... [and] Billy the black man killed one of his little babies ... Yes, he took it by his feet and dashed its brains out against a tree.*

These are terrible stories. But the worst of it is the tone in which they are discussed between a mother and her four young children, then aged between seven and thirteen, as if such occurrences and attitudes were commonplace.

It is very odd, Emma says, *that animals should know the difference between black and white people.*

I do not suppose that it is their color altogether. It may be the unpleasant smell which they have; from want of cleanliness, her loving mother replies.

I find this chapter very hard to read. That an ancestor of mine could be so callous, so racially prejudiced.

Rosemary Wighton, in her introduction to the second edition, writes: *This chapter, horrifying as its racial attitudes will appear to a modern reader, has the ring of real observation.*

One can only try to imagine the rage and grief of a people dispossessed of their long-inhabited country and ancient, vibrant culture. One can only try to understand how an intelligent, loving woman like Charlotte could have been so blind.

It helps to put her within the context of her times.

In 1788, one of the First Fleeters wrote that Indigenous Australians were *to all appearances the Lowest in Rank Among the Human Race*, and another that they were *more like monk[e]ys than warriors.*

William Stones wrote in 1858 (17 years after the publication of *A Mother's Offering*): *low down in the scale of humanity, the native Australians hardly rise to the intelligence of many forest brutes.*

Louisa Anne Meredith, an émigré to Australia, wrote in 1880 (39 years after the publication of *A Mother's Offering*): *[Australian Aborigines] were certainly the very lowest type of humanity; the ugliest, least intelligent and least teachable of savages.*

Sigmund Freud, the Austrian-born father of psychoanalysis, wrote in *Totem and Taboo: Resemblances Between the Mental Lives of Savages and Neurotics*, published in 1913 (72 years after the publication of *A Mother's Offering*): *[those] tribes which have been described ... as the most backward and miserable of savages, the Aborigines of Australia.*

The English-Australian biologist and anthropologist Sir Baldwin Spencer wrote in 1927 (86 years after the publication of *A Mother's Offering*): *Australia is the present home and refuge of creatures, often crude and quaint, that have elsewhere passed away and given place to higher forms. This applies equally to the aboriginal as to the platypus and kangaroo.*

It's shameful.

I know that the Atkinsons were greatly respected by the local Indigenous people, and Louisa Atkinson was acutely aware of the harm done by colonisation.

The men were severe to their wives, striking and even killing them when under the influence of anger; but I believe these cases were far less frequent when they had not lost virtues and acquired vices from the so-called Christian people who invaded them ... A great sin lies on us as a people, for much has been done to injure, and little to benefit the poor original possessors of our farms and runs.

She is right. A great sin does lie on us as a people.

Stan Grant has written:

Being good and great does not absolve you from a terrible sin and a pain inflicted on a people who did nothing to deserve it. Remember that: the first people of this land who have suffered for your greatness did nothing to deserve it. A truly great country— if we truly believe that—should be held to great account.

We must recognise the first injustice, the original act of dispossession. When my ancestor James Atkinson came to Australia in 1820, it was because he wanted land. He occupied a stretch of terrain that stood in the lee of Mount Gingenbullen, protected from the cold winds that blew from the southern alps, near a freshwater creek so that he would have water. In 1822, Governor Macquarie granted him 1,500 acres of this rich, rolling landscape. James felled trees and cleared pastures and built a house.

It was not, and never had been, empty land. It had been lived in for 60,000 years, by *a people who made the first seafaring journey in the history of mankind. A people of law, a people of lore, a people of music and art and dance and politics,* as Stan Grant said in his iconic talk on the IQ2 stage in 2015.

I take comfort in knowing that my ancestors were more enlightened than many other colonists of the time, and that James wrote to the Colonial Secretary to express his concerns about the sharp decrease in the number of local Indigenous people living nearby. I know that his concern and goodwill was much appreciated, and that the Aboriginal Elder Errombee saved his life when they were lost together in the bush. I'm glad that Louisa was clear-sighted enough to see that the 'settling' of Australia was an invasion. I'm desperately sorry that my ancestors were complicit in white acts of dispossession and destruction, and so hopeful

I can be part of a process of reconciliation and resolution. I love this beautiful and ancient country, and feel so proud of being Australian, even if only for six generations and not a thousand.

It is hard to know what amends to make. To acknowledge the truth of the harm that has been done is one small step. To apologise and ask for forgiveness is another. To try and be an agent of healing and understanding is yet another, tiny yet immeasurable.

In 2019, I was a guest at the Bendigo Writers Festival. I went to listen to a panel called 'Inspirational Landscapes', in which Peter Doherty, Kim Mahood and Charles Massy discussed their deep connection to the Australian landscape and how it inspires them in their work. The panel was chaired by Gemma Rayner, who began with one of the most beautiful acknowledgements of country I've ever heard. It paid respects to the Dja Dja Wurrung and Taungurung people, on whose traditional lands the festival was being held, and the words were provided by the Dja Dja Wurrung Clans Aboriginal Corporation as part of their Recognition and Settlement Agreement.

I would like to paraphrase it here, addressed to the Wodi Wodi people of the Dharawal Nation, traditional owners of the land on which my ancestors lived and where the dust of their bodies now lies.

I would like to demonstrate my respect by acknowledging the traditional owners of the Wodi Wodi people of the Dharawal Nation, and pay respect to the Elders past, present and emerging, for they hold the memories, the traditions, the culture and the hopes of all Dharawal peoples. I express my gratitude for the sharing of this land, my sorrow for the personal, spiritual and cultural costs of that sharing, and my hope that we may walk forward together in harmony and in the spirit of healing.

Every time I read these words, my throat thickens and my eyes sting with tears.

After the Bendigo Writers Festival, I spend a week on the road, travelling from library to library, sharing stories about my latest published novel. As I drive the long empty highways of the Australian outback, the fields on either side brown and bare in the pale winter sun, I listen to music and think about what I want to write about my great-great-great-great-grandmother's book. I do not know how to say what I am feeling. I am so afraid of offending, of hurting, of causing more harm.

In Echuca, a man in the audience rises to ask me a question. He is tall and wiry and brown, with dark eyes and beard. He wears feathers in his hair.

'When you write, do you feel as if you are the vessel of that story?' he asks. 'And if you do not serve the story, it will leave you?'

I am surprised. 'Yes,' I reply. 'I feel like I'm a conduit and that the story runs through me like a charge of electricity. I must submit myself to it, and not allow my own fears or ambitions to hold me back from telling my story.'

My answer pleases him. He nods in acknowledgement. 'Are your stories like a fire dance?' he asks.

'Yes,' I answer, 'and I dance them to try to change the world.'

Again I have pleased him. He nods and smiles at me, and we talk about the mysterious power of stories to open up eyes and hearts as if we have known each other a very long time, as if we are building a private chrysalis of words. The audience listens quietly, entranced.

Afterwards, as I sit signing books and chatting, he returns with a branch of sweet-smelling eucalyptus leaves and a feather. The branch was to welcome me to his country, he tells me, and to make sure I travelled safely through it. The feather represented my sea eagle spirit, a force of strength and courage and spiritual healing in me.

I am inexpressibly moved.

Chapter 16

WISHING FOR WINGS

Written by Kate

so ready and free in using your beautiful wings
'Peter Prattle'

—⧳◆⧴—

Every year, when I go to the UK to run my writers' retreat in the Cotswolds, I make some kind of literary pilgrimage.

One place I have always wanted to visit is Jane Austen's house in Chawton, where she lived while she wrote her novels. Since Jane was only 21 years older than Charlotte and came from a similar background, it seemed like a perfect opportunity to make an obeisance at the holy shrine of one of my literary idols, as well as gain some insight into how women writers of the early nineteenth century lived and wrote.

So, after our week in Kent, we head west into Hampshire.

Chawton is the most gorgeous village. We wander down the street, taking photos of every thatched roof and rain-heavy rose. I am breathless with excitement, so glad to be sharing this special moment with Binny, Emily and Ella—normally I have to make my journeys of literary homage alone.

When I see Jane Austen's tiny writing desk in the dining parlour, tears rush into my eyes. She sat here, a slender young woman with spectacles perched on the end of her nose, writing with a quill pen, using ink she probably made herself from oak galls. The dining room door was left unoiled so that it creaked when it opened, giving her time to hide her manuscript under a napkin. It is incredibly humbling, to think how she wrote such masterpieces as *Pride and Prejudice*, *Emma* and *Persuasion*, scratching them out with a pen cut from a feather, writing any major additions or alterations on spare scraps of paper and skewering them in place with pins.

Emily and Ella practise writing with a quill in the museum's kitchen while Belinda and I examine every single artefact on display. I weep again when I read the letter that her sister Cassandra wrote upon Jane's death:

> *I* have *lost a treasure, such a sister, such a friend as never can have been surpassed. She was the sun of my life, the gilder of every pleasure, the soother of every sorrow; I had not a thought concealed from her, and it is as if I had lost a part of myself.*

Binny finds me rubbing away tears, and gives me a hug. We are very much aware of how lucky we are to have each other.

I'm interested in knowing how Jane Austen spent her day, and so I go to the museum bookshop and browse through the dozens of books written about her. I pick up Lucy Worsley's *Jane Austen at Home* and am soon absorbed.

I discover that Jane was responsible for preparing the morning meal: *breakfast … was* her *part of the household work—The tea and sugar stores were under* her *charge*—and *the wine ... Cassandra did the rest.*

Jane also practised her music, and then there was what Lucy Worsley calls *the never-ending duty of needlework, that busy-work symbolising gentility and obligation.* In the afternoon, Jane and Cassandra walked, sometimes to Alton for shopping, sometimes to visit a neighbour or their brother at Chawton House. *I went up to the Gt. House between three and four, and dawdled away an hour very comfortably,* Jane wrote in 1814.

Then she ate supper with her mother, her sister, and their friend and companion Martha Lloyd, unfashionably early so that the cook could work without needing to light any candles. Then the ladies would sit and sew or read—or in Jane's case, write—until bedtime.

Most of the hard work, of course, was done by servants. Lucy Worsley estimates the Austens had as many as nine different members of staff, though most did not live with the family or work full-time. Even when the family lived in reduced circumstances in Bath in 1801, they had help in the house. Jane wrote to her sister, Cassandra: *My mother looks forward with as much certainty as you can do to our keeping two maids ... We plan having a steady cook and a young, giddy housemaid, with a sedate, middle-aged man, who is to undertake the double office of husband to the former and sweetheart to the latter.*

In contrast, while Charlotte was writing her book, she had to do all the cooking, cleaning and caring for her children. From the moment she woke in the morning to the moment she fell into bed at night, she would have been hard at work. Ashes and cinders from the cold wood stove had to be swept away, kindling chopped, the fire laid. Water had to be fetched, and the chamber pots emptied and cleaned. Soap was made by filtering the raw urine through the ashes to make lye. The floor had to be swept, the rugs beaten, the kerosene lamps cleaned and their wicks trimmed, the windows washed, the beds made, the stove lead-blackened.

Charlotte would have had to do the shopping before she could prepare her children a meal. If she bought a chicken, it would need to be killed, plucked and gutted before it could then be chopped up and cooked. Fish needed to be scaled. Loaves of sugar had to be pounded, coffee ground, flour sifted, nuts shelled and raisins seeded.

It was a very different life from that to which she had once been used.

Jane Austen lived at Chawton for the last eight years of her life, and during that time she wrote four novels. All except *Pride and Prejudice* were published by Thomas Egerton 'on commission', which means at the author's own financial risk. Publishers paid the costs of publication and then repaid themselves through a ten per cent commission for each book sold. Once they had earned back their investment, the rest was paid to the author. If a novel did not recover its costs through sales, the author was responsible for them.

Jane Austen sold the copyright to *Pride and Prejudice*, and so received a one-time payment of £110 from the publisher for the manuscript.

This was probably how Charlotte sold *A Mother's Offering* to the publisher and bookseller G.W. Evans, in 1841. George Evans had been an early explorer, and was the first European to cross the Great Dividing Range. He was for some time the drawing master at The King's School in Parramatta, while his wife Lucy ran a finishing school for young ladies. It is probably this shared interest in art and education that drew Charlotte and Evans together.

Print runs at this time were small—usually 500 copies or fewer, to reduce the risks to the publisher and the novelist. Jane Austen's early popularity meant that *Emma*—the last book published in her lifetime—had a print run of 2,000 copies. We do not know how many copies of *A Mother's Offering* were printed, but the likelihood is the run was even smaller than 500 copies.

Only a handful remain.

※

After a week in the Cotswolds, we drive on to Yorkshire. We have a double purpose: to follow some faint clues to our family ancestry and—of course—to visit Haworth Parsonage, where the genius of the Brontë sisters flared so briefly and so fiercely.

I love the landscape. Cloud shadows race over the green dales and the high bare fells, all dissected by low walls of hand-hewn rock. It has a wildness that stirs my blood.

We had discovered, in the brief family memoir Louisa Atkinson wrote for her daughter in 1872, that her father James' family had originated in Yorkshire, where they were an *estated and wealthy family*. I had not known this before, and I find my love for the landscape is intensified by this knowledge.

We visit Ripon Cathedral, where many of the family are said to be buried, and go down into the Saxon crypt. Descending into its dim depths is like going back in time; I feel as if I might hear monks chanting at any moment. The crypt was built in imitation of Christ's tomb, and is very pure and simple, with whitewashed walls with small niches for candles.

It is an uncanny place, where the deep past and death seem very close.

On our drive to Haworth, an impenetrable white mist falls upon the moors. We can see nothing but the faint blur of an occasional pair of headlamps. Belinda slows the car down to a crawl. It is eerie and atmospheric. Somehow we find our way to our hotel, at the base of the steep cobblestoned lane that leads up to the church and the parsonage—and the Black Bull pub where Branwell Brontë was known to enjoy a pint or ten, escaping out the back door when his long-suffering sisters came through the front door, seeking to drag him home.

Despite the drizzle, we cannot wait to walk on the moors. Rugged up in new jumpers and coats, we climb the hill, walk through the churchyard—fittingly gloomy and Gothic in the fog and rain—and squelch through the mud till we are as damp and cold and shivery as any Brontë heroine.

We eat at Haworth Old Hall, as always choosing the most authentic nineteenth-century food we can find—in this case belly pork with slow-roasted apples with sage and honey, rather than the brown rice and lentils with masala-spiced roast chickpeas and tempura-battered okra also on offer.

Binny and I can't wait to show Haworth Parsonage to our girls the next day. Emily has been before, as a tiny baby, but this is my daughter Ella's first visit.

We are all exhausted after our long day, so we retire early to our hotel. Ella and I are sharing a gorgeous four-poster bed with piles of warm blankets and soft pillows. I have a long, slow, hot bath, reading my book on Jane Austen and discovering—much to my astonishment—that she may have died of arsenic poisoning.

When I come out of the bathroom, all clean and pink and flushed in my pyjamas, I find Ella in bed, fast asleep. Her phone is in her hand, tucked up next to her cheek like a beloved soft toy.

The next morning, it is raining again.

We wrap ourselves up warmly and head up the hill. I pick a bunch of elderflowers from the churchyard, and lay them on the memorial plaque for Charlotte and Emily. They both died so tragically young. I wish Anne's grave was there too. I always feel she is unfairly forgotten.

Then on to the museum, each room so poignant—the couch where Emily died, Charlotte's tiny wedding dress, the pretty pebbles Anne collected at the seaside. I think a lot about our Charlotte and ourselves as I wander through the tiny rooms.

The museum has a quote from Charlotte Brontë on the wall that reads:

> *I hardly know what swelled to my throat as I read her letter: such a vehement impatience of restraint and steady work; such a strong wish for wings.*

I know exactly what she meant by that. I too have always wished for wings.

Charlotte Brontë's sketchbooks amaze me—her drawings are so like our Charlotte's! An information panel informs me that the basic method of teaching art to young women at the time was to bid them to copy from engraved plates in popular magazines and drawing manuals, and that Charlotte Brontë practised diligently so that she might be better equipped as a governess. I did not know this, and it helps explain some of the more artificial-looking drawings in our Charlotte's sketchbooks.

I am particularly drawn to the teeny-tiny handmade books that the Brontë children made when they were in their early teens. Measuring roughly 1 x 2 inches, they were made from scraps of paper sewn together with thread and covered with Lilliputian handwriting.

Charlotte (then aged 13) and Branwell (aged 12) created at least 20 miniature books together, set in their fantasy world of Angria. Similar books created by younger siblings Emily and Anne have all been lost.

I love these books because they are so similar to the ones I created when I was a child. Mine weren't tiny—I wrote them in old school exercise books—but I also tried to make them look as much like published books as possible.

Jane Austen did the same. From the age of 11 to 17, she wrote poems, plays and stories and bound them into three notebooks, which she called 'Miscellanious Morsels'.

What made us do it?

I cannot speak for Jane Austen or the Brontë siblings, but I did it for fun. For the joy of writing, and for the dream of creating a real published book one day.

Did our Charlotte scribble down stories as a child too? It is impossible to know, but I think it is likely.

One of the things that has puzzled us in our search for Charlotte's life and work is the number of references to her having published *several useful works for children*. We wonder if there were other books and stories written by Charlotte, now lost. Once again we curse the bonfire that burned so many precious treasures when Oldbury was sold.

Then I find a handwritten note by Marcie Muir in her research folders on Charlotte's life and writing, in the archives at the National Library of Australia. It concerns a book review found in *The Sydney Gazette*, 2 February 1837. The annotation reads: *very entertaining & instructive little work for children entitled P.P.'s Tales.*

The note suggests that Marcie Muir had been investigating the possibility that this book—*P.P.'s Tales*—may have been written by Charlotte. So I do a little digging to find out more about other early books published in or about Australia.

In Maurice Saxby's *Books in the Life of a Child*, I discover that one of the earliest known mentions of Australia appeared in a small chapbook entitled *Amusing and Instructive Tales by Peter Prattle*. A copy is held at the Mitchell Library, and so I ask for it to be brought to the Special Collections room for me. The title page states that it was published in London by T.H. Mundy, but it is clear to me that this is a misprint of 'T.H. Munday', a well-known children's publisher of the time. There is no publication date, but the book was given to a girl named Ada Louisa Smith by her Grandpapa in 1832.

In 1832, Charlotte was living at Oldbury farm and had given birth to her first three children. Charlotte Elizabeth was four, Jane Emily was two, and James John was a newborn.

I read the slim chapbook, wondering if it could have been written and illustrated by Charlotte.

Gradually I begin to grow excited. There are powerful resonances between *Amusing and Instructive Tales by Peter Prattle* and *A Mother's Offering*. I start making notes.

The first story is entitled 'The Way Charles and His Two Brothers Amused Themselves on a Visit to Their Cousins William & Mary', and tells the story of three English boys named Charles, Alfred and Edgar. It explores themes of kindness to animals, and shows an interest in insects and science, issues close to Charlotte's heart. At one point, the author writes: *the gratitude of brutes is a strong testimony to the kindness of their owners.* This echoes *A Mother's Offering*, in which Charlotte describes herself saving a swallow from a cat and a beetle from spiders. Kindness to animals was by no means a widespread philosophy at the time, with the first Cruelty to Animals Act not passing in Britain until 1835.

The next story is 'The Happy Grandmother and Her Grandchildren Who Went to Australia', which Saxby describes as *a … lively … early mention of Australia.* It tells the story of Dame Trueman who is struggling to care for the four children of her dead daughter in a small English village. Her grandchildren are named Meg, James, John and William. Is it a coincidence, I wonder, that two of the boys have the same name as Charlotte's husband and brother-in-law, the names she christened her own son?

James and John are, of course, very popular English names.

Dame Trueman's long-lost son comes to visit and tells her of the wonders of Australia where he has settled. They decide to emigrate to Van Diemen's Land. On the journey Dame Trueman is *unpleasantly affected by the smell of the bilge water,* a detail that echoes Charlotte's experience on her own journey to Australia. She wrote in her journal on Monday 25 September: *The water is so dreadfully putrid with being kept up close they say it will get better. It is much to be hoped it will or I think there will be nothing left of me.*

Once in Tasmania, the children are delighted by a tame kangaroo that *lapped tea* from a bowl and *picked a bone like a monkey.* Some literary critics have taken this as proof that the author had never visited Australia, as kangaroos are, of course, herbivores.

However, I remember Christabel, the baby wallaby we cared for when we were children. Every morning Belinda and I had to feed the animals before we went to school. We had a pony, two dogs, three cats and some budgerigars (mine was named Barnaby, and was so tame I could walk up to the corner shop with him sitting on my shoulder). It was like feeding time at the zoo. The dogs would want to eat the cats' food, the pony would want to eat the wallaby's food, and the wallaby always tried to eat the dogs' food, which usually contained meat scraps.

So I googled to see if there was any evidence of kangaroos eating meat. I found an *Australian Geographic* article that examines an amateur video showing a kangaroo eating a bird. Professor Tim Flannery was interviewed, saying, 'most herbivores will eat some protein if it's available.' Professor Graeme Coulson agreed, stating that 'captive macropods are known to eat a wide range of food, including chicken and lamb chops.'

So the description of a tame kangaroo with a bone in its paws is not as ill-informed as it seems.

Marcie Muir writes: *There is a similarly foreign air about the happy grandmother's family in Peter Prattle … the introduction of kangaroos, parrots and palm trees into a cottage garden scene adds an exotic and luxuriant air quite inconsistent with the atmosphere of Sydney as it was then.*

Except that kangaroos, parrots and palm trees are all native to Australia. It is the roses around the cottage door that are foreign. Also, the story is set not in Sydney, but in Van Diemen's Land. Charles Darwin visited Hobart Town in February 1836—four or five years after the tale was written—and recorded: *The bases of these mountains, following the edges of the bay, are cleared & cultivated; the bright yellow fields of corn & dark green ones of potato crops appear very luxuriant … I was chiefly struck with the comparative fewness of the large houses.*

Perhaps the tree roughly sketched in the background of the picture in *Amusing and Instructive Tales* is a soft tree fern, often called the man fern because of its height. In addition, the illustration of the kangaroo actually looks much more like a kangaroo than other early drawings, many of which were drawn from skins.

The story also mentions cockatoos, parrots and parroquets (an archaic form of 'parakeet'), which shows an unusually in-depth acquaintance with Australia's birdlife, given that John Gould's seven-volume *The Birds of Australia* was not published until 1848.

A poem called 'Human Happiness' follows, which examines whether Nature, Youth, Love, Friendship, Vice or Virtue could provide happiness and concludes, rather morbidly, that only Death is happiness, *If Virtue guides thee here!*

This seems to echo the paragraph in *A Mother's Offering* in which Mrs Saville says: *May the remainder [of his life] be as happy, as the former has been unfortunate; and above all my dear children, we should pray, that the uncertainty and fleeting nature of all worldly happiness, may be so fixed in his mind, as to ensure him a happy eternity.*

Mind you, a great deal of early nineteenth-century literature personifies death as a kind of spiritual solace for those who are grieving.

The next story is set in the 'American forests', and features a brave little dog who saves three boys from a panther (with the accompanying illustration showing what looks more like a leopard). It does not seem as if the author could have been to America.

A poem entitled 'The Caterpillar, the Chrysalis and the Butterfly' follows, and then a little story called 'Foolish Fears' in which a child named Clara learns not to be afraid of spiders, moths and beetles. Clara is, of course, the pseudonym given to the eldest Atkinson daughter, Charlotte Elizabeth, in *A Mother's Offering*.

The book finishes with a poem entitled 'The Escape of the Doves', which begins:

Come back, pretty doves! Oh! Come back from the tree,
You bright, little, fugitive things!
We would not have thought you so ready and free
In using your beautiful wings.

This poem reminds me of Charlotte's story about the swallows in *A Mother's Offering: the little birds were accustomed to alight on the window … and there with loud warblings, pour forth the gratitude which glowed in their little hearts.*

Another compelling piece of evidence is the name of the publisher, T.H. Munday. He was one half of Dean & Munday, one of the most famous publishers of children's books in Great Britain. His father William Munday and his uncle Thomas Dean were both apprentices in the family-owned printing house of Baileys; both married daughters of the house. They took over the business and renamed it Dean & Munday in 1811, living and working together closely at the business' premises on Threadneedle Street in London, and publishing popular children's books, illustrated with hand-coloured lithographs and wood engravings.

Thomas H. Munday was the eldest son of William Munday and his wife Anna Maria Bailey. He and his cousin, Thomas Dean junior, began apprenticeships with their fathers as teenagers and were later partners in the firm, but could not work together. Their collaboration was officially dissolved in 1838.

Charlotte may have had a personal connection to T.H. Munday. Her elder sister Letitia had married a man named Charles Munday in August 1822, ten years before the publication of *Amusing and Instructive Tales by Peter Prattle*. It seems possible that Charles Munday was related to Thomas H. Munday, and may have introduced Charlotte's work to him.

The Mitchell Library has two books by Peter Prattle in its catalogue, and so I call up the other edition to compare. It is called *Instructive Tales by Peter Prattle*, and is much thicker. It contains all the tales and poems of the first copy, along with the addition of a few longer, more light-hearted, tales.

Again there is no publication date, but a quick internet search shows the book listed under 'new publications' in *The Edinburgh Review* and *The Literary Gazette* in 1842. This is the year after the publication of *A Mother's Offering*. If Charlotte had written previously under the pseudonym of 'Peter Prattle', perhaps she persuaded the publisher of the first edition to reissue it with added material in order to earn more income from it?

The new tales are in much the same style as those in the first Peter Prattle book. The first story is called 'The Flower Garden or Alfred's Amusement', and again frames a lesson in natural science within conversations between a father and his son. The language is as lyrical as Charlotte's: bees' honeycomb is described as *fairy fabric*, for example.

Later, the audience of the story is addressed directly:

Children! The best volume of instruction is that which is offered to your view in every walk you take. In everything around you, from the humble moss that grows upon the thatched cottage of the labourer to the majestic oak that adorns the extended park of more wealthy neighbours, are objects of pure and innocent delight to be found.

This reminds me of two passages in *A Mother's Offering*.

In one chapter, Mrs Saville cries: *Oh! my children! how very, very fatal is this habit of putting off from day to day, what should be done immediately; for we know not the day, nor the hour, when time may cease for us; and we be summoned into eternity.*

In another, she describes a beautiful forest of firs in which *numerous mosses of every shade and variety … clothe the ground: while the trees are frequently covered with beautiful lichens.*

Later in the same story, Peter Prattle writes: *Alfred had several sisters. Some of them were botanists, and they occasionally made little excursions in a pony-chaise into the country ... to procure specimens of various plants.*

These botanist-sisters are called Caroline and Louisa, which are of course the names of Caroline Louisa Atkinson, who grew up to be Australia's first woman botanist, her name given to the species *Erechtites atkinsoniae, Xanthosia atkinsoniana* and *Doodia atkinsonii*, among others.

In 1842, our great-great-great-great-aunt Louisa was only eight years old. But, as Elizabeth Lawson writes in *The Natural Art of Louisa Atkinson*: *it is likely that Louisa, just turning six, was already sketching and writing with her sisters at Budgong [in 1839]*. Perhaps Charlotte named the botanist-sisters in the story as a compliment to her own botany-loving little girl.

The next tale, 'The Lost Holiday; or the Boys and the Butterfly', describes the misadventures of three boys who try to catch a butterfly and end up with torn clothes, cuts, bruises, and a crushed and mangled insect. The father of one of the boys says:

> *My dear boy ... the troubles you brought on yourself are entirely for want of a little forethought; for had you considered before you began the chase after the butterfly, that it was very wicked and cruel, I am sure you would have left the poor butterfly to pursue its way unmolested.*

Compare this sentiment with a passage from *A Mother's Offering*:

> *Julius—When I am going to catch a butterfly. or perhaps any other pretty insect, some of those things which you teach us come into my mind, and then I do not do it, Mamma; for fear I should kill them.*

Mrs. S.—I am glad to hear you apply so well what you learn, my dear boy; for that is the use of all learning: to make us wiser and better. It is not merely acquiring a great many things by rote, that will make us better; unless we apply what we learn, as we have an opportunity; and by checking yourself from catching a beautiful butterfly (which I have no doubt you much wished to have), because you thought it would not be right, is a sacrifice well pleasing to the Being who formed it, as well as you.

The next new Peter Prattle story is a long one about a boy and his beloved pony, conducted mainly in instructive dialogue, and has a vivid description and illustration of a shipwreck, one of the major subjects of *A Mother's Offering*.

Another story, later in the book, explains how a kaleidoscope is made, in a conversation between Alfred and his father, in much the same question-and-answer construction as Charlotte's book.

In addition, the book is illustrated with hand-coloured engravings, some of which look like drawings in Charlotte's sketchbooks.

It's all circumstantial evidence, but suggestive nonetheless. And if Charlotte was Peter Prattle, then she is the author and illustrator of one of the first children's stories ever set in Australia, as well as the author of the first children's book published here.

The English literary critic and writer Cyril Connolly famously wrote in 1938: *There is no more sombre enemy of good art than the pram in the hall.*

It is true that most nineteenth-century women writers were childless. Jane Austen, the Brontë sisters, George Eliot, Christina Rossetti, Emily Dickinson and Louisa May Alcott were all without offspring. Mary Shelley had five pregnancies, but only one of her babies survived childhood.

I can attest myself to the difficulties of being both a writer and a mother. Only one of my books was written before my children were born. After giving birth to my darling sons, Ben and Tim, I began to write children's books, partly because I wanted to write for my own boys and partly because I had so little time and energy left for writing after running around after them all day—and children's books have considerably fewer words in them!

So I want to turn Cyril Connolly's statement inside out. For my great-great-great-great-grandmother and for my sister and me, the pram in the hall is not a sombre enemy, but a source of joy and love and life.

After all, Charlotte wrote her stories for her children—both for their pleasure and for their salvation—and she chose to name her book *A Mother's Offering to Her Children*.

Afterword

SONGSPIRALS

Written by Kate

and become at last heirs to immortality
Charlotte Waring Atkinson

━━▸◆◂━━

On a beautiful balmy day in spring, the constellation of the Seven Sisters shining faintly in the sky, my family come together to celebrate my mother's birthday.

Fairy lights are strung through the trees, and the back garden of my brother's house in Warrawee is filled with people talking and laughing, glasses of sparkling wine in their hands. Our children are busy mixing drinks, carrying around platters laden with delicious food, and talking to Mum's friends. My father is here, looking so much stronger and healthier after months of Binny's good food and loving care. Our newly discovered sister Emma Jane and her husband Aldo are here too, my mother always having room in her heart for more people to love.

On her wrist, my mother wears the charm bracelet that has been handed down to the women of my family for six generations. The golden links of its chain, hung with tiny tinkling charms, seem to me like a metaphor for the miraculous spiral of our DNA, the coiling ladder that connects us all, both to our far-distant ancestors and to our unborn descendants.

It is also a metaphor for our family, each of us clasped hand-in-hand, connected by our shared histories.

Researching and writing this book about our great-great-great-great-grandmother Charlotte Waring has been a journey of profound discovery for both me and Belinda.

We found that stories we had been brought up to believe in were untrue; and that other long-doubted stories carried within them an astonishing kernel of truth. We uncovered long-hidden secrets that rattled our sense of who we were; and we have built new bridges of empathy and understanding that we hope will bring us much closer to those we love.

While I was working on this book, I spoke about it at a literary event. I was proud of our clever, courageous Charlotte, and proud to be writing a book about her with my sister.

A woman I did not know said to me, in a tone of disparagement, 'it's not like she was Charlotte Brontë.'

'No,' I replied. 'But who is?'

I was hurt at the time, and chastened, but as the evening went on I found myself growing angry. It is true that our Charlotte did not write a book that is incandescent with genius like the work of the Brontë sisters, writers whom Binny and I admire so much. But does that mean that her life does not matter? I think it is so important to record and celebrate the lives of ordinary people, all struggling and suffering and sorrowing the best they can, striving to move through this difficult world with strength and courage and grace.

Charlotte Waring Atkinson was just an ordinary woman. She loved a man and gave birth to children, then tried her best to raise them and care for them, even though she was ground down by grief and harmed in both body and spirit by cruelty and violence. She fought for her children, she found her voice, and she stood up and spoke out at a time when many women were kept mute.

I am immeasurably proud to be descended from her.

All of my life I have been fascinated by the idea of songlines, songspirals, Dreaming tracks that sing the country to life.

Songlines are not just sung poems. They are spells, rites of passage, memory palaces, systems of navigation, ancestry trees, creation myths, tales of wonder, lists of ancestral laws, moral codes, oral archives, the living narrative of our nation. Singing up one's country is a way of knowing that animates and connects country and kin.

So, figuratively speaking, this book has been a way for me and my sister to sing the country of our past to life, to sing the songlines of our forebears.

It is our offering to our brave ancestor.

Acknowledgements

We would like to thank many people who have helped us with the research for this book, including Patricia Clarke, author of *Pioneer Writer*, and Linda Emery, Archivist of the Berrima District Historical and Family History Society. Jan Gow and Neil McCormack spent numerous hours helping us check facts and sharing their extensive family archives, and Neil kindly gave us permission to use exquisite images from Charlotte's 1843 sketchbook, which he owns.

Many other members of our extended family shared their anecdotes and research with us, particularly Jen Paterson, Robin Corban, Elaine Holdom, Paula MacMillan-Perich, Kaye McBride, Essie Whiteman, Mark Watson, Dennis Foley and Elaine Johns.

Our family shared the challenging journey with us over two years, so we owe them a huge thank you for their love, encouragement and support: Gilly and Glyn Evans; Rob, Nick, Emily and Lachie Murrell; Greg, Ben, Tim and Ella Forsyth; Nick, Victoria, Tom, Meg and Gus Humphrey; Gerry Humphrey; Emma, Aldo, Siena and Stella Barbato.

In England, we gained valuable insights from Nicola Crichton-Brown; Emma Darwin; Brenda Copus; James Saynor, Shoreham and District Historical Society; Max Batten and Tudor Davies, Bromley Borough Local History Society; and historian Gillian Rickard.

A huge thank you to our wonderful publishing team at the National Library of Australia, who had such passion for this story from the beginning, including Susan Hall; Amelia Hartney; Juliet Rogers; Bobby Graham; Katherine Crane; Jemma Posch; Zoe Caley; Kathryn Favelle; our rigorous proofreader Tessa Wooldridge; and designer Lisa White, who created our gorgeous cover. Rebecca Bateman, Indigenous curator at the National Library, carefully checked all our references to Indigenous Australian culture and history. Our editor, Diana Hill, was brilliant, and we are immensely grateful for her meticulous fact-checking, hard work and patient wisdom.

Kate would also like to thank the State Library of New South Wales for awarding her the prestigious 2019 Nancy Keesing Fellowship, which helped fund the research for this book, particularly Richard Neville, Dr Rachel Franks and Megan Atkins.

Apology

In the nineteenth century, most European Australians used disparaging and patronising terms to describe the Indigenous Australians. These terms and attitudes are now considered racist. We have included some of these attitudes and terms, not with the intent to offend any readers but to provide a reflection of attitudes prevalent during that time.

We acknowledge that our ancestors settled on land of the Wodi Wodi people. We would like to pay our respects to the Wodi Wodi people, both living and dead.

List of illustrations

Front cover: composite of illustrations from album of watercolour drawings by Charlotte Atkinson, 1843, courtesy Neil McCormack; **p.3:** self-portrait, Charlotte Waring, page from Jane Emily Atkinson album, 1848, drawings attributed to Charlotte Waring, Mitchell Library, State Library of New South Wales, PXA 579. **Picture section images:** portrait of Charlotte Elizabeth Atkinson, page from Jane Emily Atkinson album of watercolours and drawings, 1848, drawings attributed to Charlotte Waring, Mitchell Library, State Library of New South Wales, PXA 579; portrait of Jane Emily Atkinson, page from Jane Emily Atkinson album of watercolours and drawings, 1848, drawings attributed to Charlotte Waring, Mitchell Library, State Library of New South Wales, PXA 579; portrait of Caroline Louisa Atkinson, page from Jane Emily Atkinson album of watercolours and drawings, 1848, drawings attributed to Charlotte Waring, Mitchell Library, State Library of New South Wales, PXA 579; butterflies and flowers, page from album of watercolour drawings by Charlotte Atkinson, 1843, courtesy Neil McCormack; dedication, page from album of watercolour drawings by Charlotte Atkinson, 1843, courtesy Neil McCormack; flowers, page from album of watercolour drawings by Charlotte Atkinson, 1843, courtesy Neil McCormack; cat, page from album of watercolour drawings by Charlotte Atkinson, 1843, courtesy Neil McCormack; possum, page from album of watercolour drawings by Charlotte Atkinson, 1843, courtesy Neil McCormack; robin, page from album of watercolour drawings by Charlotte Atkinson, 1843, courtesy Neil McCormack; owl, page from album of watercolour drawings by Charlotte Atkinson, 1843, courtesy Neil McCormack; insects, including moths, butterflies and grasshoppers, page from album of watercolour drawings by Charlotte Atkinson, 1843, courtesy Neil McCormack; sailing ships, page from Jane Emily Atkinson album of watercolours and drawings, 1848, drawings attributed to Charlotte Waring, Mitchell Library, State Library of New South Wales, PXA 579; 'Hunting the Giraffe', page from Jane Emily Atkinson album of watercolours and drawings, 1848, drawings attributed to Charlotte Waring, Mitchell Library, State Library of New South Wales, PXA 579; bird and frog, page from Jane Emily Atkinson album of watercolours and drawings, 1848, drawings attributed to Charlotte Waring, Mitchell Library, State Library of New South Wales, PXA 579; (top) portrait of Jane Emily Atkinson, c.1844, Mitchell Library, State Library of New South Wales, P2/369; (centre) portrait of James John Oldbury Atkinson, c.1844, State Library of New South Wales, P2/370; (bottom) portrait of Caroline Louisa Waring Atkinson, c.1844, State Library of New South Wales, P2/371; Charlotte Atkinson, *View at Oldbury*, c.1826, Mitchell Library, State Library of New South Wales, SV1B/Sut F/1; Louisa Atkinson, *View of Oldbury from Dairy Hill*, between 1849 and 1872, Mitchell Library, State Library of New South Wales, PX*D 640; photographs of Oldbury House, New South Wales, and Oldbury House, Kent, by Belinda Murrell; personal photographs courtesy of the authors.

Notes

p.7   *I dare say there are many wonderful things*: Charlotte Waring Atkinson, *A Mother's Offering to Her Children by a Lady Long Resident in New South Wales*, online at setis.library.usyd.edu.au/ozlit/pdf/barmoth.pdf (prepared by University of Sydney Library, 2003, from the print source published by *The Gaz ette*, Sydney, 1841) , p.10

Prologue: A Family of Storytellers

p.11   *for that is the use*: ibid., p.64

p.14   *one of the most accomplished women*: Steve Meacham, 'Unearthed Australiana Could Fetch $90,000', *The Sydney Morning Herald*, 26 May 2011, p.9

Chapter 1 Almost an Orphan

p.18   *I was a tender-hearted child*: Waring Atkinson, *A Mother's Offering*, online at setis.library.usyd.edu.au/ozlit/pdf/barmoth.pdf, p.66

p.22   *was 17 the day she married*: Louisa Atkinson Calvert, 'Notes on the Waring Family', c.1872, Papers of the Cosh and Atkinson families, 1842–1928, Mitchell Library, ML MSS 3849, Box 1

p.22   *was able to carry her about*: ibid.

p.22   *was remarkable*: ibid.

p.22   *a man of fortune*: ibid.

p.22   *lived in London*: ibid.

p.24   *when driving*: ibid.

p.25   *handsome & stately*: ibid.

p.27   *The Warings are descended*: ibid.

p.27   *an ancient family*: *The Gentleman's Magazine*, May 1793, part 1, vol.43, no.5, p.391

p.29   *a man of property*: ibid.

Chapter 2 A Kentish Man

p.32   *In the midst of their boyish pursuits*: 'Peter Prattle', Charlotte Waring Atkinson presumed author, 'The Way Charles & His Two Brothers Amused Themselves', in *Amusing and Instructive Tales by Peter Prattle*. London: T.H. Mundy [Munday], 1832, n.p.

p.35   *the best of times*: Charles Dickens, *A Tale of Two Cities*. New York: Vintage Books, 1990 [1859], p.3

p.36   *To be rooted*: Simone Weil, *The Need for Roots*. London: Routledge, 2002 [1949], p.43

p.38   *the aunts*: Letter to Janet Cosh from Lucy (no surname), 22 March 1967, Papers of Janet L. Cosh, 1826–1983, National Library of Australia, NLA MS 8018, Box 2, File 15

p.40   *I have a fair daughter*: Sappho, translated by Edward Marion Cox, *The Poems of Sappho*. London: Williams and Norgate, London, 1925, n.p.

p.44   *to dig a hole through*: E. (Edith) Nesbit, *Five Children & It*. London: Puffin Books, 2008 [1902], p.7

p.45   *Many a noble fortune*: Jane Austen, *Persuasion*. Harmondsworth, UK: Penguin Books Ltd, 1982 [1818], p.47

Chapter 3 The Governess Trade

p.50   *I was very fond of rambling about*: Waring Atkinson, *A Mother's Offering*, online at setis.library.usyd.edu.au/ozlit/pdf/barmoth.pdf, p.62

p.50   *Where shall you change horses?*: Jane Austen, *Pride and Prejudice*. London: Penguin, 2008 [1813], p.206

p.52   *When I was a little girl*: Waring Atkinson, *A Mother's Offering*, online at setis.library.usyd.edu.au/ozlit/pdf/barmoth.pdf, p.66

p.53   *instructed not only in the general branches*: Charlotte Waring Atkinson's deposition, 18 March 1841, Papers of Patricia Clarke, 1887–2010, National Library of Australia, NLA MS 8363, Box 20, File 19

p.53   *she attained*: Charlotte Waring Atkinson's deposition, 18 March 1841

p.56   *five feet 1½ inches in height*: Atkinson Calvert, 'Notes on the Waring Family'

p.58   *during that period*: Charlotte Waring Atkinson's deposition, 18 March 1841

p.63   *I was very fond of rambling*: Waring Atkinson, *A Mother's Offering*, online at setis.library.usyd.edu.au/ozlit/pdf/barmoth.pdf, p.62

p.64   *inexpressible misery*: Charlotte Brontë, quoted in Clement K. Shorter, *Charlotte Brontë and Her Circle*. London: Hodder and Stoughton, 1896, p.378

p.64   *was obliged to retire*: Charlotte Waring Atkinson's deposition, 18 March 1841 p.64 *that having spent*: Charlotte Waring Atkinson's deposition, 18 March 1841

p.64 *highly recommended*: Harriet King, letter to Phillip Parker King, quoted in Harriet Lethbridge King, *The Admiral's Wife: Mrs Phillip Parker King, A Selection of Letters 1817–56*. Edited by Dorothy Walsh. Melbourne: Hawthorn Press, 1967, p.36

Chapter 4 Seeking Adventures Abroad

p.65 *It required much perseverance*: Waring Atkinson, *A Mother's Offering*, online at setis.library.usyd.edu.au/ozlit/pdf/barmoth.pdf, p.14

p.67 *I believe we have procured a Governess*: Harriet King, letter to Phillip Parker King, quoted in King, *The Admiral's Wife*, p.32

p.68 *Came on board the Cumberland*: Charlotte Waring, Journal Kept on Board the 'Cumberland' Bound from England to New South Wales, 1826, National Library of Australia, NLA MS 8997

p.68 *a pen was made for the sheep*: Charlotte E. McNeilly, 'Saxon Merino', *Australian Town and Country Journal*, 9 August 1905, p.26

p.70 *Saturday … what with*: Waring, Journal Kept on Board the 'Cumberland'

p.71 *Sunday 3. Fine day*: ibid.

p.72 *Monday … Mr A escorted us*: ibid.

p.74 *Tuesday … Mrs W had joked me*: ibid.

p.75 *the time of my embarkation*: ibid.

p.75 *our passage hitherto*: ibid.

p.75 *You are the best sailor ever*: ibid.

p.75 *coast of Devon*: ibid.

p.76 *very arbitrary*: ibid.

p.76 *They insisted*: ibid.

p.76 *We caught a sight of each other*: ibid.

p.77 *the captain wished to sail*: ibid.

p.77 *we paced the deck*: ibid.

p.77 *Charles is returned*: Harriet King, letter to Phillip Parker King, quoted in King, *The Admiral's Wife*, p.17

p.78 *We think Captn C behaved very temperately*: ibid., p.46

Chapter 5 Courtship

p.79 *I must be mistress of my own actions*: Charlotte Waring, as reported by Harriet King in a letter to Phillip Parker King, quoted in ibid., p.49

p.79   *left of a former voyage*: Waring, Journal Kept on Board the 'Cumberland'

p.80   *Very sick dressing*: ibid.

p.81   *such a sea as is seldom seen*: ibid.

p.81   *when we heard the captain calling*: ibid.

p.82   'Lines Written During a Storm in the Bay of Biscay': Waring Atkinson, *A Mother's Offering*, online at setis.library.usyd.edu.au/ozlit/pdf/barmoth.pdf, p.139

p.85   *handsome and brilliant*: Atkinson Calvert, 'Notes on the Waring Family'

p.86   *I am very much disappointed in Miss Waring*: Harriet King, letter to Phillip Parker King, quoted in King, *The Admiral's Wife*, p.48

p.86   *He is a gentleman*: Austen, *Pride and Prejudice*, p.337

p.87   *the children were delighted*: Harriet King, letter to Phillip Parker King, quoted in King, *The Admiral's Wife*, p.50

p.88   *It is impossible*: ibid., p.52

p.88   *Charles and James arrived*: ibid., p.64

p.89   *A plank was placed*: McNeilly, 'Saxon Merino', p.26

Chapter 6 Betrothed

p.90   *enjoying the blessings*: Waring Atkinson, *A Mother's Offering*, online at setis.library.usyd.edu.au/ozlit/pdf/barmoth.pdf, p.59

p.91   *You would be astonished*: Harriet King, letter to Phillip Parker King, quoted in King, *The Admiral's Wife*, p.53

p.91   *Those who would*: *The Sydney Gazette and NSW Advertiser*, 23 January 1827, p.3

p.92   *rude and miserable*: James Atkinson, *An Account of the State of Agriculture & Grazing in New South Wales*. Sydney: Sydney University Press, 1975 [1826], p.28

p.92   *A ... governess who had come from a noble house*: Emmeline Maria Macarthur, 'Recollections of Emmeline Leslie (nee Macarthur), 1909', online at *The Gordons of Manar*, manar.org.uk/emmelineleslierecollections001.htm, p.11

p.93   *I must say*: Alexander Berry, letter to Edward Wollstonecraft, 16 April 1827, transcribed by Patricia Clarke, Charlotte Barton—Transcription of Letters Received, 1839, from Alexander Berry and John Coghill, Mitchell Library, ML MSS 6836

p.93   *Our Jim ... his intended*: Alexander Berry, letter to Edward Wollstonecraft, 22 April 1827, transcribed by Patricia Clarke, Charlotte Barton—Transcription of Letters Received, 1839, from Alexander Berry and John Coghill, Mitchell Library, ML MSS 6836

p.95   *Miss Waring has left them*: Harriet King, letter to Phillip Parker King, quoted in King, *The Admiral's Wife*, p.74

p.95   *One can understand Mrs King's chagrin*: Marcie Muir, *Charlotte Barton: Australia's First Children's Author*. Sydney: Wentworth Press, 1980, p.22

p.96   *A few miserable huts*: 'Notes of a Pedestrian Journey from Bathurst to Bong Bong …', *The Sydney Gazette and NSW Advertiser*, 17 March 1832, p.3

p.97   *a rustic little white cottage*: Waring Atkinson, *A Mother's Offering*, online at setis.library.usyd.edu.au/ozlit/pdf/barmoth.pdf, p.58

p.98   *The grave on the side of our hill*: ibid., p.134

p.100   *It was one of those lovely days*: ibid., p.59

p.102   *Kindness*: Atkinson, *An Account*, p.116

p.103   *The Black Tribes*: James Atkinson, letter, Return of the Aborigines of the Sutton Forest district AONSW, Colonial Secretary's Correspondence 4/2045, Letter 28/4074, quoted in Michael K. Organ, *Illawarra and South Coast Aborigines 1770–1900*. Wollongong, NSW: University of Wollongong, 1993, p.75

p.103   *what was before a Wild and Worthless wilderness*: James Atkinson, letter, quoted in Brian H. Fletcher, 'Introduction', in Atkinson, *An Account*, p.10

p.103   *are a mild, cheerful and inoffensive race*: ibid., p.145

p.103   *have seldom been*: ibid., pp.145–146

p.104   *This Tribe*: James Atkinson, letter, quoted in Organ, *Illawarra*, p.75

p.105   *feloniously and burglariously*: Judith Gilpin and Fred McGrath, 'Hollands Family History', 1994, p.4, provided by Jen Paterson

Chapter 7 Oldbury

p.108   *All seemed peace and serenity*: Waring Atkinson, *A Mother's Offering*, online at setis.library.usyd.edu.au/ozlit/pdf/barmoth.pdf, p.59

p.109   Information about Ambrose Brian, the stonemason who built the house, obtained from an interview with Linda Emery, Archivist of the Berrima District Historical and Family Historical Society

p.112   *pious, clever, amiable*: Atkinson Calvert, 'Notes on the Waring Family'

p.113   *Mr Atkinson was considered*: Randolph Want, 'Diary 1829', Papers of Janet L. Cosh, 1826–1983, National Library of Australia, NLA MS 8018, Box 1, File 1

p.113   *in the kitchen … a large fire*: ibid.

p.115   *with which he expressed himself most pleased*: 'Advance Australia', *The Sydney Gazette and NSW Advertiser*, 19 June 1832, p.2

p.115   *in the evening a large party dined at Oldbury*: ibid.

p.117   *to enquire after James Atkinson*: George Bell's diary, 5 February 1834, online at Nic Haygarth website, nichaygarth.com/index.php/tag/bargo-brush/

p.117 *James Atkinson was*: Atkinson Calvert, 'Notes on the Waring Family'

p.118 *after a painful*: Family Notices, *The Sydney Herald*, 5 May 1834, p.3

p.122 *The most compelling*: Narelle Bowern, *The Aborigines of the Southern Highlands, New South Wales (1820–1850)*. Moss Vale, NSW: Narelle Bowern, 2018, p.53

p.122 *The grave on the side of our hill*: Waring Atkinson, *A Mother's Offering*, online at setis.library.usyd.edu.au/ozlit/pdf/barmoth.pdf, p.134

p.122 *forty-four years*: Louisa Atkinson, 'A Voice from the Country: Recollections of the Aborigines, Sydney', *The Sydney Mail*, 19 September 1863, quoted in Organ, *Illawarra*, p.136

p.122 *the presence of carved trees*: Bowern, *The Aborigines*, p.55

p.123 *It is clear that they trusted him*: ibid., p.59

Chapter 8 Grief

p.124 *This my loves*: Waring Atkinson, *A Mother's Offering*, online at setis.library.usyd.edu.au/ozlit/pdf/barmoth.pdf, p.118

p.131 *Charlotte … professed*: Atkinson Calvert, 'Notes on the Waring Family'

p.131 *In a plain dress*: Louisa Atkinson, *Gertrude the Emigrant: A Tale of Colonial Life*. Edited by Elizabeth Lawson. Canberra: School of English and Australian Scholarly Editions Centre, 1998 [1857], p.20

p.132 *Mrs Doherty was seated*: ibid., p.83

p.132 *'You could not reason…'*: ibid., p.84

p.132 *Several times during the morning*: ibid., p.20

p.133 *most diabolical language*: 'Flogging of an Emigrant Settler by Runaway Convicts', *The Sydney Herald*, 11 February 1836, p.2

p.133 *uncommonly thick*: ibid.

p.133 *with all his strength*: ibid.

p.137 *usually regarded as the most callous*: George E. Boxall, *The Story of the Australian Bushrangers*. London: Swan Sonnenschein & Co., 1899, p.60

p.138 *in such a state of intemperance*: R. Therry, 'Crime in Penal Settlements— Remarkable Criminals', Papers of Patricia Clarke, 1887–2010, National Library of Australia, NLA MS 8363, Box 21, File 24

p.139 John Lynch's spree of brutal murders: see *The Sydney Herald*, 15 March 1854, p.3

p.139 *more robberies*: *The Sydney Monitor*, 18 November 1839, p.2

p.139 *three times within a few months*: John Godden Colyer, letter to the editor, *The Sydney Gazette*, 7 March 1840, p.2

p.140 *two years after the death*: Atkinson Calvert, 'Notes on the Waring Family'

Chapter 9 Changing the World

p.143 *to endeavour to discover*: Waring Atkinson, *A Mother's Offering*,
online at setis.library.usyd.edu.au/ozlit/pdf/barmoth.pdf, p.46

p.143 *There is nothing like geology*: Charles Darwin, letter to his sister
Catherine Darwin, 6 April 1834, online at University of Cambridge,
Darwin Correspondence Project, darwinproject.ac.uk/letter/DCP-LETT-242.xml

p.144 *We all on board*: Charles Darwin, letter to his sister Susan Darwin,
3 September 1834, online at darwinproject.ac.uk/letter/DCP-LETT-286.xml

p.144 *In the evening I walked through the town*: Charles Darwin,
Beagle diary, 12 January 1836, online at *Charles Darwin's Beagle Diary*,
darwinbeagle.blogspot.com/2011/01/12th-january-1836.html

p.144 *probably, when we reach England*: Charles Darwin, letter to his sister
Susan Darwin, 28 January 1836, online at darwinproject.ac.uk/
letter/?docId=letters/DCP-LETT-294.xml

p.145 *the first stage*: Charles Darwin, *Beagle* diary, 16 January 1836,
online at darwinbeagle.blogspot.com/2011/01/16th-january-1836.html

p.145 *most beautiful*: Charles Darwin, *Beagle* diary, 19 January 1836,
online at darwinbeagle.blogspot.com/2011/01/19th-january-1836.html

p.145 *In the dusk*: ibid.

p.146 *on the strange character of the Animals*: ibid.

p.146 *The house would be considered*: Charles Darwin, *Beagle* diary, 27 January 1836,
online at darwinbeagle.blogspot.com/2011/01/27th-january-1836.html

p.148 *On the whole*: Charles Darwin, *Beagle* diary, 28 January 1836, online at
darwinbeagle.blogspot.com/2011/01/28th-january-1836.html

p.150 *And blame not*: Elijah Waring, 'The Poet's Apology', *The Poetical Magazine 2*, 1809

p.150 *the Warings were originally*: Susan Darwin, letter to her brother
Charles Darwin, c. 24 October 1839, online at darwinproject.ac.uk/
letter/?docId=letters/DCP-LETT-472.xml

p.151 *the boys'*: 'Youth Travel Plain Judging', *The Advertiser* (Adelaide), 10 February
1953, p.3

p.152 *London, 3rd June, 1953*: *Narracoorte Herald*, 15 June 1953, p.2

p.157 *In the distant future*: Charles Darwin, *On the Origin of Species by Means
of Natural Selection*. London: John Murray, 1859, p.488

Chapter 10 Trapped

p.159 *Oh! dear! poor things*: Waring Atkinson, *A Mother's Offering*,
online at setis.library.usyd.edu.au/ozlit/pdf/barmoth.pdf, p.23

p.160 *it is entirely on account of Mr Barton*: Alexander Berry, letter to Charlotte Barton, 1 June 1839, transcribed by Patricia Clarke, Charlotte Barton— Transcription of Letters Received, 1839, from Alexander Berry and John Coghill, Mitchell Library, ML MSS 6836

p.160 *I consider him ready*: Alexander Berry, letter to Charlotte Barton, 26 October 1839, transcribed by Patricia Clarke, Charlotte Barton—Transcription of Letters Received, 1839, from Alexander Berry and John Coghill, Mitchell Library, ML MSS 6836

p.161 *strung painfully*: Emma Darwin, *This Is Not a Book about Charles Darwin: A Writer's Journey through My Family*. Newbury, UK: Holland House Books, 2018, p.4

p.162 *On every shelf*: ibid., p.130

p.165 *The ordinary response*: Judith L. Herman, *Trauma and Recovery: The Aftermath of Violence—From Domestic Abuse to Political Terror*. New York: Basic Books, 1997, online at whatnow727.files.wordpress.com/2018/04/herman_trauma-and-recovery.pdf, n.p.

p.166 *double consciousness*: Sigmund Freud, quoted in ibid., n.p.

p.166 *This altered state*: ibid., n.p.

p.166 *the repetition compulsion*: Sigmund Freud, quoted in ibid., n.p.

p.168 *a raving lunatic*: quoted in Patricia Clarke, *Pioneer Writer: The Life of Louisa Atkinson, Novelist, Journalist, Naturalist*. Sydney: Allen & Unwin, 1990, p.28

p.168 *In order to gain*: Herman, *Trauma and Recovery*, n.p.

p.168 *Oh! when I think*: Anne Brontë, *The Tenant of Wildfell Hall*. London: Smith, Elder & Co., 1871 [1848], pp.230–231

p.170 *The Grounds adjoining*: Lachlan Macquarie, diary, 18 and 19 October 1836, online at Macquarie University, *Journeys in Time*, mq.edu.au/macquarie-archive/journeys/1820/1820a/oct18.html and mq.edu.au/macquarie-archive/journeys/1820/1820a/oct19.html

p.171 *The pass had been improved*: Louisa Atkinson, 'A Night Adventure in the Bush', in *A Voice from the Country*. Canberra: Mulini Press, 1978, pp.28–30

p.173 *I remember a little Gentleman*: Waring Atkinson, *A Mother's Offering*, online at setis.library.usyd.edu.au/ozlit/pdf/barmoth.pdf, pp.14–15

p.174 *Recovery unfolds*: Herman, *Trauma and Recovery*, n.p.

p.175 *The [local] tribe*: Waring Atkinson, *A Mother's Offering*, online at setis.library.usyd.edu.au/ozlit/pdf/barmoth.pdf, pp.131–132

p.175 *free and safe at last!*: Brontë, *The Tenant of Wildfell Hall*, p.290

Chapter 11 A Notable She-Dragon

p.176 *Our future destiny*: Waring Atkinson, *A Mother's Offering*, online at
setis.library.usyd.edu.au/ozlit/pdf/barmoth.pdf, p.18

p.177 *Her situation is extremely distressing*: Charlotte Waring Atkinson's
deposition, 1 September 1840, Papers of Patricia Clarke, 1887–2010,
National Library of Australia, NLA MS 8363, Box 20, File 19, quoted in
Clarke, *Pioneer Writer*, pp.37–38

p.177 *incapable*: Petition by Alexander Berry and John Coghill, 6 March 1841,
Papers of Patricia Clarke, 1887–2010, National Library of Australia, NLA
MS 8363, Box 20, File 19

p.177 *legal prostitution*: Mary Wollstonecraft, *A Vindication of the Rights of Woman:
With Strictures on Political and Moral Subjects*. London: T.F. Unwin, 1891
[1792], p.222

p.177 *As it stands at present*: John Temple Leader, address to the House of
Commons, 14 December 1837, quoted in *The Mirror of Parliament*,
Volume 1. London: Longman, Orme, Brown, Green, & Longmans,
1838, p.740

p.178 *By marriage, the husband and wife*: William Blackstone, *Commentaries
on the Laws of England*. Oxford: Clarendon Press, 1765–1769, p.430

p.179 *It was not Caroline who was being sued*: Lucinda Hawksley, *March, Women,
March*. London: Andre Deutsche Ltd, 2013, p.24

p.180 *fit and proper*: Petition by Alexander Berry and John Coghill, 6 March 1841

p.180 *The legal system*: Herman, *Trauma and Recovery*, n.p.

p.181 *[he] had every reason*: George Barton's deposition to the NSW Supreme Court,
23 November 1841, quoted in Clarke, *Pioneer Writer*, p.26

p.182 *in order to escape*: Herman, *Trauma and Recovery*, n.p.

p.182 a *blistering petition*: Clarke, *Pioneer Writer*, p.39

p.182 *his habits*: Charlotte Waring Atkinson's deposition, 6 March 1841, Papers
of Patricia Clarke, 1887–2010, National Library of Australia, NLA MS 8363,
Box 20, File 19

p.182 *his intemperate habits*: ibid.

p.182 *violent and dangerous*: ibid.

p.182 *not consider that Ladies*: Charlotte Waring Atkinson's deposition,
18 March 1841

p.183 *peculiar circumstances*: quoted in Clarke, *Pioneer Writer*, p.40

p.183 *His youth ... his local inexperience*: ibid.

p.183 *children ... were often*: ibid.

p.184 *a bill had been filed*: Atkinson v. Barton, Supreme Court of New South Wales, *The Sydney Herald*, 3 July 1841, online at Macquarie University, *Decisions of the Superior Courts of New South Wales, 1788–1899*, law.mq.edu.au/research/colonial_case_law/nsw/cases/case_index/1841/atkinson_v_barton/

p.184 *impertinent and scandalous*: Master in Equity Order Book, 9 July 1841, quoted in Clarke, *Pioneer Writer*, p.41

p.185 *irrespective … of any personal demerit*: Atkinson v. Barton, Supreme Court of New South Wales, *The Sydney Herald*, 3 July 1841, online at law.mq.edu.au/research/colonial_case_law/nsw/cases/case_index/1841/atkinson_v_barton/

p.185 *it would require a state*: Atkinson v. Barton, Supreme Court of New South Wales, *The Sydney Herald*, 10 July 1841, online at law.mq.edu.au/research/colonial_case_law/nsw/cases/case_index/1841/atkinson_v_barton/

p.185 *then at the breast*: Caroline Sheridan Norton, *Observations on the Natural Claim of the Mother to the Custody of Her Infant Children*. London: James Ridgeway, 1837, p.7

p.186 *The Court is apprised*: quoted in Dr Kathleen Kelley Reardon and Christopher T. Noblet, *Childhood Denied*. Thousand Oaks, CA: SAGE Publications, 2009, p.88

p.186 *eight years after his death!*: Clarke, *Pioneer Writer*, p.42

p.186 *The whole is a fine specimen*: Letter from Alexander Berry to John Coghill, 14 July 1842, quoted in ibid., p.43

p.186 *a notable she-dragon*: ibid.

p.187 *We should never*: Waring Atkinson, *A Mother's Offering*, online at setis.library.usyd.edu.au/ozlit/pdf/barmoth.pdf, p.114

Chapter 12 Return to Oldbury

p.188 *it would afford us much delight*: ibid., p.10

p.189 *to substitute*: Advertising, *The Sydney Morning Herald*, 20 December 1842, p.3

p.189 cost of schooling, two guineas per quarter: see Advertising, 'Miss Rennie's School', *The Colonial Observer*, 23 December 1841, p.8

p.192 *it was then empty*: Louisa Atkinson, *Cowanda, the Veteran's Grant*. Canberra: Mulini Press, 1995 [1859], p.51

p.192 *So strong*: Louisa Atkinson, 'The Wallaby Rocks', in *Excursions from Berrima and a Trip to Manaro and Molonglo in the 1870s*. Canberra: Mulini Press, 1980, p.12

p.193 *Jem Vaugh*: Louisa Atkinson, 'A Voice from the Country: Recollections of the Aborigines', *The Sydney Morning Herald*, 22 September 1863, p.3

p.194 *winning ways*: 'Interview with Essie Whiteman', in Clarke, *Pioneer Writer*, p.65

p.195 *beloved*: Family Notices, *The Sydney Morning Herald*, 4 February 1853, p.3

p.195 *aged nearly thirteen months*: ibid.

p.196 *at Oldbury, the residence of her mother*: Family Notices, *The Sydney Morning Herald*, 29 August 1854, p.5

p.197 *the mistress ... now I have got the axe*: Law: Bathurst Circuit Court, *The Sydney Morning Herald*, 8 March 1854, p.3

p.199 *delightful, romantically situated*: Advertising, *The Sydney Morning Herald*, 9 February 1865, p.7

p.199 *a sound English education*: Advertising, *The Sydney Morning Herald*, 20 December 1861, p.8

p.200 *a saddle [for] a down pillow*: Louisa Atkinson, 'The Day's End', in *A Voice from the Country*. Canberra: Mulini Press, 1978, p.31

p.201 *To earn an independent*: Louisa Atkinson, *Debatable Ground, or, the Carlillawarra Claimants*. Canberra: Mulini Press, 1992 [1861], p.100

Chapter 13 Charlotte's Legacy

p.202 *the cheering hope*: Waring Atkinson, *A Mother's Offering*, online at setis.library.usyd.edu.au/ozlit/pdf/barmoth.pdf, p.126

p.202 *the smooth white stone*: Louisa Atkinson, 'A Voice from the Country: Recollections of the Aborigines', *The Sydney Mail*, 19 September 1863, quoted in Organ, *Illawarra*, p.140

p.203 *full of hope*: Fitzroy Iron Works Heritage sign, *Thomas McNeilly shopkeeper and Labourer*, Mittagong, NSW

p.203 *rough slab hut*: Atkinson, *Excursions from Berrima*, p.17

p.207 *The bride is a niece*: 'Wedding Bruck-Garlick', *The Molong Argus*, 9 April 1909, p.4

p.207 *confirmed invalid*: Louisa Atkinson, letter to her solicitor, quoted in Clarke, *Pioneer Writer*, p.183

p.208 *I have a helpless family*: Fitzroy Iron Works Heritage sign, *Thomas McNeilly shopkeeper and Labourer*, Mittagong, NSW

p.208 *at Oldbury, after a long and painful illness*: Family Notices, *The Sydney Morning Herald*, 16 October 1867, p.1

p.213 *many will have reason*: 'Death of Mrs C.E. McNeilly', *Leader* (Orange), 18 March 1911, p.2

p.214 *a real solicitor*: Interview with Bertha Bruck, Papers of Janet L. Cosh, 1826–1983, National Library of Australia, NLA MS 8018, Box 3, File 18

p.215 *idling about*: Charlotte McNeilly's deposition, Petition 1, Case of McNeilly vs McNeilly, Archives of the NSW Supreme Court, Divorce Petition number 0053, 30 September 1876 p.215 *so violently*: ibid.

p.215 *left with her children*: ibid.

p.215 *managed to keep her children alive*: ibid.

p.215 *to murder her*: 'Remarkable Divorce Case', *Australian Town and Country Journal*, 3 March 1877, p.21

p.216 *from that time*: Charlotte McNeilly's deposition, 30 September 1876

p.216 *wielded a facile, graceful pen*: 'Death of Mrs C.E. McNeilly'

p.217 *was very beautiful*: Jan Gow, letter to Janet Cosh, Papers of Janet L. Cosh, 1826–1983, National Library of Australia, NLA MS 8018, Box 3, File 18

p.218 *Mrs. McNeilly was that type of woman*: 'Death of Mrs. C.E. McNeilly'

p.218 *The roots of his spiritual life*: 'Death of Ald. E.T. McNeilly Foremost Citizen of Orange', *Leader* (Orange), 19 June 1929, p.2

p.219 *bright, sweet and loveable*: 'Obituary Mrs H.C. Wood', *The Gosford Times and Wyong District Advocate*, 11 June 1915, p.12

Chapter 14 Anon.

p.222 *Tell us some little story then*: Waring Atkinson, *A Mother's Offering*, online at setis.library.usyd.edu.au/ozlit/pdf/barmoth.pdf, p.58

p.223 *The old south land*: Patricia Wrightson, *The Ice Is Coming*. Melbourne: Hutchinson Group (Australia) Pty Ltd, 1977, pp.11–12

p.228 *Nearly a century*: Rosemary Wighton, 'Introduction', in Charlotte Waring Atkinson, *A Mother's Offering to Her Children by a Lady Long Resident in New South Wales*, facsimile edition. Milton, Qld: Jacaranda Press, 1979 [1841], p.vii

p.228 *For many years it was believed*: Wighton, 'Introduction', in *A Mother's Offering*, p.ix

p.230 *Genius of a sort*: Virginia Woolf, *A Room of One's Own*. London: The Folio Society, 2000 [1929], p.56

p.230 *did not like to declare ourselves women*: Charlotte Brontë, 'Biographical Notice of Ellis and Acton Bell', introduction to *Wuthering Heights and Agnes Grey by Ellis and Acton Bell*. London: Smith, Elder & Co., 1850, p.ix, online at bl.uk/collection-items/charlotte-bronts-1850-preface-to-wuthering-heights

p.230 *Writing for money*: Amanda Foreman, 'Historically Speaking: Austen, Anonymous Writers and History', *The Wall Street Journal*, 27 July 2017, online at dramandaforeman.com/3408-2/#more-3408

p.231 *I have already mentioned*: Wighton, 'Introduction', in *A Mother's Offering*, p.vii p.231 *children living in Australia*: ibid.

p.233 *[A Mother's Offering to Her Children] which embraces a variety*: *The Sydney Gazette*, 23 December 1841, p.3, quoted in Muir, *Charlotte Barton*, p.13

p.234 *It seemed hopeless*: ibid., p.17

p.234 *[Louisa Atkinson's] mother appears*: Margaret Swann, 'Mrs. Meredith and Miss Atkinson, Writers and Naturalists', *Journal of the Royal Australian Historical Society*, vol.15, part 1, 1929, quoted in ibid., p.32

p.235 *One of Australia's deepest*: *The Age*, 31 October 1980, Papers of Janet L. Cosh, 1826–1983, National Library of Australia, NLA MS 8018, Box 4, File 24

p.235 *brilliant feat*: ibid.

p.236 *it wasn't easy to swap Puck for pot-koruck*: Patricia Wrightson, 'When Cultures Meet', IBBY Conference, 19 May 1978, quoted in Patricia and Peter Wrightson, *The Wrightson List*. Sydney: Random House Australia, 1998, p.ix (NB: Patricia Wrightson defines '*pot-koruck*' as *mischievous spirits who inhabit watercourses and play tricks on fishermen*: Wrightson, *The Wrightson List*, p.125)

p.236 *as a vitalising force*: ibid., p.xii

p.236 *There has been enough violation*: ibid., p.xiii

p.236 *an electrifying moment*: 'Publisher's Note', ibid., p.vii

p.236 *in ringing tones*: Maurice Saxby, 'Author Delved into World of Children', obituary for Patricia Wrightson, *The Sydney Morning Herald*, 2 April 2010, online at smh. com.au/national/author-delved-into-world-of-children-20100401-ri05.html

Chapter 15 Fire Dance

p.238 *This little work*: Waring Atkinson, *A Mother's Offering*, online at setis.library.usyd.edu.au/ozlit/pdf/barmoth.pdf, Preface, p.3

p.238 *Master Reginald Gipps*: ibid.

p.239 *engaged at her needle*: ibid., p.5

p.239 *You are afraid*: Jean-Jacques Rousseau, *Emile, or On Education*. The Floating Press, 2009 [1762], online at books.google.com.au/books?id=nWj_ZbVcwgIC& printsec=frontcover&dq=Jean-Jacques+Rousseau,+Emile,+or+On+Education, p.156

p.240 *a place where young ladies sat in the stocks*: Charlotte Brontë, *Jane Eyre: An Autobiography*. Leipzig: Bernhard Tauchnitz, 1850, p.27

p.240 *was published for*: Maurice Saxby, *Offered to Children: A History of Children's Literature 1841–1941*. Sydney: Scholastic Australia, 1998, p.39

p.240 *it was a conservative book even then*: Wighton, 'Introduction', in *A Mother's Offering*, p.xi p.241 *didacticism*: Dinny Culican-Ward, 'Charlotte Barton: Australia's First Writer for Children', *Margin: Life and Letters of Early Australia*, no.55, November 2001, p.12

p.241 *not a failed novel*: Brenda Niall and Frances O'Neill, *Australia through the Looking-Glass: Children's Fiction, 1830–1980*. Melbourne: Melbourne University Press, 1984, p.58.

p.241 *But tho' I like praise*: Jane Austen, letter to Fanny Knight, 30 November 1814, online at pemberley.com/janeinfo/brablt15.html

p.242 *secretly, subtly*: Lucy Worsley, *Jane Austen at Home: A Biography*. London: Hodder & Stoughton, 2017, p.129

p.242 *What little I know*: Waring Atkinson, *A Mother's Offering*, online at setis.library.usyd.edu.au/ozlit/pdf/barmoth.pdf, p.5

p.242 *had belonged to Animals*: ibid., p.15

p.243 *sedate [and] genteel*: Saxby, *Offered to Children*, p.41

p.243 *This is a trochus*: Waring Atkinson, *A Mother's Offering*, online at setis.library.usyd.edu.au/ozlit/pdf/barmoth.pdf, p.105

p.243 *poor little white slug*: ibid., p.63

p.244 *Take not the life*: ibid., pp.63–64

p.244 *while* A Mother's Offering *stops short*: Saxby, *Offered to Children*, p.20

p.244 *Swan Lake appears*: Waring Atkinson, *A Mother's Offering*, online at setis.library.usyd.edu.au/ozlit/pdf/barmoth.pdf, p.16

p.244 *Nothing can be more ingenious*: ibid., p.60

p.244 *drawn from printed sources*: ibid., p.3

p.244 *[John] Ireland told the Captain*: ibid., p.36

p.244 *dreadful savages*: ibid., p.38

p.244 *wretched blacks*: ibid., p.39

p.245 *About as near as I can guess*: John Ireland, *The Shipwrecked Orphans*. New Haven: S. Babcock, 1844, pp.24, 27, online at gutenberg.org/files/57515/57515-h/57515-h.htm

p.246 *Mrs. S.—They remained*: ibid., pp.26–27

p.246 *One of the most bloodthirsty scenes*: Saxby, *Offered to Children*, p.24

p.247 *Mrs. Fraser was very ill*: Waring Atkinson, *A Mother's Offering*, online at setis.library.usyd.edu.au/ozlit/pdf/barmoth.pdf, p.112

p.247 *inhuman savages*: ibid., p.114

p.247 *no other food*: ibid., p.115

p.248 *as soon as she arrived in England*: ibid., p.118

p.248 *These poor uncivilized people*: ibid., p.128

p.248 *Jane ... a young married woman*: ibid., p.129

p.248 *naturally much distressed*: ibid.

p.248 *and poor little sorrowing Sally*: ibid.

p.248 *little Sally went and stood outside*: ibid., pp.129–130

p.248 *Oh! Mamma that is just what I should do*: ibid., p.130

p.248 *the tribe came again*: ibid.

p.248 *sent her child*: ibid.

p.249 *Ah! Mamma, I am very sorry*: ibid.

p.249 *was very blamable*: ibid.

p.249 *a black man named Woombi*: ibid., p.131

p.249 *The Blacks have a great objection*: ibid., pp.134–135

p.249 *Mamma, it seems unnatural*: ibid., p.131

p.249 *In a savage state*: ibid., p.132

p.250 *It is very odd*: ibid., p.133

p.250 *This chapter*: Wighton, 'Introduction', in *A Mother's Offering*, p.x

p.250 *to all appearances*: David Blackburn (First Fleet naval officer), letter
       to Richard Knight, 12 July 1788, Blackburn Letters, State Library of
       New South Wales

p.250 *more like monk[e]ys than warriors*: Daniel Southwell, letter to Mrs Southwell,
       5 May 1788, 'Journal and Letters of Daniel Southwell', in *Historical Records of
       New South Wales*, vol.2, appendix D

p.250 *low down in the scale*: William Stones, *My First Voyage: A Book for Youth*.
       London: Simpkin, Marshall & Co, 1858, p.162

p.251 *[Australian Aborigines] were*: Louisa Anne Meredith, *Tasmanian Friends and
       Foes: Feathered, Furred, and Finned ...* Hobart Town: J. Walch & Sons, 1880, p.81

p.251 *[those] tribes which have been described*: Sigmund Freud, *Totem and Taboo*.
       London: Routledge, 1999 [1913], p.1

p.251 *Australia is the present home*: Baldwin Spencer and Francis James Gillen,
       The Arunta: A Study of a Stone Age People. London: Macmillan & Co., 1927, p.vii

p.251 *The men*: Louisa Atkinson, 'A Voice from the Country: Recollections of
       the Aborigines', *The Sydney Mail*, 12 September 1863, quoted in Organ,
       Illawarra, p.135

p.252 *Being good and great*: Stan Grant, *Talking to My Country*. Sydney: HarperCollins,
       2017, p.26

p.252 *a people who made the first seafaring journey*: Stan Grant, 'Racism Is Destroying
       the Australian Dream', speech at the IQ2 Racism Debate, 27 October 2015, City
       Recital Hall, Sydney, Australia, online at youtube.com/watch?v=eA3UsF8yyho

p.253 *I would like to demonstrate*: Acknowledgement of Country, the City of
Greater Bendigo, online at bendigo.vic.gov.au/Acknowledgement_of_Country

Chapter 16 Wishing for Wings

p.256 *so ready and free*: Waring Atkinson presumed author, 'The Escape of the Doves',
in *Amusing and Instructive Tales by Peter Prattle*, n.p.

p.257 *I have lost*: Cassandra Austen, letter to Fanny Knight on the death of her sister
Jane, 18 July 1817, online at pemberley.com/janeinfo/brablt17.html#toc

p.257 *breakfast … was her part*: Caroline Austen, *My Aunt Jane Austen:
A Memoir*. Hampshire: Jane Austen Society, 1952, quoted in Worsley,
Jane Austen at Home, p.298

p.258 *the never-ending duty*: ibid., p.299

p.258 *I went up to the Gt. House*: Jane Austen, letter to Cassandra Austen,
13 June 1814, online at pemberley.com/janeinfo/brablt13.html#letter73

p.258 *My mother*: Jane Austen, letter to Cassandra Austen, 3 January 1801, quoted
in Helen Amy, *The Jane Austen Files: A Complete Anthology of Letters & Family
Recollections*. Stroud, UK: Amberley Publishing Limited, 2015, p.261

p.260 *estated and wealthy family*: Atkinson Calvert, 'Notes on the Waring Family'

p.262 *I hardly know*: Charlotte Brontë, letter to Ellen Nussey, 7 August 1841,
quoted in exhibition, Brontë Parsonage Museum (Hayworth, UK),
June 2019

p.263 *several useful works*: article regarding Louisa Atkinson in *Australian Town
and Country Journal*, 30 November 1878, Papers of Janet L. Cosh, 1826–1983,
National Library of Australia, NLA MS 8018, Box 3, File 16

p.263 *very entertaining*: Handwritten annotation to *The Sydney Gazette*,
2 February 1837, p.2, Papers of Marcie Muir Relating to Margaret Horder
and Charlotte Barton, National Library of Australia, NLA MS Acc09.199,
Box 12B

p.264 *the gratitude*: Waring Atkinson presumed author, 'The Way Charles &
His Two Brothers Amused Themselves', n.p.

p.265 *a … lively …*: Maurice Saxby, *Books in the Life of a Child: Bridges to Literature
and Learning*. Melbourne: Macmillan Education Australia, 1997, p.91

p.265 *unpleasantly affected*: Waring Atkinson presumed author, 'The Happy
Grandmother and Her Grandchildren Who Went to Australia', in
Amusing and Instructive Tales by Peter Prattle, n.p.

p.265 *The water is*: Waring, Journal Kept on Board the 'Cumberland'

p.265 *lapped tea … picked a bone*: Waring Atkinson presumed author,
'The Happy Grandmother', n.p.

p.266 Video of kangaroo eating a bird, australiangeographic.com.au/topics/
wildlife/2014/02/video-kangaroo-eats-a-bird/

p.266 *There is a similarly foreign air*: Marcie Muir, *A History of Australian Children's
Book Illustration*. Melbourne: Oxford University Press, 1982, p.12

p.266 *The bases of these mountains*: Charles Darwin, *Beagle* diary, 5 February 1836,
online at darwinbeagle.blogspot.com/2011/02/5th-february-1836.html

p.267 *If Virtue guides thee here!*: Waring Atkinson presumed author, 'Human
Happiness', in *Amusing and Instructive Tales by Peter Prattle*, n.p.

p.267 *May the remainder*: Waring Atkinson, *A Mother's Offering*, online at
setis.library.usyd.edu.au/ozlit/pdf/barmoth.pdf, p.56

p.267 *Come back, pretty doves!*: Waring Atkinson presumed author,
'The Escape of the Doves', n.p.

p.268 *the little birds*: Waring Atkinson, *A Mother's Offering*, online at
setis.library.usyd.edu.au/ozlit/pdf/barmoth.pdf, p.59

p.269 *fairy fabric*: 'Peter Prattle', Charlotte Waring Atkinson presumed author,
'The Flower Garden or Alfred's Amusement', in *Instructive Tales by Peter
Prattle*, London: T.H. Munday, c.1842, n.p.

p.269 *Children! The best volume*: ibid.

p.269 *Oh! my children! how very, very fatal*: Waring Atkinson, *A Mother's Offering*,
online at setis.library.usyd.edu.au/ozlit/pdf/barmoth.pdf, p.137

p.269 *numerous mosses*: ibid., p.62

p.270 *Alfred had several sisters*: Waring Atkinson presumed author, 'The Flower
Garden', n.p.

p.270 *it is likely that Louisa*: Elizabeth Lawson, *The Natural Art of Louisa Atkinson*.
Sydney: State Library of New South Wales Press, 1995, p.35

p.270 *My dear boy*: Waring Atkinson presumed author, 'The Lost Holiday; or the
Boys and the Butterfly', in *Instructive Tales by Peter Prattle*, n.p.

p.270 *Julius—When I am going*: Waring Atkinson, *A Mother's Offering*, online at
setis.library.usyd.edu.au/ozlit/pdf/barmoth.pdf, p.64

p.271 *There is no more sombre*: Cyril Connolly, *Enemies of Promise*. Chicago:
University of Chicago Press, 2008 [1938], p.116

Afterword: Songspirals

p.273 *and become at last heirs*: Waring Atkinson, *A Mother's Offering*, online at
setis.library.usyd.edu.au/ozlit/pdf/barmoth.pdf, p.138

Select bibliography

Amy, Helen, *The Jane Austen Files: A Complete Anthology of Letters & Family Recollections*. Stroud, UK: Amberley Publishing Limited, 2015

Atkinson, Charlotte Waring, *A Mother's Offering to Her Children by a Lady Long Resident in New South Wales*. Sydney: G.W. Evans, 1841, online at setis.library.usyd.edu.au/ozlit/pdf/barmoth.pdf (prepared by University of Sydney Library, 2003, from the print source published by *The Gazette*, Sydney, 1841)

—— (presumed author), *Amusing and Instructive Tales by Peter Prattle*. London: T.H. Mundy [Munday], 1832

—— (presumed author), *Instructive Tales by Peter Prattle*. London: T.H. Munday, c.1842

Atkinson, James, *An Account of the State of Agriculture & Grazing in New South Wales*. Sydney: Sydney University Press, 1975 [first published 1826]

Atkinson, Louisa, *A Voice from the Country*. Canberra: Mulini Press, 1978

——, *Excursions from Berrima and a Trip to Manaro and Molonglo in the 1870s*. Canberra: Mulini Press, 1980

——, *Tom Hellicar's Children*. Canberra: Mulini Press, 1983 [first published as a serial 1871]

——, *Debatable Ground, or, the Carlillawarra Claimants*. Canberra: Mulini Press, 1992 [first published as a serial 1861]

——, *Cowanda, the Veteran's Grant*. Canberra: Mulini Press, 1995 [first published 1859]

——, *Gertrude the Emigrant: A Tale of Colonial Life*. Edited by Elizabeth Lawson. Canberra: School of English and Australian Scholarly Editions Centre, 1998 [first published 1857]

Bennett, Francis James, *Ightham: The Story of a Kentish Village and Its Surroundings*. London: Homeland Association, 1907

Blackstone, William, *Commentaries on the Laws of England*. Oxford: Clarendon Press, 1765–1769

Bowern, Narelle, *The Aborigines of the Southern Highlands, New South Wales (1820–1850)*. Moss Vale, NSW: Narelle Bowern, 2018

Select Bibliography

Bridges, Barry John, 'Aspects of the Career of Alexander Berry, 1781–1873'. PhD thesis, University of Wollongong, 1992, online at ro.uow.edu.au/theses/1432/

Brontë, Anne, *The Tenant of Wildfell Hall*. London: Smith, Elder & Co., 1871 [first published 1848]

Brontë, Charlotte, 'Biographical Notice of Ellis and Acton Bell', introduction to *Wuthering Heights and Agnes Grey by Ellis and Acton Bell*. London: Smith, Elder & Co., 1850, online at www.bl.uk/collection-items/charlotte-bronts-1850-preface-to-wuthering-heights

——, *Jane Eyre: An Autobiography*. Leipzig: Bernhard Tauchnitz, 1850

Caesar, Muriel Waring, 'The Warings of the Lea', *The Black Countryman*, 1980, no.3

Calvert, Louisa Atkinson, 'Notes on the Waring Family', c.1872, Papers of the Cosh and Atkinson families, 1842–1928, Mitchell Library, ML MSS 3849, Box 1

Clarke, Patricia, *Pioneer Writer: The Life of Louisa Atkinson, Novelist, Journalist, Naturalist*. Sydney: Allen & Unwin, 1990

Connolly, Cyril, *Enemies of Promise*. Chicago: University of Chicago Press, 2008 [first published 1938]

Costa, James T., *Darwin's Backyard: How Small Experiments Led to a Big Theory*. New York: W.W. Norton & Company, 2017

Crichton-Brown, Nicola, *Cavan Station: Its Early History, the Riley Legacy and the Murdoch Vision*. Sydney: HarperCollins, 2019

Culican-Ward, Dinny, 'Charlotte Barton: Australia's First Writer for Children', *Margin: Life and Letters of Early Australia*, no.55, November 2001

Darwin, Emma, *This Is Not a Book about Charles Darwin: A Writer's Journey through My Family*. Newbury, UK: Holland House Books, 2018

Emery, Linda, *Tales from a Churchyard: All Saints Church and Cemetery, Sutton Forest*. Exeter, NSW: Linda Emery, 2004

Fletcher, Brian H., 'Introduction', in James Atkinson, *An Account of the State of Agriculture & Grazing in New South Wales*. Sydney: Sydney University Press, 1975

Frost, Lucy, *No Place for A Nervous Lady: Voices from the Australian Bush*. Melbourne: McPhee Gribble Publishers, 1984

Grant, Stan, *Talking to My Country*. Sydney: HarperCollins, 2017

Hawksley, Lucinda, *March, Women, March*. London: Andre Deutsche Ltd, 2013

Henning, Rachel, *The Letters of Rachel Henning*. Sydney: Angus & Robertson, 1986

Herman, Judith L., *Trauma and Recovery: The Aftermath of Violence—From Domestic Abuse to Political Terror*. New York: Basic Books, 1997, online at whatnow727.files.wordpress.com/2018/04/herman_trauma-and-recovery.pdf

Hume, Robert D., 'The Value of Money in Eighteenth-Century England: Incomes, Prices, Buying Power—and Some Problems in Cultural Economics', *Huntington Library Quarterly*, vol.77, no.4, online at Huntingdon Library Quarterly – Penn Press, hlq.pennpress.org/media/34098/hlq-774_p373_hume.pdf

Ireland, John, *The Shipwrecked Orphans: A True Narrative of the Shipwreck and Sufferings of John Ireland and William Doyley, Who Were Wrecked in the Ship Charles Eaton, on an Island in the South Seas*. New Haven, CT: S. Babcock, 1844, online at gutenberg.org/files/57515/57515-h/57515-h.htm

Keynes, Randal, *Creation: The True Story of Charles Darwin*. London: John Murray, 2009

King, Harriet Lethbridge, *The Admiral's Wife: Mrs Phillip Parker King, A Selection of Letters 1817–56*. Edited by Dorothy Walsh. Melbourne: Hawthorn Press, 1967

Lawson, Elizabeth, *The Natural Art of Louisa Atkinson*. Sydney: State Library of New South Wales Press, 1995

Macarthur Onslow, Sibella, *Some Early Records of the Macarthurs of Camden*. Sydney: Angus & Robertson, 1914

Muir, Marcie, *Charlotte Barton: Australia's First Children's Author*. Sydney: Wentworth Press, 1980

——, *A History of Australian Children's Book Illustration*. Melbourne: Oxford University Press, 1982

Murrell, Belinda, *The River Charm*. Sydney: Random House Australia, 2013

Niall, Brenda, and O'Neill, Frances, *Australia through the Looking-Glass: Children's Fiction, 1830–1980*. Melbourne: Melbourne University Press, 1984

Nicholas, F.W., and Nicholas, J.M., *Charles Darwin in Australia*. Melbourne: Cambridge University Press, 2002

Norman, Philip, 'Notes on Bromley and the Neighbourhood', *Archaeologia Cantiana* (journal of the Kent Archaeological Society), vol.24, 1900, online at kentarchaeology.org.uk/Research/Pub/ArchCant/Vol.024%20-%201900/024-08.pdf

Norton, Caroline Sheridan, *Observations on the Natural Claim of the Mother to the Custody of Her Infant Children*. London: James Ridgeway, 1837

Olsen, Penny, *Louisa Atkinson's Nature Notes*. Canberra: National Library of Australia, 2015

Organ, Michael K., *Illawarra and South Coast Aborigines 1770–1900*. Wollongong, NSW: University of Wollongong, 1993

Pool, Daniel, *What Jane Austen Ate and Charles Dickens Knew: From Fox Hunting to Whist*. New York: Touchstone, 1993

Reardon, Dr Kathleen Kelley, and Noblet, Christopher T., *Childhood Denied: Ending the Nightmare of Child Abuse and Neglect.* Thousand Oaks, CA: SAGE Publications, 2009

Rousseau, Jean-Jacques, *Emile, or On Education.* The Floating Press, 2009 [first published 1762], online at books.google.com.au/books?id=nWj_ZbVcwgIC&prints ec=frontcover&dq=Jean-Jacques+Rousseau,+Emile,+or+On+Education

Saxby, Maurice, *Books in the Life of a Child: Bridges to Literature and Learning.* Melbourne: Macmillan Education Australia, 1997

——, *Offered to Children: A History of Children's Literature 1841–1941.* Sydney: Scholastic Australia, 1998

Waring, Charlotte, Journal Kept on Board the 'Cumberland' Bound from England to New South Wales, 1826, National Library of Australia, NLA MS 8997

Weil, Simone, *The Need for Roots.* London: Routledge, 2002 [first published 1949]

Wighton, Rosemary, 'Introduction', in Charlotte Waring Atkinson, *A Mother's Offering to Her Children by a Lady Long Resident in New South Wales*, facsimile edition. Milton, Qld: Jacaranda Press, 1979 [first published 1841]

Wollstonecraft, Mary, *A Vindication of the Rights of Woman: With Strictures on Political and Moral Subjects.* London: T.F. Unwin, 1891 [first published 1792]

Woolf, Virginia, *A Room of One's Own.* Cambridge, UK: The Folio Society, 2000 [first published 1929]

Worsley, Lucy, *Jane Austen at Home: A Biography.* London: Hodder & Stoughton, 2017

Wrightson, Patricia, and Wrightson, Peter, *The Wrightson List.* Sydney: Random House Australia, 1998

Index

Page numbers for illustrations are in *italic*.
Illustrations that appear between pages 96 and
97 are shown as '*b96–97*' and those between
pages 224 and 225 are shown as '*b224–225*'.
Places are in New South Wales unless
otherwise indicated.

Index

McNeilly, Ted (Edwin), 203, 215, 217–218
McNeilly, Thomas, 194–195, 203, 208, 213–217
Mecklenburg Square, London, UK, 55–56, 57
Mereworth, Kent, UK, 43–49
Mereworth, NSW, 94, 111–112, 139, 140, 194, 196
Mitchell Library, Atkinson Papers, 27, 83–85, 213
A Mother's Offering to Her Children, 52, 59, 98, 100
    anonymity of author, 228–235
    commentary on, 237–250
    first published, 14–15, 187, 259–260
    pedagogical purpose, 239–244
    re-published, 228–232
    see also Waring, Charlotte
Muir, Marcie, 95, 204, 206, 232–235, 263–264, 266
Murrell, Belinda ('Binny'), *b224–225*
    home schooling of children, 189–191
    writing, 16, 110, 163–164, 227–228
Murrell, Emily, 16, 29–30, 40, 84, 127, 128, 221, *b224–225*
Murrell family, 127–129

National Library of Australia archives, 38, 69, 204, 205–207, 213, 217, 233, 263
New South Wales, 65–66, 90–95, 114–115
    census, 102–103
    child mortality, 196–197
    Darwin's visit, 144–150
Norton, Caroline, 179–180

Oldbury, Kent, 14, 34–43, 75, *b224–225*
Oldbury, Sutton Forest, 113–115, 118, 130
    Aboriginal massacre (alleged but refuted), 121–123
    Charlotte's departures from, 167–175, 197
    Charlotte's returns to, 192–194, 202, 207
    description, 70, 97–99, 104–105, 109, 110–111, *b224–225*
    homestead and residences, 13–14, 48, 49, 97–98, 104, 108–112, 195, 211
    James John in charge, 196, 197
    life at, 99–102, 111–119, 192–194
    roads and travel to, 95–97
    sale and bonfire, 212–213, 263
    theft and violence at, 115–116
    workforce, 70, 104–107, 115–116, 121, 129, 139, 159–160
Orange, 213–218

plaid cloak, James Atkinson's, 3, 74, 81, 82, 84–85
plants *see* botany

population, 102–103, 123
post-traumatic stress disorders, 165–167, 168
Prattle, Peter, books by, 263–271

rape, 116, 137, 142, 165–167
Ritchie, Robert and Ann, 105
Roberts, Jane (later Waring) *see* Waring, Thomas and Jane
Roberts, Maria (later Waring), 54
Robinson, Letitia, 24, 25, 26

Saxby, Maurice, 240, 243, 244, 246, 264, 265
Shelley, Mary Wollstonecraft, 58, 59, 229, 272
shipwrecks, 245–248, 271
Shoreham, Kent, UK, 22, 28–29, 30, 48–49, 52, 53, 75, 193
Smith, Thomas, 138, 139, 141
Southern Highlands, 13, 108, 139, 169–173
    see also Berrima and district; Bong Bong
Sutton Forest, 13, 70, 96
    All Saints Church, 13, 114, 118, 137, 139, 140–142, 195, 196, 209, 211
    see also Oldbury, Sutton Forest
Swanton Cottage, Kent, UK, 48
Swanton Cottage, Oldbury, Sutton Forest, 48, 195, 211

theft, 115–116, 133, 136, 139
Throsby, Betsey Broughton, 71–72
Throsby, Charles, 71, 72, 101, 134–137, 170
Throsby, Dr Charles, 71, 96
Throsby, Mary, 70–71, 72, 73, 74, 76, 88
Throsby Park, Moss Vale, 139, 170
Trafford family, 62–64
Turner, Elizabeth *see* Waring, Elizabeth Turner

Venner family, 52
Vincent, John and family, 114, 139
The Vineyard, Rydalmere, 90–91, 146, 149
violence
    Aboriginal massacre (alleged but refuted), 121–123
    aftermath, 165–167, 168, 174, 180, 182
    Barton's behaviour, 138–140, 168, 176, 182, 183, 197
    bushranger attacks, 133–139, 141–142
    by Oldbury convicts, 139, 159–160
    rape, 116, 137, 142, 165–167
    settler–Aboriginal conflict, 103–104
von Mueller, Baron Ferdinand, 201

Want, Randolph, 113
Waring, Albert (Thomas Albert), 22–26, 29, 31, 53–55
Waring, Albert (Thomas Albert) junior, 54, 55
Waring, Ann Mayern, 206

303